ECONOMISTS AT BAY

*why the
experts
will never
solve
your
problems*

ECONOMIS

McGraw-Hill Book Company
New York   St. Louis
San Francisco   Toronto
Mexico   Düsseldorf

AT BAY

*why the
experts
will never
solve
your
problems*

—◆◆—

Robert Lekachman

For
David Ricardo Lekachman
and
Samuel Bailey Lekachman

Book design by Lynn Braswell.

Copyright © 1976 by Robert Lekachman.

All rights reserved. Printed in the United States of America.
No part of this publication may be reproduced, stored in a retrieval
system, or transmitted, in any form or by any means, electronic,
mechanical, photocopying, recording, or otherwise, without the prior
written permission of the publisher.

23456789 BPBP 798765

Library of Congress Cataloging in Publication Data

Lekachman, Robert.
  Economists at bay.

  Includes bibliographical references and index.
  1. Economics.   2. Economists.   I. Title.
HB71.L45   330   75-30759
ISBN 0-07-037153-9

Other books by Robert Lekachman

History of Economic Ideas

The Age of Keynes

Varieties of Economics: Documents, Examples and Manifestoes

Inflation: The Permanent Problem of Boom and Bust

Edited by Robert Lekachman

National Policy for Economic Welfare at Home and Abroad

Keynes and the Classics

Keynes' General Theory: Reports of Three Decades

National Income and Public Welfare

contents

introduction

As a group, economists are slightly more entertaining than bankers and a trifle duller than lawyers. The excuse for perpetrating an entire volume about their shortcomings is only this: when respectable economists are wrong en masse, other people usually suffer the consequences. The economists who encouraged Richard Nixon in early 1973 to dismantle a comparatively effective set of wage and price controls neither expected nor desired the price explosion that immediately followed this dash for freedom. That explosion, however, was the pretext for the Nixon-Ford actions which deliberately deepened and prolonged the 1974–75 mini-depression. Various people, most of them black, poor, female, or young or sufficiently unfortunate to combine in themselves several of these attributes, lost employment and income because reputable economic advisers urged a pair of conservative presidents first to restore "free markets" and then to counter the inflation which this action stimulated with high unemployment.

At no point were the economists either prescient or helpful. When President Ford, fresh to his great office, summoned a horde of economists to a Washington summit conference in September 1974, none of those assembled warned of the sharp collapse of production and employment which began almost as soon as they left town. It was then easier, accordingly, for Mr. Ford to persist in the folly of asking for higher taxes instead of lower taxes and more federal spending, just as though inflation were the country's major problem.

It is not surprising that an intensely conservative soul like President Ford has fretted more sincerely about prices than about jobs. But the economists did give the president's choice of priorities the seal of professional approval and frightened Congress away from adequate job-creation legislation. Public acquiescence in the economy's worst slide since 1937 is explained in part by the suddenness of economic calamity. Supplementary unemployment benefits, unemployment compensation, and food stamps cushioned the shock of layoff for many of those affected. It is likely all the same that if mainstream economists had more quickly agreed that unemployment was a more serious problem than inflation, liberal and moderate congressmen would have been encouraged to press more stimulative spending and tax reductions upon their colleagues and the president than they felt politically safe in doing.

The world is full of happenings which defy prophecy: OPEC, revolution in Portugal, oil in the North Sea, to cite three at random. No one is likely to be invariably correct about the future whether he relies upon giant computers, intuition, or astrology. However in recent times economists have been so seldom correct that the suspicion is abroad in the land that something must be seriously awry with economics itself.

I share the popular suspicion. What follows is an attempt in chapter 1 to sketch in broad strokes the current condition of economics as a policy science. The next chapter is devoted to recent blunders in the management of inflation and unemployment. Chapter 3 explains how innocent young people of good character and decent mental capacity nevertheless become economists. The succeeding two chapters deal respectively with large corporations and trade unions, two important institutions which economists, handicapped by their training, have seldom adequately interpreted and never incorporated fully into their theoretical models. Chapter 6 harks back to better days when economists spoke in mighty voices on topics larger than the outlook for the first quarter of the New Year. I suggest that Adam Smith, Karl Marx, Thorstein Veblen, and John Maynard Keynes have important things to say even in the 1970s to the holders of doctorates in economics who have never been required to read them. My concluding chapter argues that economics will never return to its former glories until economists take their courage in both hands, retreat from their inconsequential roles as "neutral" technicians, and once again act like social scientists in search of understanding and social change.

Economists are no worse than other people. They have livings to earn, children to educate, mortgages to pay, and promotions to seek. In the 1950s when the world was quiet, Eisenhower the Good benevolently reigned in the White

House, and the writ of American imperial power ran without effective contradiction throughout the "free world," the errors of economists were trivial matters. Our days are different and more dangerous. Daring is called for, not intellectual timidity. Ours is a universe of shrinking resources, teeming population, and incessant conflict within and among nations.

I never thought that economists would save the world, but they may yet help preserve it from total disaster. The diseases of economics are not terminal. There are signs of self-renewal. J. K. Galbraith has declared himself a socialist. Wassily Leontieff, a Nobel Laureate, travels the land extolling the merits of democratic planning. The Union for Radical Political Economy enrolls a growing percentage of graduate students, young economists, and even a few middle-aged fellow travelers. Other dissidents in the Veblenian tradition operate the Association for Evolutionary Economics. An occasional Marxist even secures tenure.

I hope that this book modestly contributes to the discontent of economists with their own subject. The emotion is entirely healthy.

1

the sad state of economics

Despite the fact that he (Labor Secretary John Dunlop) is an economist, basically, I have great confidence in him.

—George Meany

When bright people say stupid things, the question inevitably arises, why is their perception of reality so blurred? Good economists are bright men and women. They are possessed of splendid academic credentials and arcane analytical techniques. They speak in tongues as difficult to comprehend as the dialects of nuclear physicists, molecular biologists, structural linguists, or respectable literary critics. Moreover, most economists are individuals of good will, eager to extirpate poverty, redeem the cities, diminish pollution, feed the hungry, heal the sick, and house the unsheltered. All the same, economists do make the oddest statements and promulgate undue quantities of faulty prophecy and policy prescription.

Thus when, on January 11, 1973, President Nixon announced the end of a comparatively successful Phase II program of wage and price controls and the substitution of a vague and ambiguous Phase III set of voluntary guideposts, Walter Heller, Gardner Ackley, and Arthur Okun, the three Kennedy-Johnson Council of Economic Advisers chairmen, all supported Mr. Nixon's dash toward economic freedom. As *The New York Times* of January 13 headlined their position, "3 Democratic Economists Back Phase 3 Structure and Principles." The subhead noted that "Heller, Ackley and Okun are Joined by Dr. Burns, Who Voices Full Support."

Why were these three respected liberal economists as well as their venerable conservative colleague, Federal Reserve Chairman Arthur Burns, so embarrassingly mistaken in their reading of events?

Or, for that matter, how could their somewhat less distinguished professional colleagues on Nixon's Council of Economic Advisers have possibly said in black and white that the rate of inflation "as measured by the consumer price index" would "be reduced to 2½ percent or less by the end of 1973"? Just for good measure the council insisted that unemployment would be in "the neighborhood of 4½ percent by the end of the year."[1] In point of fact, the consumer price index rose between December 1972 and December 1973 from 127.3 to 138.5, something like quadruple the predicted increase. By December 1973, unemployment was at 4.8 percent, and rising—not declining. Contrary to the council's cheerful expectations, the economy was sinking into the second Nixon recession.

I suppose that a cynic might say that government economists, like secretaries of state, are paid to lie for their country's sake. At the least, these ladies and gentlemen are prone to interpret their president's policies and programs in the most favorable way. Still, academic and business economists have done little if any better as guides to the perplexed. If in the waning days of 1973 an unwary soul had followed the advice of the *Institutional Investor*, a well-regarded Wall Street publication, he or she would have purchased such securities as Raytheon, United Airlines, American Motors, Citicorp, ABC, Sohio, Marriott, Kodak, and AT & T. Here is how such a person would have fared.[2]

Stock	Predicted Price	December 16 Closing Price
Raytheon	50	24⅞
United Airlines	mid-30s	13⅞
American Motors	midteens	3¾
Citicorp	60–72	27¼
ABC	50–100 percent increase over present price (28)	12⅞
Sohio	"could peak at $225 later this year"	59⅛
Marriott	mid-30s	6½
Kodak	$170 by year-end	58¼
AT & T	"$65 per share in a recessionary environment"	43⅝

Well, who can expect objectivity from people involved in the stock market? They are almost bound to be bullish. Wall Street's health depends upon a heavy volume of business generated by greedy souls eager to double and treble their investment stakes.

Unfortunately independent and business economists (whose jobs require reasonable acuity of frontal vision) did little better than their colleagues. At the end of 1973, *Business Week*'s sample of projections by computer models and

independent analysts produced a consensus inflation outlook: 6 percent for the coming year. Instead the gross national product deflator, the most comprehensive of the
indexes, soared by a sickening 10 percent and the consumer
price index ballooned even more. These same forecasters
were confident that output of goods and services would
be up by 1½ percent. It was down by 2 percent. Prophecies
of 1974 profits, interest rates, and national employment
were similarly off their targets. As one business economist
temperately put it, "We did not provide advance warning
to our managements of the distressing situation into which
the American economy has drifted over the past several
years."[3]

When one economist told an audience in passing that he
wondered why anyone bothered to listen to economists
any more, *The New York Times* featured the comment as
the Quotation of the Day, an honor that that economist had
never been granted for anything else he might have said
that was a trifle more respectful to his colleagues'
pretensions.*

Economists are as sensitive as anybody else. Thus in the
spring of 1975 Soma Golden, *The New York Times*' well-
informed business and economics specialist, reported something like a failure of nerve among the economists. "Most
analysts today," she concluded, "believe that 5.5 to 6 percent unemployment is probably the lowest that the Government can achieve without stirring up virulent inflation
again. And even that job target is a long way from attainment—1979 at the earliest, according to most forecasters."[4]

---

* The occasion was a February 1975 conference on full employment at
the City University of New York. I was the economist in question.

The Wall Street Journal sampled the views of economists and arrived at very similar conclusions. Economists have a bad case of "future fear," which "takes varying forms: A feeling that the U.S. is sliding down the British path of decline toward economic stagnation. A belief that resource scarcities point toward slow growth and political strife over how to slice up a static national-income pie. A conviction that a political system that rewards politicians who deliver short-term benefits can't cope with long-term economic problems requiring sacrifice. A fear that we haven't learned from our past economic blunders and are doomed to repeat them."[5]

Whatever was wrong with the economists in 1975, it must have amazed ordinary folk that the experts were still fretting about inflation when measured unemployment was hovering around 9 percent and rising with each month's glum bulletin from the Bureau of Labor Statistics.* If the well-known man in the street had been paying any attention to the utterings of the learned, he might have been angered by a tendency to focus on wages as a potential source of inflation. As blue- and white-collar families realize from daily experience, wages have lagged steadily behind the cost of living since sometime in 1971. In early 1975 the average factory worker was worse off than he had been nine years earlier. In two years he had lost more than 8 percent of his purchasing power.

The bewilderment of the economists was the more striking because the major causes of inflation were quite easy to

---

* For a variety of technical reasons, including the unpopularity in low-income neighborhoods of men equipped with ties, jackets, and clipboards, the true rate of unemployment is at least 2–3 percent higher than the government statisticians allege it to be.

identify. They include the quadrupling of oil prices by OPEC, two devaluations of the dollar, Federal Reserve expansion of the money supply during the 1972 presidential election,* swelling world demand for American food and raw materials, and the well-known habit of dominant corporations of raising prices in both recessions and booms.† Inflation, in short, relates to issues of shifting world power, the maneuvers of mysterious multinationals, the time on the political clock, the exigencies of détente, and the profit targets set by our own domestic corporate giants. As members of a middle-class meritocracy, economists are no more tutored in the higher mysteries of corporate boardrooms than the public at large. Certainly few economists have much of interest to say about the intricate interplay of public politics, private financial power, and the prosperity of the American economy.

To put the matter mildly, economists who ignore the politics of economic decision are subject to repeated embarrassment. As Paul Samuelson has suggested, "I think the greatest error in forecasting is not realizing how important are the probabilities of events other than those everyone is agreeing upon."[6] Is the world simply too unpredictable a place to make sense of? Should economists stop forecasting? Is Norman Robertson, a Mellon Bank economist, justified in blaming everything, including the mistakes of his colleagues, on the OPEC cartel? "Few events," he asserted, "in the 20th century have tested so severely the smooth

---

* Some have charged and others have denied that Chairman Burns deliberately pumped up an economic boom to help his great and good friend Richard Nixon get reelected.
† GM and its friendly rivals raised prices $1,000 per chariot in 1974, despite rapidly declining sales and spreading factory layoffs.

functioning of international trade and finance or have resulted in such abrupt and radical changes in economic power relationships."[7] Was OPEC action really that unexpected? One might more readily accept the plea were it not that economists ignored the evidence of energy depletion in the United States which the Paley Commission emphasized back in the Eisenhower Era, failed to take into account the booming world demand for petroleum in Japan, Western Europe, and the United States, and, above all, neglected the politics of the Middle East and the rest of the oil-producing Third World. The increasing militancy of OPEC *before* the 1973 Yom Kippur war and the probability that such a war would occur should have alerted economists to looming "abrupt and radical changes in economic power relationships." But economists don't believe that cartels can hold together. The conventional wisdom focuses on differences of interest among the members, tendencies for states to cheat, and switches by the customers to substitutes. What such analysis neglects is the sheer power of shared political objectives, among them revenge on the advanced countries and victory against Israel.

As I shall argue in detail in chapter 3, the trouble with economics is the profession's addiction to techniques diminishingly relevant to the institutions and interests which determine prices, employment, growth, and prosperity and depression. The world will continue to astonish economists so long as they concentrate upon the small, incremental changes in purely economic magnitudes to which their training has habituated them. Undaunted by forecasting blunders in 1972, 1973, and 1974, the prophets again projected small changes in 1975 and an upturn in the middle of the year. According to *Fortune*, the most unvaryingly cheerful of the business media, "What will probably be in many ways the worst U.S. recession since the Depression has lately struck with such stunning speed and severity that it has already run more than half its course."[8] The reasoning seems to be that since depressions are of course impossible (why?), the recession must soon end or else it will turn into a forbidden depression.

The business-cycle experts these days have dropped the very word *depression* out of their technical lexicons. Out there in the real world, there are only expansions and contractions, prosperities and recessions. The laity, understandably influenced by losses in jobs and earnings and rising prices in supermarkets, doctors' offices, restaurants, department stores, auto showrooms, and appliance stores, do know what to call a labor market in which no jobs are available for 20 percent of all teenagers, over 40 percent of black teenagers, 6 percent of male heads of families, 11 percent of New Yorkers, and nearly 25 percent of the unhappy residents of Detroit. Mayor Beame spent much of the unmerry month of May 1975 begging Governor Carey, Secretary Simon, and David Rockefeller, his friend at the Chase Manhattan, to give, guarantee, or lend New York City enough money to pay its bills and meet its payrolls. In Detroit, a race riot very nearly broke out between black and white police officers over the issue of how police layoffs were to be distributed. At the same time the Treasury was mailing out tax rebates, mayors and governors were firing public employees in droves and raising state and local property and sales taxes.

In April and May of 1975, sales in the auto industry, which directly or indirectly provides jobs and incomes for nearly a fifth of the population, were running far below the already depressed levels of the preceding year. Although money for mortgages was available, few Americans could afford a new or old house. The median price of a new home was over $39,000. A family needed an income somewhere between $20,000 and $25,000 to be able to acquire an average house. Just 15 percent of all American families in 1975 had incomes larger than $23,000.

One might readily forgive ordinary Americans who took evidence of this nature as sufficient indication that their country was in a genuine depression. In the Keynesian era, it would be reasonable to expect a coalition of economists and politicians to unite behind vigorous stimulation of the depressed economy. Really deep tax cuts, extensive public job creation, aid to the bankrupt cities, public housing, attention to mass transit, a start on comprehensive health care, a return to a more generous version of Nixon's Family Assistance Plan, and full funding of environmental protection programs: these should have been a tempting array of choices.

Unfortunately, economists and politicians, like generals and admirals, prefer to refight old battles. For at a time when inflation was slowing down, many economists, bankers, and Wall Street types fretted about the danger of renewed inflation. If the federal deficit got too big, wouldn't the Treasury have to borrow so much that corporations would be crowded out of the capital markets? How could the economy recover if corporations couldn't borrow? If the Federal Reserve pumped in enough credit for both the Treasury and the private sector, then inflation would surely follow.

Prudence suggested that we move slowly. Nine percent unemployment was no doubt too much, but, looking on the bright side, 91 percent of the labor force still had jobs, at least if we didn't count the million or two men and women who were so discouraged that they had given up looking for work, and we *did* count as employed people on short hours and laboring at jobs far below their qualifications. In other words, the creation of full employment and the simultaneous control of inflation were seen as possible but too painful to undertake by either economists or politicians. Inflation, like unemployment and income distribution, is rooted in concentrations of power and power relationships. A cure of inflation, consistent with high employment, requires the limitation of private discretion and the substitution of public for corporate discretion. In a society dominated by large corporations, the agents of inflation are, naturally, the men who run these corporations. By an extraordinary feat of self-deception, most economists construe price and profit controls on the operations of these monstrous organizations as interference with the free markets with which they have been conducting a durable romance ever since in 1776 Adam Smith published *The Wealth of Nations*. Politicians who as practical people might favor controls, hesitate because it is exceedingly difficult to curb the avarice of the very organizations which finance your campaign for reelection and, often, helped you get elected in the first place.

It is instructive to glance at that short Golden Age of economic policy which lasted from early 1961 until the middle of 1965, when a deliberate national effort was made to combine rapid growth and a reasonable degree of price stability. During this half-decade, the cost of living rose a mere 1 or 2 percent annually, unemployment steadily diminished, and the economy grew at the 3–4 percent per capita rate each year which conformed to the long-run historical trend. Unions settled for modest 5 percent wage increases. Although corporate profits (encouraged by the investment tax credit and liberalized depreciation allowances) did substantially better than wages, corporate price setters contented themselves with relatively stable prices. Other marvelous events dazzled the electorate. In 1964 and 1965, Lyndon Johnson cajoled Congress into enacting the War on Poverty, medicare, Model Cities, and an expensive Elementary and Secondary Education Act. This program amounted to the first major social welfare progress since the New Deal. As president of all the people, Mr. Johnson did not neglect the prosperous. In 1964, Congress substantially reduced taxes on personal and corporate income. All this and stable prices too. Americans, who are really no worse than other people, were more than happy to feed some of the hungry, heal a few of the sick, attempt to educate the ignorant, and house a discreet fraction of the poorly sheltered—and pay lower taxes.

The Democratic economists who presided over this modern version of the miracle of the loaves and the fishes were not oblivious of the inflation hazard. The preventive medicine which they prescribed was mild, unlikely to diminish existing inequalities of income and wealth, but politically sophisticated. In their 1962 *Economic Report*, Walter Heller and his colleagues on the Kennedy Council of Economic Advisers, operating independently of congressional authorization, defined an appropriate code of conduct for union negotiators and corporate price fixers, the famous wage-price guidelines. "There are," the *Economic Report* began, "important segments of the economy in which large firms or well-organized groups of employees have some discretionary ability to affect the levels of their prices and wages."[9] The danger was always present that these decision makers might greedily raise their demands beyond the capacity of the economy to generate more goods and services. If the economy produces this year only 3 percent more goods and services than last year, wages and profits cannot rise by 5 percent without inflationary consequences. If, as the statistical record revealed, worker productivity tended to increase 3 percent each year, then wages could appropriately rise 3 percent without justifying any price increase.

In some industries productivity increased faster than 3 percent and in other industries more slowly. Less efficient industries were urged to raise wages by the standard 3 percent which measured the national experience and increase their prices just enough to compensate them for increased real labor costs. But in the really efficient industries whose per capita productivity improvements were running at 5 or 6 percent rates, the guidelines recommended division of the loot between employees and customers. A 6 percent improvement in efficiency should be split evenly—a 3 percent wage hike and a 3 percent price cut. Hence price stability was attainable whenever unions settled for no more than average productivity gains, when less efficient corporations raised prices only when they had to, and when more efficient enterprises actually cut prices. At the end of this process, both wages and profits were slightly higher in real terms and, although the guideposts did nothing to remedy existing inequalities of income distribution, at least they did not widen them. So long as all parties obeyed the rules, high employment and stable prices could live in harmony.

When early in 1967, the Council of Economic Advisers mused upon five years of experience with the guidelines, it identified as a major shortcoming the reluctance of efficient corporations *ever* to reduce their prices. The 1–2 percent annual inflation which marked the price record was thus explained by this upward but never downward price flexibility. A smaller contributing influence was the result of occasional unwillingness by unions to adhere to the wage guideline.

Whatever had been accomplished during this period rested on presidential willingness to intervene strongly against the corporations which threatened to post inflationary price increases. The most picturesque of these episodes occurred in April 1962. As an exercise in political economy, it deserves retelling. During the autumn and winter of 1961, the steelworkers and the steel industry bargained to an extremely moderate wage settlement. During the 1950s this industry had had a bad record of both strikes and inflationary pricing. Here was a chance for the industry, blessed by union restraint and afflicted by growing competition from substitute materials and foreign steel producers, to engage without risk in a little price discipline. All the omens were favorable. Since union gains were limited to fringe benefits which, for the most part, went into effect a year or more after the beginning of the new contract, the contract imposed almost no additional costs upon U.S. Steel and the other companies. Unlike the settlements of the 1950s, this one came without a strike, but only after much personal persuasion directed toward his former union associates by Labor Secretary Arthur Goldberg. Mr. Goldberg and President Kennedy interpreted the new contract as bringing into force a personal promise by Roger Blough, head of U.S. Steel, that the union's reasonable behavior would be matched by price restraint on the part of the industry.

What followed afforded a dramatic test of the *actual* as

distinguished from the legal powers of any president. On April 10, 1962, shortly after the last steel executive had initialed the contract, U.S. Steel's board of directors met in New York City and raised steel prices 3.5 percent, approximately six dollars per ton. *After* this decision was enacted, Blough on short notice arranged a late-afternoon appointment with the president in the course of which he handed his host a four-page mimeographed statement of the company's action. In a bitter evening of discussion with his aides, hard upon the meeting, Mr. Kennedy delivered himself of a remark that subsequently resounded through the business community: "My father always told me that all businessmen were sons of bitches, but I never believed it till now."[10]

For all his colorful language, the president was in a tight spot. If he treated the industry's action as a *fait accompli*, the guidelines would in short order become a laughingstock and the effort to combine price stability and rapid growth would fail. Neither unions nor corporations would heed appeals from Washington if they came to believe that they were all talk and no action. Unfortunately, Congress had enacted no price control statute and the president appeared to possess no legal right to compel U.S. Steel and the companies prepared to follow its lead to retract their action. It was a measure of the significance that John Kennedy attached both to promoting economic expansion and restraining inflation that he decided to take the risk of throwing the prestige of his office into balance and losing. That evening he committed all his chips.

These resources were considerable. In the next forty-eight hours, the administration threatened antitrust suits and grand jury inquiries, began to divert defense contracts, announced the drafting of unfriendly legislation, unleashed Senator Estes Kefauver, the leading congressional scourge of the monopolists, leaked stories to friendly columnists of Internal Revenue audits,* and made personal appeals to the chief executives of some of the smaller steel companies to refrain from emulating U.S. Steel.

Briefly the issue hung in doubt, especially since during the next day, April 11, the major steel companies, Bethlehem, Republic, Youngstown, and Jones & Laughlin, dutifully matched their price leader's action. Indeed by the end of the day, only five of the smaller companies, representing 14 percent of industry capacity, had failed to act. Fortunately for Mr. Kennedy and his helpers, a single key figure was among the five sluggards. The maverick was Joseph L. Block, chairman of Inland Steel, who even before this confrontation between industry and White House had already expressed a sympathy, heretical among his associates, for government guidance of price and wage decisions. In Block's opinion, "A contest of strength where the stronger side wins doesn't prove a thing. Each side has to represent its own interests but neither side must be unmindful of the needs of the nation. Who else can point out those needs but the Government?" Swayed by his own instincts as much as by a concentrated telephone campaign of persuasion by the White House, Block declared that "We did not feel that it was in the national interest to raise prices at this time. We felt this very strongly."[11]

---

* After Watergate, many of these maneuvers seem far less commendable and much more hostile to legal due process than they did at the time (at least for good Democrats who enjoyed the spectacle of their young president harrying the wicked steel magnates).

Block's decision, taken in Japan where he was visiting, was crucial. Possibly influenced by Inland's rivalry in several of its markets, Bethlehem rescinded its price increase, and U.S. Steel reluctantly followed suit. The parade of companies which had cheerfully clambered up the price ladder behind their leader now sullenly clattered down that ladder. The moral of it all according to the president when he was interviewed on television late in 1962 was this:

... though I don't like to rake over old fires, I think it would have been a serious situation if I had not attempted with all my influence to try to get a rollback, because there was an issue of good faith involved.... If I had not attempted, after asking the unions to accept the noninflationary settlement, if I had not attempted to use my influence to have the companies hold their prices stable, I think the union could have rightfully felt that they had been misled. In my opinion it would have endangered the whole bargaining between labor and management, would have made it impossible for us to exert any influence ... in the future ... on the great labor-management disputes. So I have no regrets.[12]

Roger Blough's interpretation of the episode was rather different. The president, he charged, acted not in the public interest but simply in his administration's political interest. "I believe," Blough asserted, "that he and Secretary Goldberg felt an increase in steel prices ... would be viewed as evidence that the Administration's policies were adverse to labor's interests."[13] Administration economists, though by no means eager to repeat the episode in the same or other industries, drew from this famous victory the encouraging lesson that a determined president could discipline a recalcitrant industry even in the absence of statutory authority over wages and prices. The economists drew back from the stronger conclusion that permanent political control over powerful private economic institutions was the prerequisite to noninflationary prosperity.

The sixties support an additional generalization. The relative success of economic policy in the first half of that decade was facilitated by the terms of a social contract at once implicit and fragile. In Western Europe, Japan, and the United States, corporations and unions tacitly agreed to refrain from serious attempts to alter existing distributions of income, wealth, and economic influence, at least so long as generally high employment, marginally improved social services, and sustained economic growth generated annual improvement in living standards for average families. All the Western governments in one way or another* promised the voters that the horrors of the 1930s would never be repeated. Everybody was a winner out of each year's dividend of economic growth. Prizes for all!

The postwar climate of diminished class warfare forced radical unions and socialist political parties in Europe and Japan to surrender or soften their earlier programmatic emphasis upon redistributive taxation and confiscatory inheritance levies. Daniel Bell's celebrated argument that we were passing through the end of ideology was really based upon the diminishing capacity of Marxism as a fighting faith to attract mass support in parliamentary democracies. Save in England (a somewhat special case), unions began to drift in the direction of strictly limited business objectives—more money, shorter hours, new fringe benefits, and

---

* In the United States, the Employment Act of 1946, watered down though it was, did register a novel American commitment to national action against unemployment and depression.

so on, that since the time of Samuel Gompers have constituted the program of the official American labor movement.

The Labor Party in England and the Social Democrats in West Germany discovered that it was expedient, indeed essential, that they shed their traditional ideological baggage. The electoral record demonstrates that before blue- and white-collar voters were willing to set Harold Wilson and Willy Brandt at the head of their respective political tables, they wanted to be reassured that their prosperity would not be endangered by destructive alterations in the arrangements which generated floods of cars, appliances, and vacations in Spain and Italy.

Two decades of comparative social harmony depended upon the promise of steady economic growth—more profits, and more wages. In Japan and West Germany, the process of postwar reconstruction stimulated a long boom and so did the injections of Marshall Plan and other aid by the U.S. Banking and fiscal policy were equally supportive of prosperity. Our Federal Reserve and central banks in other countries tacitly agreed to validate dollar claims against gross national product slightly in excess of their economies' capacity to spew out new goods and services. Corporate profit targets and union wage demands added up to a total 1 or 2 percent larger than the sum of the price tags attached to new output. However, so long as the central bankers printed the money and supplied the credit, and the excess claims were moderate, nearly everybody got what he sought in dollar terms and slightly less than he had hoped for in real terms. The slight inflationary tilt imparted to prices was tolerable to consumers and encouraging to businessmen. Merchants traditionally prefer rising to falling prices.

In the 1950s and the 1960s, favorable terms of trade between advanced and developing nations enhanced the favorable context of growth. The Middle East, Africa, Malaysia,
and Latin America sold their oil, tin, rubber, coffee, copper, chrome, bananas, and bauxite at low prices to the industrial countries who were their major customers. These
customers were frequently able to place in the bargaining
scales the threat of military or covert intervention against
radical or greedy politicians in the raw-material-exporting
lands. CIA-engineered coups against the Mossadegh government in Iran and the Arbenz regime in Guatemala signalized
the latent power of buyers over sellers.

For their part the industrial countries sold machines, computers, gadgets, and appliances to the developing nations at
relatively high prices. The citizens of the advanced countries had to work relatively little in order to get quite a
lot of the raw materials they needed. The West became
affluent in part at least because the Third World stayed
poor. One need not endorse OPEC politics and Arab hostility to Israel to recognize that a strong and substantially
justified sense of historical grievance is at work.

It is as difficult to interpret the economic events of the
last decade without attention to the politics in which they
are embedded as to understand what happened between
1945 and 1965. It was no accident that in our own country
the inflationary demons began to breathe fire and flame after
mid-1965. It was in the middle of that year that Lyndon
Johnson made his calamitous decision to escalate the war in
Vietnam and bring back that old coonskin to nail to the
living-room wall. Recollections of World War II and the

Korean conflict should have reminded the president that the only way to fight wars without inflation is to raise taxes, ration scarce items, set national production priorities, and regulate wages and prices. But Lyndon Johnson had good reasons not to emulate Franklin Roosevelt and Harry Truman. He expected the war to end quickly and cost comparatively little. He wanted to increase funding for Great Society programs. Finally he seriously questioned public assent to higher taxes. In 1964 the voters thought that they had elected the peace candidate.* They were startled by peak $30 billion annual expenditure on Vietnam and war costs which totaled some $150 billion.

Vietnam expenditures were piled on top of consumer and business spending already close to full-employment levels. Johnson's political calculation set in motion a classic demand-pull inflation, a typical pursuit of too few goods by too many dollars. In short order, unions began to disregard the wage guideline, and prices, long quiescent, began to rise. The familiar wage-price-wage spiral was reactivated. By 1967, when Mr. Johnson at length reluctantly asked Congress to impose a tax surcharge on profits and other incomes, the inflation had picked up speed. Congress, playing its own brand of politics, failed to help when it delayed its consent until early 1968. By refusing to ask his constituents to choose between guns and butter, Lyndon Johnson compelled the Federal Reserve to print enough money to finance both. That money steadily lost value. Workers and employers, seeking to preserve their purchasing power,

---

* Old political joke: They warned me that if I voted for Goldwater we'd have a big war in Asia. I voted for Goldwater and sure enough that is just what happened.

sought even more dollars. Their efforts stimulated still more inflation. In the game of catch-up the winners are the adroit and the powerful.

War and inflation are traditional old friends, but never more intimate than when the war is unpopular, the politicians are particularly deceptive, and hard allocations of resources between civilians and generals are evaded. In short, the beginnings of inflation in the 1970s had little to do with failures of economic understanding, unusual corporate or union greed, or even political ignorance. Lyndon Johnson's economists urged him to raise taxes at the beginning of 1966 when the size of the Vietnam commitment was becoming clear.* Vietnam shot and bombed away much of the growth dividend which had purchased two decades of social and political détente.

For veterans of the 12 and 14 percent inflation rates of recent experience, the 6 percent rate which greeted Richard Nixon on Inauguration Day in January 1969 probably seems trivial. It was enough, however, to alarm a country which had accustomed itself to the quasi stability of the early 1960s. The president's response to the problem drew upon political calculation and personal history. Burned by his narrow loss to John Kennedy in 1960 during the third Eisenhower recession, Mr. Nixon resolved to check inflation without paying the price of recession. Accordingly he

---

* In another time and another country, Dr. Ackley and his two colleagues on the Council of Economic Advisers would have resigned over so large a departure from their professional judgment of necessary economic policy. Instead the 1966 *Economic Report*, accepting dubious Pentagon estimates of forthcoming Vietnam costs, refrained from direct advocacy of fiscal restraint. The episode casts no particular credit on the individuals involved.

advertised a preference for gradualism. Budgetary restraint and tighter credit, the president and his advisers hoped, would reduce consumer and business borrowing, curtail aggregate demand, and gently diminish rates of increase in wholesale and consumer price indexes.

During 1969 and 1970 the United States obligingly embarked upon the fourth Republican recession of the postwar era. If conventional economic wisdom were correct, rising unemployment would soon generate lower rates of wage increase, less price inflation, and renewed economic growth.* The scenario was painfully slow in unfolding. By early 1971, when Richard Nixon, battered by a poor Republican performance in the 1970 congressional elections, declared himself to the consternation of friend and foe a Keynesian,† the impact of recession was far more visible upon employment and personal income than upon prices. Only administration economists, looking upon the data with eyes of hope and longing, noticed improvement in the monthly price measurements.

Politically the need for something new was urgent. Economically the situation was different. If Nixon and his unmerry men had allowed recession to persist another twelve or eighteen months, it is probable that inflation would have been vanquished. For despite the conventional reluctance of dominant corporations to cut the prices of autos, appliances, pharmaceuticals, breakfast foods, and most of the

---

* The alleged trade-off between inflation and unemployment is embodied in the Phillips curve, of which much more will be said in the next chapter.

† Cynics took this endorsement as strong evidence that Keynes must now be obsolete.

rest of the average American's shopping list, the message of the vanishing customer in time penetrates the skulls of even the lords of the corporate turf. If enough customers stop buying for a long enough time, even the stickiest of prices begin to respond. As with businessmen, so also with tightly organized tradesmen in construction and public employment. When 25 percent of the electricians, carpenters, and plumbers are jobless, when cities fire policemen, and private employers pare their payrolls, sales drop and prices follow their downward course. Even when dominant corporations and, in a few situations, strong unions are as important as they are in the United States, a good, deep recession breaks into the wage-price spiral. And when both wages and prices stop rising or rise much more slowly, the excuse which each provides for the escalation of the other no longer remains available.

In the good old days when capitalism was young and John Maynard Keynes was unheard of, recurrent depression was accepted even by its victims as an act of God. The moralistic treated depression as condign punishment for overindulgence in the fleshpots of prosperity. Economists pointed to the beneficial side effects. Depression shook the weaker brethren out of the economy. Inefficient entrepreneurs, bankers, and merchants closed their doors and put up their shutters. They released their resources for more productive use by better managers and more gifted entrepreneurs. No doubt bankruptcy was hard on employers and even harder on their employees: it was simply splendid from the standpoint of economic efficiency and renewed growth. Soon or late, after a spell of painful business readjustment and general unemployment, the economy, now purified of its excesses of waste and speculation, would recover, the business-cycle upswing would begin, and full employment of harder-working men and women in better managed enterprise would ensue.*

In those days the life of the politician was simpler than it has become in the wake of the Keynesian revolution. Unfortunately for the politicians, the voters now judge depression and unemployment as the results of political mismanagement. Revenge at the polls is the obvious punishment for congressmen, senators, and especially presidents who make life harder than it has to be. It must be small consolation for defeated politicians that the voters' intuition is perfectly correct.

In early 1971 the economy was recovering far too slowly to suit a president lusting for 1972 reelection. Unemployment continued to rise and on all sides, including even the friendly business community, clamor mounted for decisive presidential action. The president's declaration of faith in Keynes was accompanied by the release of impounded congressional appropriations and encouragement to the Federal Reserve, headed by Dr. Arthur F. Burns, a long-time friend and Nixon counselor, to ease credit and reduce interest rates.

Nothing helped. In January 1971, unemployment was an even 6 percent, alarming for politicians who had started

---

* Say's law (named after J. B. Say, a French follower of Adam Smith) held that a competitive economy naturally moved toward a full-employment equilibrium. Twentieth-century followers of Say explained continued mass unemployment not as disproof of this "law" but as evidence of business monopoly, union interference with necessary wage adjustments, and meddling on the part of the politicians in natural adjustment processes.

from a 3.4 percent level only two years earlier. According to invariable American custom, the black rate was 9.5 percent and the teenage rate 17.3 percent. Unthrilled by the president's conversion to fiscal and monetary liberalism, the economy remained sluggish during the first six months of 1971. Unemployment, still 6 percent in May, actually reached its peak (after economic recovery had already begun) in August at 6.1 percent. The consumer price index, 119.2 in January, reached 122.1 in August. In the context of recent experience, the inflation was less than dreadful, but it disappointed general expectations.

What to do? The electoral clock was ticking ominously toward November 1972. Wise men in Nixon's official entourage and legions of outside commentators offered the president a great deal of solicited and unsolicited advice. As late as June, when the President convened his economists and economic officials at Camp David, spokesmen professed gratification with existing policies. George Schultz, at the time director of the Office of Management and Budget, assured press and public that the game plan was working and the appropriate watchword was "steady as you go." Not yet a Republican but then Treasury Secretary John Connally told the world in bold Texas accents that the administration had no plan to intervene directly in wages, prices, and profits and thus abridge the economic liberty held in uniquely high esteem in the Lone Star State. In July the unlucky Paul McCracken, still Chairman of the Council of Economic Advisers, wrote a sharp *Washington Post* article specifically attacking J. K. Galbraith's plea for controls. He insisted that controls, always an inferior policy, were particularly ill-advised in the summer of 1971 because most of the inflation had occurred either in competitive industries or services* rather than in the concentrated industries identified by Galbraith as the major culprits.

Administration reassurances did nothing to soothe public concern. If anything, the cries for controls got shriller. Business periodicals like *Business Week* editorially endorsed controls. George Meany reiterated his approval of "equitable" restraints upon wages, other forms of income, and prices. In politics even more than in other spheres of human activity, appearances count more than realities. Appearances were dead against an administration which, fairly or not, was perceived as inactive and indifferent to its citizens' distress, just as much in its current Keynesian garb as in its previous suit designed by Milton Friedman.

As readers of *Six Crises* and connoisseurs of its author's speeches know, President Nixon detested controls and recalled with horror his brief spell of service as a compliance attorney during World War II in the Office of Price Administration. August 15, 1971 was the day on which these sentiments became inoperative. Nixon's plans to visit Peking and Moscow were maturing. In spirit he now reached out to Cambridge, Massachusetts and drafted John Kenneth Galbraith for his reelection campaign. Not that the dreadful name was uttered aloud in the president's circle. Inescapably, however, the public record included Dr. Galbraith, that inveterate Democrat, as one of the few economists of reputation who in season and out argued for permanent controls over the numerous industries in which giant corporations exercised decisive influence over market prices. On that enchanted August Sunday, Mr. Nixon went even

---

* An equally logical implication of McCracken's position was extension of price controls to medical and legal services.

further than his unacknowledged guide had counseled. For ninety days he imposed a total freeze on incomes and prices, and promised a detailed set of regulations to follow the freeze.* For good measure, he devalued the dollar by suspending gold sales, imposed a 10 percent surcharge on imports, revived the investment tax credit (renamed the Job Development Credit), reduced auto excise taxes, and proposed additional tax benefits for individuals.

The effect was much as though the president, stung into action by political necessity, decided to bewilder the universe by accepting simultaneously all of his critics' nostrums: import surcharges for the protectionists, substitution of a dollar float for fixed currency parities as sustenance for Milton Friedman's legion of free marketeers, fiscal stimulation via tax reduction as a nod to the Keynesians, and controls for Galbraith and his supporters in the business and labor community. No wonder, as *The New York Times'* Leonard Silk amiably phrased it, that administration policies struck him as "the most comprehensive economics in the history of the world,"[14] spacious enough to house under one White House roof "Friedmanism and Keynesianism, laissez faire and price controls, mercantilism and free trade, the ideologies of free enterprise and social responsibilities."[15]

In its politics, Phase I, as this policy collage was christened, was the high point of the president's first-term economic policy. Mr. Nixon took bold action. The action appeared to be equitable: everything was controlled. As

---

* The joke was on the congressional Democrats who had passed an Economic Stabilization Act which the administration did not want. The thought was that the White House would never invoke its authority and Congress could enjoy blaming the president for inflation and other ills.

might have been predicted by the sophisticated, later analysis implied that benefits flowed mostly to corporations and stockholders and wage restraints were noticeably more effective than curbs on prices and profits. At the time, however, most Americans were relieved that, however belatedly, the administration was doing something effective to alleviate public concern over prices and jobs. George Meany grumbled and his representatives walked out of the Pay Board. But George was a notorious grouch.*

After the freeze ran its course, political considerations continued to guide control policies. Phase II, starting November 1971, featured one of those bureaucratic contrivances of which management types seem fond. There was a seven-person Price Commission, presided over by a Texas business-school dean, C. Jackson Grayson, who demonstrated unexpected public relations flair. The commission required prenotification of planned price increases by large corporations, detailed justification of their necessity, and profit margins no wider than those of the best two of the three preceding years. Smaller fry were instructed to post lists of base-period prices and keep accurate records of changes in them that they actually made.

Complementing the Price Commission was a Pay Board, headed by an elderly federal judge totally innocent of previous experience in labor-management relations. Its members were drawn from labor, business, and the general public. Its key action was promulgation of a 5.5 percent wage

---

* Meany had something to grumble about. Arnold Weber, one of the controllers, conceded after he returned to the University of Chicago that the controls had been designed to "zap" (Weber's word) the unions. So they did.

increase standard. As time passed, this guideline was frequently bent and jesuitically interpreted but never quite destroyed as a check on union demands and the cost of contract settlements. Supervising both agencies, prescribing the limits of their jurisdiction, and exerting quiet White House control, was a Cost of Living Council headed by Donald Rumsfeld,* former congressman and director of the Office of Economic Opportunity.

Despite the withdrawal from the Pay Board of most of the labor representatives,† Phase II controls worked well enough in late 1971 and during the 1972 election year so that most economic observers assumed (and urged) that they be continued into 1973.

Something different actually happened. Until the relevant tapes are played, one can only surmise why on January 11, 1973, the president abruptly terminated Phase II and substituted a much vaguer set of Phase III standards. Phase III dispensed with further price prenotification and restated the 5.5 percent wage guideline only with great ambiguity. It was a sign of administration confusion that John Ehrlichman implied that the guideline no longer applied, but Ron Ziegler promptly insisted that his superior had misspoken and the guideline still lived. For his part George Meany sounded as though the junking of the 5.5 percent restraint was part of what the president had promised in return for the AFL-CIO's benign neutrality during the presidential race.

---

* In the Ford administration, Mr. Rumsfeld reappeared in Haldeman's old chief-of-staff position.
† Frank Fitzsimmons of the teamsters, a close political ally of the administration, remained on the Pay Board.

One can only guess. Swollen with the euphoria of his landslide triumph, the president might simply have been indulging his own conservative instincts. Although the controls had been reasonably effective, they had served their purpose in allowing the stimulation of a preelection boom while preventing more rapid inflation. Like the president, Herbert Stein and other influential administration economists always disliked controls as interferences with free markets. The conservative economists who had reluctantly but loyally designed and administered the freeze and Phase II now got their reward.

Gratitude may have reinforced ideology. As the boom gathered momentum, Phase II controls began to annoy large corporations whose profits soon seemed likely to exceed the best-two-out-of-three-year standard. Proud to lead a business administration, Mr. Nixon had ample reason to be grateful to the corporate paymasters who sometimes beyond the limits of law had financed his electoral sweep.

The joy conveyed by this dash to freedom was unfortunately limited to economists, ideologues, corporative executives, and stockholders. As the stock market plummeted, the Dow Jones averages daily registered investor fears that renewed inflation would soon result and carry in its train another savage credit squeeze and a new recession. Corporate behavior gave daily support to these apprehensions, for major companies promptly interpreted Phase III as full of sound and fury, signifying nothing. Accordingly they jostled each other in the rush to post new and higher prices. A new run on American currency, led by American multinational firms, international banks, and the oil sheiks of the Middle East, soon compelled Washington to devalue the dollar for the second time in fourteen months.

Nothing went well. The bills for détente began to come in. The impact of massive grain sales to the Russians in 1972 caused bread and meat prices to soar. Rich from their booming export sales of cars, cameras, appliances, and textiles, the carnivorous Japanese were widely suspected of collaring the supply of high-grade American beef. It helped not at all that the administration pointed out as a silver lining that the Japanese left behind more of the cheaper cuts which they had been in the habit of buying when they were poorer.

The politics of food were domestic as well as international. Ever the commercial farmer's champion, Agriculture Secretary Earl Butz refused to remove acreage restrictions on plantings until 1973. Bad weather, the politics of détente, 1972 election maneuvers, escalating world demand for American farm products, and Washington preference for Republican farmers over urban Democratic consumers, all spelled the end of cheap food on the American table. Nonfood prices promptly joined the parade and industrial materials began to climb at 12 percent annual rates. An impending energy crisis (months before the Yom Kippur war!) and the complaints of businessmen persuaded the president to postpone application of the antipollution standards set by the Clean Air Act.

In the spring of 1973, six or eight months before the OPEC oil embargo gave its fillip to world inflation, no one in his right mind could seriously have argued that prices were behaving acceptably.

The farce of the first Nixon administration which had featured one economic guru after another had culminated in the staged recovery from the 1969–70 recession. Along with television spectaculars in the Kremlin and at the Great

Wall of China, the dedicated activities of CREEP, and the misfortunes of the McGovern campaign, the 1972 economic boom had done its bit to keep Richard Nixon in the White House.

In October 1973 the world changed.

Until then, American inflation could be analyzed, as I have just treated it, as an affair of domestic politics and corporate policy. The Vietnam war generated an inflationary degree of excess demand because Lyndon Johnson refused to seek the taxes needed to pay for the bombs and soldiers that he ordered into the conflict. The market power of concentrated industries and the minimum fee schedules of lawyers and escalating charges by doctors and hospitals, contributed to the inflationary pressures. Although international trading relationships and the growing competition in world markets of West Germans and Japanese rivals increasingly influenced American policy, one could reasonably have argued that for the most part Americans had the power to correct domestic unemployment and domestic inflation.

I have earlier argued that this condition was changing as American energy sources diminished and American energy demands rapidly continued to rise. October 1973 accelerated these changes and made them spectacularly visible to every motorist waiting in long lines to get his small ration of gasoline. When OPEC proved that it could administer an effective embargo and make a 400 percent hike in the price of crude petroleum stick, inflation became an international phenomenon and politics took an abrupt turn in this country and elsewhere.

The new politics of scarcity, enacted upon a global stage, enormously complicate economic management even in the absence of immediate electoral considerations. This reordered universe is one of rapidly shifting landmarks, not least in our notions of which countries are rich, which not so rich, and which poor. It is a sign of new times that Kuwait is the richest nation on the globe: few people, lots of oil. For Americans, born into a vision of abundance, the hardest reorientation involves realization that lavishness in the use of inexhaustible resources is a luxury of the past.

Americans feel poorer than they used to be. They *are* poorer even if they still have their jobs. Vast transfers of resources, most of them unfavorable to most Americans, have been taking place. The most obvious is the extra $25 billion paid to OPEC. These billions are a genuine subtraction from the goods and services available to Americans. When the Shah of Iran buys a large piece of Pan Am, dividends in the future will flow to him rather than American stockholders. The billions of dollars of military hardware we are selling to Iran, Saudi Arabia, and other Persian Gulf oil polities use labor and raw materials which otherwise would be available to make consumer goods for the home folks. Twenty-five billion dollars worth of lost resources represent a substantial fraction of the growth dividend which in good times permits steady improvement in living standards.

Resources are also being shifted from most Americans to a very few of their fellow citizens. Stockholders in the energy companies, handling coal as well as oil, are reaping profit windfalls from the higher prices paid by homeowners for heating fuel and motorists for gasoline. Urban consumers pay a third toll to farmers and food processors whose prices have been driven up by famines in Southeast Asia, the Sahel, and elsewhere.

Matters are likely to get worse. Other raw-material-producing countries are inevitably trying to emulate OPEC. It remains to be seen how successful they will be. Much depends on the importance of the commodity, the availability of substitutes, and the political cohesion of the producers. Among them Bolivia, Thailand, Indonesia, and Malaysia export four-fifths of the world's tin. Four other poor countries, Surinam, Guinea, Jamaica, and Guyana, mine a third of the globe's bauxite. Timber supplies are concentrated in a relatively small number of nations. Cartel possibilities exist also for copper, coffee, tea, uranium, and other metals.

Americans are unlikely in the knowable future to starve or even face serious decline in material standards of life. The cartels, actual or potential, may dissolve or never materialize. Science and technology, in the nick of time, may provide inexpensive substitutes for oil and other raw materials. But on present evidence, it is more likely that long-run growth in the American economy will decline. If it does, there will be no way to simultaneously meet the expectations of the public for general improvement in their real income. When real growth is zero or even 1 or 2 percent, arithmetic does not allow wages and profits to rise by 5 percent.

Economists, like the public at large, must come to grips with the politics and economics of redistribution. The only alternatives to conscious choice by democratic process of groups to be rewarded and others to be denied is galloping inflation* or deep depression. Either is likely to dissolve the flimsy bonds which keep groups with disparate interests at peace with each other in a single political community.

The Ford administration appears to prefer depression to inflation. Such seems to be the persistent message of Treasury Secretary William Simon. Fretting early in 1975 about deficits and inflation, Mr. Simon told the House Ways and Means Committee that we didn't dare do too much about unemployment and recession. He put it this way:

There is no way to escape the basic dilemma presented by large government deficits. On the one hand, if the deficits cause a significant increase in the money supply, we shall have further inflation. On the other hand, if deficits are not permitted to increase the money supply, we must be prepared to endure tight credit and high interest rates.

What to do?

This is a very difficult circle to break. The only solution is to take a long-term view and resist the temptation to deal with each painful aspect of the cure as a crisis to be solved by short-term remedies, i.e., by more deficits.[16]

Even for an administration less hidebound than the Ford White House, the politics of redistribution are exceedingly

---

* The condition of England, where in mid-1975 inflation was running at 36 percent annual rates and economic growth was zero, reflects an inability of Englishmen to agree upon the proper distribution of a static national product. As all groups grab for more real income, prices rise, everybody is disappointed, and even larger new demands are made.

difficult for democratic communities to handle. As the British economist Rudolf Klein has well explained its intractability,

Immediately the competition for resources becomes a zero-sum game. One man's prize is another man's loss. If the blacks want to improve their share of desirable goods, it can only be at the expense of whites. If the over-65's are to be given higher pensions, or improved medical services, it can only be at the expense of the working population or the young.

If this is the inevitable reaction of a market economy to zero or slow growth, then Klein is right to fear that

It would seem only too likely that the haves would man the barricades to defend their share of resources, against the have-nots. The politics of compromise would be replaced by the politics of revolution, because the have-nots would be forced to challenge the whole basis of society, and its distribution of wealth and power.[17]

Democratic societies have engaged in successful redistributions during major wars. It remains to be seen whether traditional processes of debate and compromise can handle a permanent requirement for lowered expectations.

Klein's reliance upon renewed growth may be justified by the probable disastrous consequences of its alternative. Pessimists like Robert Heilbroner who are convinced that population pressure and resource limitation make renewed growth highly unlikely may be equally correct in their speculation that only authoritarian governments are capable of making hard choices of benefits for some and none for others.[18] Return to "normality" if the word is construed to mean 1945–72 economic and political relationships is implausible. Green Revolution or no, food supplies expand more slowly than the number of mouths craving food. In 1974 the world cereal crop declined, but the world's population increased by eighty million. India, a few years ago on the brink of food self-sufficiency, now teeters on the edge of mass starvation. Climatologists warn of long-run weather shifts adverse to food production. Overfishing has diminished the potentiality of the oceans as a protein source. Miscellaneous environmental hazards: pollution, damage to the ozone barrier, and lowering of water tables among others, threaten, to an extent not yet thoroughly understood by the experts, the future of the human race.

The news is not entirely bad, but the good news is insufficient. New oil is being discovered in the North Sea, the South China Sea, Mexico, the Aegean, and elsewhere but it is expensive to extract. There are several promising energy substitutes available but they are either technologically speculative (solar, geothermal), potentially unsafe (nuclear), or environmentally destructive (oil from shale). It is hard logically to escape the conclusion that energy in the future will be so expensive that growth will be severely curtailed.

As with energy, so with food. Meat, sold on a world market, will stay expensive for American consumers. If we refuse to sell our meat to foreigners, we shall lose the raw materials and other goods for which we now trade our grain, broilers, soybeans, and meat. Like other industrial societies, the United States has prospered on cheap food and cheap energy. If standards of life are defined by abundant red meat, two or more cars per family, and a plenitude of energy-extravagant home appliances, then the prospects for maintaining even existing standards are exceedingly glum.

2

unemployment and poverty

Tens of thousands of black and Puerto Rican teen-agers in New York City are "piling up at the bottom" of the recession. With no jobs and no prospects of jobs, they are abandoning their dream of education, and their belief in the other institutions of a civilized society, and are slipping back toward the drugs and hustling of the "street."

—The New York Times
May 19, 1975

By the standards of other advanced societies, unemployment in the United States is routinely disgracefully high. The percentage of poor people is again larger than Scandinavians, Western Europeans, Japanese, or Australians are prepared to accept. The United States still lacks a universal

39

health-care system. Most of the countries of the world, rich or poor, capitalist or socialist, provide some form of children's allowances. Not the United States.

The United States remains, despite the buffets of recent years, an exceedingly rich community. Yet it allows large numbers of adults and teenagers to drift along unhappily without useful work or hope of finding it. Even greater numbers of men and women have been sentenced to ill-paid, uncertain, and menial jobs for life. As Gunnar Myrdal has noted, we maintain a permanent underclass of unassimilated people—a social situation usually considered typical of a developing rather than a developed nation.

It is not that there is a scarcity of useful work to be done. As long ago as 1964, President Johnson's Automation Commission estimated that five million jobs were unfilled in police, fire, sanitation, and park departments as well as schools, hospitals, museums, and libraries for want of funds. In 1975 no New York pedestrian or park bicyclist was likely to question the desirability of increased police protection. Few veterans of hospital care fail to regret the shortage of tender loving care from harried nurses and orderlies. Patrons of public libraries yearn for longer hours of service. Museums could serve a much larger public by staying open in the evening if they could afford to hire more guards and attendants. Concerts in parks, traveling art exhibits, and an array of more mundane but essential services which at their best make urban life safe, pleasant, and diversified all starve on budgets too small to support their activities.

A successful society weds idle men and women with useful and remunerative work. It offers cash grants without stigma to the minority who cannot work. In our country the same congressmen who routinely resist the funding of additional public jobs happily vote huge appropriations for weapons and highways and delightful tax benefits for large corporations and wealthy individuals.

It is well within our national resources to totally eliminate poverty as it is financially measured by Washington.* No doubt poverty is more than a mere shortage of money. But it could hardly hurt the poor to get a subsidy of cash. Before the 1974–75 mini-depression, all financial poverty could have been eliminated at the price of a modest shift of $10–15 billion to the poor from the rest of the community. Fifteen billion is less than 1.5 percent of the gross national product, about the size of one of the cheaper weapons systems after cost overruns. Of course the elimination of poverty would actually cost more than $15 billion because we would have to offer the hard-working families just above the poverty line smaller grants to keep them ahead of the poor. What's wrong with that? If families earning between $6,000 and $9,000 also got supplementary cash grants, so much the better. A modest degree of income redistribution would still leave plenty of inequality.

The creation of new public jobs would make the conservatives happy, since many people would then be taken off welfare rolls and placed on payrolls. For the unemployable, such a simple and dignified device as a negative income tax would use efficient agencies like the Internal Revenue Service or the Social Security Administration to mail checks to qualified individuals. No red tape. No home visits by case-

---

* By mid-1975 the official poverty line for families of four was approaching $6,000.

workers.* A community which can at tolerable expense eliminate human distress but refrains from doing so must either believe that it benefits from unemployment and poverty, or that the poor and unemployed are bad people, or that other more important values will be impaired by attempts to help the lower orders—or all of these statements.

In fact, as Herbert Gans has eloquently argued,[1] poverty serves numerous functions† for the nonpoor. The poor do the community's dirty work. The poor lighten the tax burdens of the affluent by paying higher percentages of their meager earnings to the revenue agents than their financial betters.‡

Policemen, social workers, criminologists, prison guards, and parole officers, as well as numbers racketeers, faith healers, pawn-shop proprietors, loan sharks, religious prophets, and drug merchants, live on the poor. So do the sellers of schlock furniture, credit jewelry, tainted canned goods, and wilted vegetables. Who save for slum dwellers will buy low-quality merchandise previously rejected by middle-class customers?

This is not the end of the benefits which the poor confer

---

* An NIT is defined by a cash grant, an offsetting tax on earnings, and the break-even point beyond which benefits vanish generated by the grant and the tax. Thus a thousand-dollar-per-person grant and a 50 percent tax on earnings would confer benefits on a family of four up to earned income of $8,000. At that point the grant would be reduced to zero.

† Gans cites Robert Merton's definition of socially functional behavior as "those observed consequences which make for the adaptation or adjustment of a given system."

‡ Benjamin Okner and Joseph Pechman concluded in their valuable Brookings study, *Who Bears the Tax Burden?*, that the poor and the *very* rich pay higher percentages of their incomes in taxes than the remainder of the taxpayers.

upon the rest of us. The indolence, dishonesty, and promiscuity traditionally imputed to economic inferiors make the prosperous feel better about their comforts and luxuries. When the rich contemplate the poor, they can cope more readily with their own deficiencies of intelligence and temperament. Because the poor are politically infirm, they, in Gans' words, can "conveniently absorb the political economic and political costs of change and growth." Urban renewal projects do not rearrange Sutton Place. Superhighways spare Scarsdale. Lincoln Center's multimillion-dollar salute to the arts displaced no luxury apartment buildings and no elegant restaurants or boutiques. When scapegoats are in season, which is most of the time, the poor are convenient targets.

It is well to be honest. The quiet, usually unstated case against full employment in the United States is entwined with residual racism and vigorous class prejudice. Respectable middle-class souls tend too often to believe that fear of destitution alone is the spur to the industry of blacks, Hispanics, and lower-class whites. As Senator Russell Long plaintively inquired during the congressional debate over Nixon's Family Assistance Plan, who will launder his shirts once incomes and opportunities rise in Louisiana and the rest of the South? Who will clean middle-class homes and apartments, wash the restaurant dishes, mop the floors, and tidy the hotel rooms?

Quite apart from menial labor, much work is unsatisfying. Even in the reputable white-collar offices of banks, life insurance companies, brokerage houses, and government—much dull typing and filing is done. Without fear of unemployment and loss of status and income, who would assemble cars, lipsticks, pens, transistors, and calculators on endless assembly lines? When Lordstowns erupt at 5 percent rates of unemployment, what will happen when unemployment drops toward 1 or 2 percent.

I have put the matter unscientifically. For the moment, let me speak like an economist. For my profession, the issue is the solemn one of work incentive. If our society guaranteed for each of its mature citizens either a job or an income, at the very least bad jobs would go begging and better ones might be filled only at wage rates which exceeded (at stable prices) the productivity of labor. In such a community, the balance of power would tilt permanently in favor of organized (and unorganized) employees.

This economic perception is formalized, possibly immortalized in the statistical relationship expressed in the Phillips curve* between wage hikes and unemployment. Phillips argued quite simply that the more unemployment diminishes, the more rapidly wage rates normally increase. Low rates of wage improvement were correspondingly associated with higher percentages of unemployment. This statistical conclusion summarized a number of labor market realities. Unions seek larger contract gains more militantly as employers bid for increasingly scarce new employees. In such tight labor markets, the new employees are likely to be lower in quality than old ones. When jobs are plentiful, absenteeism rises and discipline on the job flags. There is no need to stand for the abuse of an abrasive foreman when a short walk down the street takes one to another employer. When overtime is plentiful and hourly wage rates are going

---

* Named after the English economist A. W. Phillips, who correlated over time English wage and unemployment movements.

up, why not start the weekend Thursday afternoon and finish it Tuesday morning?

It was an easy analytical step from Phillips' wage-unemployment correlations to a price-unemployment connection, if what happened to wages soon translated itself into price movements in the same direction. If, as Paul Samuelson has explained these relationships, "large corporations who bargain with unions have been able to pass on the wage increases to the consumer and to pretty much maintain profit margins," then the impact of falling unemployment is "initially to increase wage rates faster than the rise of worker efficiency and very soon afterwards to increase prices at a pace fast enough to compensate corporate sellers for their increased labor costs and maintain undiminished their accustomed rate of earnings."[2]

Some countries have better Phillips curves than others. Either because their unions are mild or their labor forces are relatively homogeneous, unemployment can drop to very low figures before inflation begins to threaten. Not in America. Whenever monetary and fiscal policy shove unemployment below 5 percent or so, the argument runs, high rates of inflation are likely to occur. It follows that if the only way to reduce unemployment to 4 percent (the old "interim" target of the Kennedy-Johnson economists) is to accept wage and price increases of 8 or 9 percent, an analyst must infer that the social cost of reducing unemployment by a single percentage point is likely to be a 2 or 3 percent jump in the cost of living.

There is at least a rough trade-off, accordingly, between unemployment and inflation. For reasons which will emerge in the next chapter, economists are not supposed to advise their compatriots which combination of inflation and unemployment is preferable to other available packages. People who detest inflation enough will accept quite a bit of unemployment, particularly the unemployment of other people. Those who are experiencing or fearing unemployment will no doubt attach more importance to jobs and less to the cost of groceries.

This superficially neutral stance leads to important consequences. When inflation is rapid, the Phillips curve encourages conservative politicians to redefine full employment, minimize the human and material costs of unemployment, and concentrate exclusively upon the repression of inflation. During 1973 and 1974, the Nixon administration put on precisely this sort of show. Thus, testifying before the Joint Economic Committee of Congress in late July 1974, Herbert Stein (in his last month as Council of Economic Advisers chairman) and Arthur F. Burns agreed that the economy needed to be cooled, monetary growth slowed, and an unemployment rate of 6 percent accepted by the end of the year.* The beleaguered president, days away from his resignation under threat of impeachment, came out for The New Steadiness, as *The New York Times'* Leonard Silk dubbed reiterated reliance on monetary policy, mild appeals to corporations and unions to behave themselves, and nomination as Stein's successor of Alan Greenspan, a conservative business economist celebrated for his admiration of Ayn Rand. Mr. Nixon advocated "the kind of

---

* It was actually 7.2 percent and rising about half a percentage point a month, or nearly half a million new members of the army of the unemployed every thirty days.

steadiness that rejects gimmickry and that gives the enormous creative forces of the marketplace a chance to work."

It helps to make a planned recession politically tolerable if the significance of unemployment is minimized. One way to do so is to focus upon the majority who are still at work. As Herbert Stein once more asserted in severe criticism of the media's handling of economic news, "when the unemployment rate hits 7 percent . . . they do not show or describe seven jobless people and 93 people who are still working—that would be showing an excessive regard for the truth; they focus on the lines of unemployment at the unemployment insurance office."*

The unemployed minority can be shown by the inflation warriors to be somehow less important as individuals than the remainder of the labor force. Unemployment rates are invariably lowest among male heads of families and highest among blacks, women, and teenagers. Well, isn't the first category *most* important and the second category necessarily *less* important? Teenagers are notoriously restless at the best of times. They are between jobs a large part of the time even in prosperous periods. They have no family responsibilities. Women are often second wage earners whose income is marginal to the welfare of their families. Too bad no doubt that they can't find work but infinitely less painful than the unemployment of the prime male earners.†

---

* *New Society*, 24 April 1975, p. 192. Stein's predecessors during the 1930s probably consoled themselves with the thought that, after all, three out of every four workers still had some kind of job.

† Conservatives frequently blame minimum-wage statutes for much of the unemployment among the young, who, it is said, are not worth $2.50 an hour.

Partisans of the Phillips curve do offer a trifle more hope for superior combinations of stable prices and high employment to develop in the long run. As the labor force improves its education and raises the level of its marketable skills, the inflationary impact of hiring the final 1, or 2, or 3 percent of the unemployed is much reduced because the productivity gap between new and old employees is narrowed. Insofar as new jobs are generated in the public sector and responsibly financed by taxes, the inflationary impact is moderated. A Swedish model may lie in the American future. In Scandinavian society, the Phillips curve is benign because the Swedes, the Danes, and the Norwegians have fully integrated nearly every person into a single, skilled labor force. Sophisticated manpower-training programs keep worker skills abreast of changing technology and altered patterns of demand for goods and services.

The United States in the 1970s is obviously no Sweden writ large. Despite civil-rights statutes, affirmative action, and stern judicial edicts, we have done a poor job of educating and training blacks and other minorities. In the present state of affairs, our underclass of the sketchily schooled, unskilled, and poorly disciplined can be employed only at a cost in wage and price inflation which the community at large considers exorbitant. Until and unless we shrink this underclass, we must accept relatively high unemployment or relatively high inflation.

It is one thing to criticize displeasing ideas and another to disprove them. There is after all the possibility that the Phillips curve is a valid generalization, descriptive of the experience of mixed economies in the twentieth century.

One way of evaluating a statistical proposition is to see whether recent statistics support or contradict it. Here are some unemployment and consumer price figures for the same years.[3]

	Unemployment Rate	Consumer Prices (1967 = 100)
1960	5.5	88.7
1965	4.5	94.5
1968	3.6	104.2
1971	5.9	121.3
1972	5.6	125.3

Up to a point, the numbers appear to buttress the Phillips curve association of inflation and unemployment. Between 1960 and 1968 unemployment declined and prices rose, even if until mid-1965 and Vietnam escalation, price inflation never exceeded an annual 1 or 2 percent.

After 1968, however, Phillips advocates travel a rockier path. The new Nixon administration took inflation seriously enough to generate a small recession in 1969 and 1970. Indeed, unemployment stayed high in both 1971 and 1972 after the economy had officially emerged from the recession. Nevertheless, the consumer price index ascended over seventeen points between 1968 and 1971 and another four points in 1973 in spite of Phase I and Phase II controls. This annual rise in excess of five points is substantially larger than the price increases which occurred between 1965 and 1968 when unemployment was falling instead of rising and the Johnson administration was busy increasing its military expenditures in southeast Asia.

Nonetheless, with a little ingenuity, an expert can patch up almost any cherished doctrine. Economists choose from a whole menu of supplementary inflationary phenomena. Dollar devaluation enlarged foreign demand for American manufactures and farm products, drove their prices up, and created unexpected shortages in soybeans, chemical fertilizers, and other products. The coincidence of boom times simultaneously in Western Europe, Japan, and, after 1970, in this country, added to inflationary pressure. Politics and bad luck played important roles. A presidential election that featured the exigencies of détente encouraged massive wheat sales to the Russians in 1972 at concessionary prices. American food prices went up as a consequence, but the Russians had negotiated the deal to begin with because their own harvest had failed. As another item of bad fortune, the anchovies temporarily disappeared from the Peruvian coast. Since their destiny was to turn into fish meal fed to cattle, animal growers were driven to purchase soybeans as a substitute with predictable impact upon soybean prices. The October 1973 Middle Eastern war offered OPEC a splendid opportunity which was not neglected to quadruple the price of crude petroleum.

Although specialists enjoy quarreling about the comparative importance of these serious phenomena, it is hard to doubt that the inflation of the 1970s was stimulated by a malign combination of politics, business-cycle coincidence, and sheer bad luck. To say this diminishes rather than increases the practical significance of the Phillips curve trade-off. It is evident that supply shortages, dislocations of the mechanisms of international trade, shifts in power relationships between raw-material-producing and raw-material-importing countries, and random events affected global inflation far more than a universalized trade-off between inflation and unemployment.

Even if in more "normal" times, this trade-off is the centerpiece of macroeconomic policy, one must ask whether there is any reason to anticipate a spell of economic calm which will not be swamped by Middle Eastern (or middle western) politics, localized recession, international crop failures, or other large events. It is a safe axion to expect the unexpected.

There is every sensible reason then to discard Phillips curve trade-offs as explanatory of the alternations between inflation and unemployment or, as in recent years, the combination of the two states. However, as those familiar with academic mores will not need to be reminded, commonsense dismissal of treasured theoretical propositions is profoundly unsatisfactory to those who live by abstraction. As Thomas Kuhn has persuasively argued in *The Structure of Scientific Revolutions*,[4] old paradigms stubbornly swim in a sea of inconsistent phenomena until a new and better generalization wins the day. "Normal" science is performed by "men whose research is based on shared paradigms." They are committed to the "same rules and standards for scientific practice."[5] Above all they seldom disagree about fundamental assumptions, values, and methods of inquiry.

Hence it bears emphasis to say that between 1968 and 1973 the Phillips curve hypothesis received as fair a test as the imperfect politics of parliamentary democracy are ever likely to allow. By that test it ignominiously failed. During the Nixon administration, the price of rising unemployment was paid (according to tradition by those least able to afford it), but the boon of price stability was not forthcoming. When in August 1971, Mr. Nixon dramatically turned to wage and price controls, it was because the second term of the trade-off between unemployment and inflation was in

political currency too expensive and too uncertain to purchase, even if (as I speculated earlier) continued recession
in time would have broken the inflationary spiral.

Karl Popper has written that a proposition that is truly
scientific is susceptible to falsification by the test of failed
experiment. All economic experiments of necessity take
place within a political context. Insofar as economics is a
science and the Phillips curve is a scientific statement, it follows that rising unemployment (on a politically tolerable
scale) ought to be accompanied by slowing inflation (in an
electorally acceptable span of time). Even if the Phillips
trade-off were intellectually more persuasive than I find it,
the protracted combination of unemployment and inflation
in both 1969–71 and again in 1974–75 would rule it out of
practical consideration by politicians eager for reelection.

The persistent popularity of the Phillips curve in the
writings of mainstream economists attests to their tendency
to operate within narrow assumptions of reality. What has
been happening recently is quite likely to unduly influence
economists' notions of permanent reality, as in definitions of
the minimal, frictional unemployment which a free society
will encounter as the consequence of illness, accident, sea-
sonal layoff, and voluntary changes of job. The early editions of Samuelson's *Economics*, for example, defined the
minimum unemployment to be expected even at "full employment" as between 2 ½ and 3 percent. More recent editions allude cautiously to 4 percent or higher allowances at
full employment for the frictionally idle. Unemployment
as registered by the government statisticians ran higher in
the late 1950s and early 1960s than it did during the late
1940s and early 1950s.

The Second World War demonstrated memorably the

capacity of the American economy during an emergency to find productive work for pensioners, students, housewives, and men and women of irregular work habits. So many people were drawn into the labor force who usually were not counted in it, that unemployment may actually have been negative during 1944 and 1945. After VE Day the recent past influenced economists' definitions of full employment. The less happy employment scene during most of the 1950s modified these definitions. Alarmed about inflation, President Eisenhower cut federal budgets and tightened federal reserve credit (with the enthusiastic cooperation of the Federal Reserve Board) to such effect that three recessions marked his eight years of office. During this prolonged spell of sluggish growth, unemployment averaged over 5 percent. The notion spread among some economists that much of this unemployment was "structural" in nature, related either to the personal characteristics of the jobless or the places in which they sought employment. The structurally unemployed included bypassed men and women in Appalachia, northern Michigan, the Ozarks, and Maine. When the forests are ravaged and the mines exhausted, the economic base simply crumbles. Coal miners, lacking any other marketable skill and deeply attached to their familiar closed communities, may settle into permanent unemployment.*

Structural unemployment in the black community, it was argued, resulted from the poorer training, sketchier education, and inferior job discipline imputable to black workers. Possibly, as a number of labor market experts speculated,

---

* OPEC, which has revived the American coal industry, may have rescued some of the miners from idleness. It also appears to have created a number of new coal millionaires.

there is a dual labor market. In the better of the two markets in which most people operate, employment is regular, workers possess skills in high repute among employers, and union agreements, civil-service regulations, or informal institutional custom afford some degree of guaranteed tenure or, at the least, promise of recall after spells of layoff. In the second labor market jobs are casual and unpleasant, the qualifications of the workers sketchy, the prospects of advancement nil, and the traditional incidence of unemployment exceedingly high. Such is the universe of dishwashers and countermen, migrant farm laborers, ditch diggers, and car washers. John Coleman has described what life is like for men on garbage trucks and in hot restaurant kitchens in his *Blue Collar Journal.** Here today and laid-off tomorrow.

Dual labor market theorists deny that unemployment in casual labor markets is the result of deficient aggregate demand. It is the consequence of a lack of fit between available jobs and individuals qualified to meet their requirements. During the 1950s and early 1960s, job training was the therapy of choice for men and women in the secondary labor market, the medication that might lift them into the secure universe of the primary work force.

Stop a moment and consider what this hypothesis implies. The message is one of adaptation to labor markets as they

---

* (New York: W. W. Norton & Company, 1974). Coleman, a labor economist of repute, took an unusual sabbatical from his dignified position as president of Haverford College to enter for a few months the universe of the ill-paid and the unskilled. Elliott Liebow's classic *Tally's Corner* (Boston: Little, Brown and Company, 1967) evokes another segment of this market. His Washington, D.C. company of ghetto blacks do work from time to time, but their spells of idleness are far more frequent and lengthy than those suffered by members of the primary labor market.

are currently defined by private employers, who set the educational and skill requirements for job entry. Oddly enough it took that profoundly conservative institution, the Supreme Court of the United States, to challenge some of these assumptions. In its landmark decision in *Griggs* v. *Duke Power Company* (1971), the Court demanded that employers demonstrate that tests or educational credentials actually relate to the requirements of a job. In Chief Justice Warren Burger's words, "The facts of this case demonstrate the inadequacy of broad and general testing devices as well as the infirmity of using diplomas or degrees as fixed measures of capability."[6] Economists, it appears, would have done well to help civil-rights lawyers press cases which evoked this sort of helpful judicial response, rather than help design training programs unrelated to job needs.

Job training tends to reinforce the status quo, as do many other economic remedies. So also does automatic acceptance by Samuelson and others of the proposition that the wage-employment trade-off necessarily translates itself into a price-employment trade-off. As Samuelson noted, this is the result of the market control which large corporations exercise over prices and profits. Of all people why should economists, devoted by ideology to the virtues of unfettered competition, accept the existence, pervasiveness, and durability of price-setting power by a small number of influential corporations? The existence of this degree of market power ought to suggest very strongly indeed that resources are poorly allocated, less as the result of market signals and more as the effect of quasi-political power.

Market concentration extracts monopoly profit from the unorganized customers. Present levels of profit contain as a routine feature an element of stockholder reward which free markets would not generate. Hence, by their own criteria, economists ought not to sanction this profit by casually accepting corporate pass-throughs of higher wages to prices paid by customers. Moreover, insofar as economists reinforce their traditional dislike of monopoly profit by an ethical preference for a diminished inequality of income, they should consider the merits of absorption by corporate stockholders and managers of some of the additional wage cost. Who knows, such a requirement might become an actual stimulus to managerial efficiency.

Even moderate egalitarians might view suspiciously this "automatic" translation of higher wages into higher prices. If antitrust is excluded as a politically feasible response, there remain as alternative responses to potential inflation profit-margin controls on large corporations,* price ceilings which limit wage pass-through, or progressive corporate tax rates. Any one of these devices would wholesomely moderate corporate lust for ever higher profit.

For the time being, enough has been said about why economists operate as inveterate institutional conservatives. Taking for granted everything from the two-party system to corporate concentration of control, division between private and public activity, current profit margins, employer definition of job qualification, and the sanctity of existing distributions of income and wealth, they almost inevitably ratify the doctrine of trade-off between unemployment and inflation. Out of professional bias rather than

---

* In their valuable *Roots of Inflation* (New York: Burt Franklin, 1975) Gardiner Means and John Blair argue, with a good deal of evidence, that pursuit of profit targets by large corporations during recessions results in even larger price increases in industries dominated by one or two enterprises than those which occur in more prosperous times.

(in most instances) personal inclination, the profession gives undeserved aid and comfort to conservative politicians and industrialists privately happy at the chance to tighten labor discipline and tame unions with the club of recession. Economists impose upon the unemployed the burden of preparing themselves better for job markets as defined by potential employers. A most respectable guild, economists accept the major features of an economy which has rewarded them quite amply.

What if economists became really concerned about unemployment, poverty, and inequality? They might begin by concentrating less on growth in gross national product and more on the distribution of that product among rich, middling, and poor. They might appropriately continue with the perception that sometimes deliberately, often inadvertently or incidentally, and occasionally perversely, legislative and executive actions significantly shape the distribution of income and wealth. Taxes, subsidies, special benefits for shipbuilders, building developers, mineral extractors, cattle grazers, and farmers, public-welfare eligibility standards, awards by regulatory agencies of television channels, airline routes, and radio frequencies, and affirmative-action employment plans negotiated by corporations, universities, and government agencies, are among a large family of interventions into the flow of income and wealth.

Poverty may be partly the fault of the poor. But it must also have something to do with the circumstance that the richest Americans, 1 percent of the total population, own more than eight times the assets of the bottom 50 percent. Wealth notoriously confers political clout and the capacity to use that clout to enlist the authorities in the protection and enlargement of the owners' position in the world. Despite wars, a New Deal, a Fair Deal, a New Frontier, a Great Society, and a New American Revolution; despite civil-rights statutes and women's liberation, the distribution of income, wealth, and power has been remarkably impervious to change. The marks of this stability are plainly visible in routine political events.

In the summer of 1974 attentive readers of *The New York Times* would have learned that the president firmly opposed higher taxes on oil profits and favored relaxation of environmental and job safety standards. The president signed into law a loan guarantee measure for cattlemen who had mistakenly gambled on a perpetually rising beef market. Earlier in the year Mr. Nixon and Congress jointly provided compensation to chicken growers who had been compelled to destroy millions of chicks fed on carcinogenic substances. Most of these "farmers" turned out to be huge food corporations. In July the House Ways and Means Committee tentatively reduced applicable taxes on dividends and interests from a maximum of 70 percent to 50 percent. In June the Department of Agriculture purchased much of the Florida navel orange crop to support prices and in the same month for the same reason it bought huge quantities of hamburger. Anyone who cares can readily draw up for himself a current list of actions taken to assist the strong and relieve the unneedy.

In 1810 an early economist named Robert Gallman estimated that the top 1 percent of American families owned 21 percent of the nation's wealth. In 1915 the U.S. Commission on Industrial Relations reported that the top 2 percent of income recipients owned 35 percent of our country's assets. In 1962 according to still another economist, M.I.T.'s Lester Thurow, 25.8 percent of family wealth was in the possession of the top 5 percent.[7]

Income is also distributed unequally. The record for recent years is pretty much summarized in the following table.[8]

PERCENTAGE OF AGGREGATE MONEY INCOME RECEIVED
BY EACH FIFTH OF FAMILIES AND INDIVIDUALS
1962–71, BEFORE TAXES

Families ranked from lowest to highest	1962	1964	1966	1968	1970	1971
Total	100%	100%	100%	100%	100%	100%
Lowest fifth	5.1	5.2	5.5	5.7	5.5	5.5
Second fifth	12.0	12.0	12.4	12.4	12.0	11.9
Third fifth	17.5	17.7	17.7	17.7	17.4	17.4
Fourth fifth	23.7	24.0	23.7	23.7	23.5	23.7
Fifth fifth	41.7	41.1	40.7	40.6	41.6	41.6
Top 5%	16.3	15.7	14.8	14.0	14.4	N.A.

Between 1962 and 1968 the meager rewards of the lowest fifth improved for two reasons. The first was generally low unemployment. A second influence was the array of antipoverty legislation enacted in late 1964, 1965, and early 1966 before Vietnam halted further social progress. After 1968, the recession of 1969 and 1970, the antiurban bias of the Nixon administration, and the reduced funding of antipoverty initiatives combined to reverse the small progress of the early and middle sixties toward diminished inequality.

The beneficiaries of gross maldistribution naturally resist alteration of arrangements so comfortable to their interests. Nevertheless, as the Kennedy-Johnson era demonstrated, moderate redistribution is possible in favoring political circumstances. If, after Ernest Hemingway, the difference between rich and poor is purely financial, the most efficacious way to eliminate poverty* in a rich society is to take money away from citizens who have a lot and give it to those who have nothing or very little. If the community doesn't trust the poor with cash, it can offer food, medical care, housing, fuel, and transportation at reduced or zero cost. Over the years, the United States has authorized a considerable volume of these specific benefits, albeit in piecemeal, poorly articulated fashion. Food stamps are related to family size and income. Senior citizens, a large percentage of whom are poor, are in some cities and states allowed to ride the buses and subways at half fare. Medicare and medicaid reduce medical expenses for the elderly and the poor. On a sporadic basis, public housing reduces the rents of some members of the lowest fifth.

Of these noncash crutches for the impoverished, several judgments are in order. Veterans' benefits, social security, and medicare are respectable because large numbers of middle-class Americans have served in the armed forces, and even the young expect one day to be old. But other measures—those perceived as operating only in the interests of the poor—arouse the political resistance which benefits to the socially disfavored naturally evoke. These services are usually underfunded and for this and other reasons low

---

* The official poverty line, computed on the basis of minimal nutritional costs and expenditures on other necessities, was in 1975 approaching $6,000 for a family of four. However, public-opinion research suggests that most people identify poverty with incomes less than half the national median. By this standard families of four earning less than $7,000 or so were judged poor.

in quality. In large cities such as New York, public hospitals invariably are judged inferior to voluntary hospitals. Under congressional pressure, public housing has been deliberately differentiated from middle-class apartments by such regulations as prohibition of pets and air conditioners, substitution of window shades for venetian blinds, lack of closet doors, and so on. Inadequate as often it is, public housing shelters less than 10 percent of the poor.

The substitution of free or cut-rate services for cash suffers from a second severe fault. It is a substitution of political or bureaucratic preferences for the beneficiary's own choice of the things he would like to buy. Conventional economic wisdom celebrates sovereign command by consumers over their spending because, as the tale goes, only the individual can divide limited sums of money among many objects of choice in such a way as to derive maximum psychic benefit. The rational consumer after all income is spent concludes that there was no better way to spend it.

Poor men and women share the psychology of the more prosperous. Insofar as welfare is hedged about with restraints upon the conduct of its beneficiaries, it inevitably damages this utility-maximizing process. Ultimately the United States will reach a political consensus on income maintenance and decide either to continue to stigmatize welfare clients or to treat the need for public support as a human misfortune akin to illness, accident, old age, or personal handicap.

It is here that two cherished values of conventional economics clash. Well-trained economists do believe in the virtues of individual choice, at least for all sane adults. On the other hand, they share in the communal emphasis upon individual striving motivated by hope of material reward, with the grace notes added by their professional obsession with efficient use and allocation of resources. The first value supports cash grants without strings. The second fuels the fear that the grants may damage incentives to seek work and income.

The political progress of the negative income tax and the character of professional debate upon its design are illustrations of both the power and the limitations of contemporary social science. In modern form, debate begins with Milton Friedman's 1962 proposal to substitute cash grants for welfare cash grants, food stamps, subsidized housing and medical care, and miscellaneous social services. Dr. Friedman, the vigorous and gifted leader of the Chicago school of free-market theorists, explained the merits of his plan in these words:

The advantages of this arrangement are clear. It is directed specifically at the problem of poverty. It gives help in the form most useful to the individual, namely, cash. It is general and could be substituted for the host of special measures now in effect. It makes explicit the cost borne by society. It operates outside the market. Like any other measure to alleviate poverty, it reduces the incentive of those helped to help themselves, but it does not eliminate that incentive entirely, as a system of supplementing incomes up to some fixed minimum would. An extra dollar earned always means more money available for expenditure.[9]

For the free-market enthusiast, the heart of the matter is the struggle to reconcile altruism with the precious structure of personal incentive to productive effort and the equally vital personal freedom to spend as one chooses. Would men and women work, particularly if the jobs bore them, in the presence of an adequate guarantee of income in idleness?* Such concerns guided Friedman to two critical elements of his scheme. Work incentives were to be preserved by making grants small, and individuals were to be always better off financially at work than in subsidized idleness. Hence for a 1962 family of four (when the official poverty line was $3,000) Friedman's proposed grant was $1,500 when no family member was working. Suppose a recipient found a part-time or low-paid job? Then the person would pay a tax of 50 percent on his earnings. A man or woman who found a $3,000 job would surrender the entire $1,500 benefit. A $2,000 job would cost that person $1,000, and so on. It would, nevertheless, be worthwhile to accept the $2,000 job because the individual would enjoy a total income of $2,500—earnings plus $500 in remaining grant—or $1,000 more than were available in total unemployment.

The principle of consumer sovereignty proved that beneficiaries of Friedman's plan would be better off than they would be if the same number of dollars were devoted to

---

* The evidence is limited, but such as it is, is probably startling to a good many people. Leonard Goodwin's *Do the Poor Want to Work?* (Washington, D.C.: Brookings Institution, 1972) concluded that the poor share the attitudes and aspirations of the community at large, but that they are less hopeful of success than the nonpoor: "The ways in which the poor do differ from the affluent can reasonably be attributed to their different experiences of success and failure in the world." (p. 118) Evaluation of the federally sponsored New Jersey income-maintenance experiment by Joseph Pechman and others (*Work Incentives and Income Guarantees: The New Jersey Negative Income Tax Experiment*, Washington, D.C.: Brookings Institution, 1975) reinforces this conclusion. Apparently, at least under the conditions of the experiment, poor persons will see positive values in paid work even when the extra financial rewards are relatively small.

their welfare partly as cash grant and partly as free services. Free-market devotees believe that anybody, rich or poor, is better pleased to consult and pay a social worker, a counselor, or doctor than to have such "benefits" conferred (or imposed) upon him or her at the discretion of experts whose interests are unavoidably split between the client's welfare and the preservation of their own status, professional position, and income.

For conservatives the appeal of this kind of negative income tax is in the abolition of a welfare system scorned as wasteful, corrupt, and damaging to its presumed beneficiaries. Public money can be saved, the poor helped, and the sphere of private choice widened.

Ideas have consequences. During the first year of his administration when Nixon's counselor Daniel P. Moynihan had persuaded him that Disraeli was a fine model, the president advanced as his first major domestic innovation a Family Assistance Plan intended to replace existing welfare arrangements. With variations, FAP was based on Friedmanite principles.* Benefit levels were modest, work incentives were strong, and presidential rhetoric persistently stressed payrolls as happy alternatives to welfare rolls. Mr. Nixon held high hopes for FAP:

The new family assistance system I propose . . . rests essentially on these three principles: equality of treatment across the nation, a work requirement, and a work incentive.

---

* Vee and Vincent Burke's *Nixon's Good Deed* (New York: Columbia University Press, 1974) is a useful chronicle of its legislative fortunes, written from the sympathetic standpoint that the title hints at.

Its benefits would go to the working poor, as well as the non-working; to families with dependent children headed by a father, as well as to those headed by a mother; and a basic Federal minimum would be provided, the same in every state.

For a family of four now on welfare, with no outside income, the basic Federal payment would be $1,600 a year.

... this foundation would be one on which the family itself could build. Outside earnings would be encouraged, not discouraged. The new worker would keep the first $60 of outside earnings with no reduction in his benefits; then beyond that, his benefits would be reduced by only fifty cents for each dollar earned.[10]

FAP grafted onto the original Friedman proposal work or training requirements which encompassed even the mothers of young children. To receive benefits a person had to accept a "suitable" job within reasonable reach or prescribed job training. Although mothers of preschool-age youngsters were exempted, they were encouraged to seek jobs or training just as soon as daycare facilities became available.

Sensitive as always to criticism from the political right, Mr. Nixon reassured his supporters that FAP was not to be confused with a guaranteed income, since work or training was mandatory for most of the proposed beneficiaries. He emphatically rejected any implication of income redistribution as a possible consequence of his proposal. His spokesmen promised that strong work incentives would result in steadily declining costs as the roster of those eligible for benefits declined.

FAP, which twice was enacted by the House of Representatives, failed each time in the Senate. Liberals criticized meager benefits and drastic work requirements. Civil libertarians took arms against the limitation of fair hearings before benefit curtailment. Conservatives exposed FAP's failure to mesh with existing schemes like food stamps. Unlike Friedman's plan, FAP left undisturbed medicaid, medicare, and other free or subsidized services.*

Inevitably, politics during a presidential election year conspired to seal FAP's fate. Before he became his party's nominee Senator George McGovern had rather casually embraced a negative income tax plan of his own. Since the president and his campaigning "surrogates" ridiculed this so-called demogrant with remarkable success, it seemed inadvisable for Mr. Nixon to remind the public that he was himself supporting a device which bore at least superficial resemblance to the despised McGovern "giveaway."

One recalls the catastrophes of the McGovern campaign only because they conveniently emphasize the difficulties which face economists of liberal political opinions when they strive to design versions of a negative income tax more generous to the poor. McGovern's demogrant was an income redistribution scheme which took from the top third and gave to the remaining two-thirds. As such, it belongs in the family of moderately or less moderately redistributive plans some economists have constructed.

Before saying more about it, it is worth examining a much more carefully worked out design. In 1966 James Tobin, the distinguished Yale economist, sketched a schedule of grant rates which, he estimated, would cost $12.5 billion—the approximate size of that year's poverty gap. Here is how the numbers went for a family of five:[11]

---

* Daniel P. Moynihan's *The Politics of a Guaranteed Income* (New York: Random House, 1973) is a lively, partisan account of FAP's misfortunes.

MARRIED COUPLE WITH THREE CHILDREN

(1) Family Income before Federal Tax Allowance	(2) Present Tax (—)	(3) Tax Schedule Income after Tax	(4) Tax Allowance (+)	(5) Proposed Schedule of Income after Tax or Allowance
$ 0	$ 0	$ 0	$2,000	$2,000
1,000	0	1,000	1,667	2,667
2,000	0	2,000	1,333	3,333
3,000	0	3,000	1,000	4,000
3,700	0	3,700	767	4,467
4,000	— 42	3,958	667	4,667
5,000	— 185	4,815	333	5,333
6,000	— 338	5,662	0	6,000
7,000	— 501	6,449	— 333	6,667
7,963*	— 654	7,309	— 654	7,309
8,000	— 659	7,342	— 658	7,343

* As comparison of columns 3 and 5 will reveal, up to $7,963 families benefit either from grants or reduced tax payments. Above this breaking point, everybody is in the same tax situation.

Although notably more generous than FAP or Friedman's original model, Tobin left families with zero earned income well below the poverty line. Moreover, benefits depended very much indeed on geography. In New York, Massachusetts, New Jersey and other comparatively humane states, welfare grants exceeded those envisaged by Tobin. All the same, this meticulous design, by helping both the fully employed but poorly paid and the jobless, would have had the effect of lightening tax burdens on the families in the first category. In 1966 a family earning $7,000, a moderate income at the price levels of the period, would pay $501 at 1966 tax rates. Tobin would have saved such a family $168. The only way, naturally, that such savings at the lower portion of the income scale could be prudently financed was by raising the taxes of those at the upper portion of that scale. Though not considerable, neither was the degree of contemplated redistribution trivial.*

McGovern's demogrant, though more expensive than Tobin's version, embodied the defining features of negative income taxes: a combination within the same structure of taxes and grants, a basic grant level, and an offsetting tax on earned income. McGovern's basic grant was $1,000 per person rather than Tobin's $400. But the offsetting tax rate was 50 percent instead of 33⅓ percent. Tobin's family of five, receiving a basic grant of $5,000 rather than $2,000, could earn up to $15,000 before it stopped benefiting from cash grants or income tax reductions.

Fairly interpreted, the McGovern demogrant dealt more with equality and redistribution than with welfare. McGovern's own emphasis upon the $1,000 figure and the unhappy coincidence of that number with his early 1,000 percent support of his running mate Senator Eagleton after the revelations of past mental illness caused public furor, conspired to turn a serious public issue into a scene of black comedy.

The questions which linger concern the public's perception of its own interest and the role of economists in interpreting that interest. Most Americans are not rich. If they

---

* Somewhat unexpectedly, the tax reduction measure enacted by Congress in 1975 made a small start toward the principle of the negative income tax by making small grants to very low income taxpayers. In a television interview ("Meet the Press," May 25, 1975), Arthur Burns criticized Congress for taking this action without hearings. He apparently disregarded the lengthy hearings which FAP endured in 1969, 1970, and 1971.

are realistic, they know that they never will be rich. If they are very realistic, they will not expect their sons and daughters to become rich. McGovern proposed to give two out of every three Americans something to be paid for by that affluent third American. Yet, as the senator himself realized, factory audiences resented both the demogrant and McGovern's accompanying pledge to increase inheritance levies on large fortunes. The myth of unlimited opportunity survives in the land. Even if a blue-collar worker has surrendered his own dream of riches, his hopes for his children may be high. Conceivably many or most Americans believe that the rich deserve their riches.

It is fair to say that no economist of egalitarian sympathies made as cogent a case for McGovern's demogrant as followers of Professor Friedman offered for FAP. The explanation points to some of the limitations of contemporary economics. Friedman and his allies attached themselves to the objectives of efficiency, growth, and freedom of choice. Friedman's 1962 argument was effective because he based it squarely on the connection between his specific proposal and these values. It was scarcely necessary for Dr. Friedman to defend values almost universally venerated in his profession.

Disfavored policies include interference in "free" markets, damage to incentives, and rearrangements of income distribution. Egalitarian economists are on precarious ideological turf whenever their tax advice or preferences in negative income taxes reshuffle income and wealth in ways other than presumably unfettered competition has arranged. To their credit, such economists do transcend the ideological restraints of their craft, but never with an easy conscience. No wonder that consistent conservatives usually advance the strongest arguments.

Until economists grapple with the simple truth that efficient use of resources, steady economic growth, and consumer freedom are valuations no different from attachment to equity in income distribution and reconsideration of the social balance between public and private activity, they are professionally likely to remain intellectual allies of the status quo. Very little change is permissible when the institutional context is held sacred as the child of the free choices of past and present.

Is it possible to alleviate poverty with the approval of economists?

Perhaps. The clue appears to be more jobs. Of course, not all employed persons escape poverty. But aside from the idle rich, almost all the unemployed are also poor. The best way to help the minority of working poor is to improve by appropriate training their salable skills, so that their wages rise above poverty levels. The nonworking poor are a tougher problem. Economists in good conscience, without fear of labor market disturbance, recommend cash transfers for those of the poor who cannot work because they are too young, too old, too infirm, or too mentally or physically handicapped to compete effectively with better equipped members of the labor force.

There remain idle adult males, hordes of teenagers, and quantities of women eager and qualified to work. High economic growth and persistent prosperity are the traditional resolutions of their situation. When the demand for hands is strong enough, employers lower their hiring standards and enlist people whom they train and discipline on the job.

Here, however, the American record has been dismal since 1945.

Even following the logic of the Phillips curve, where full employment is possible only in the company of high inflation, why not simply create by public action the jobs which private employers do not furnish? Even if government workers are genuinely less productive than their private-sector colleagues, they will surely add something to the gross national product and something is preferable to nothing. In this country the challenge appears to be permanent. In 1972, a good year for most people, 5.4 million men and women were jobless—1974 and particularly 1975 were far worse.

Moreover, the burden was distributed in ways which had much more to do with the history of racial and sexual discrimination than with the impersonal judgments of competitive labor markets. Black Americans were unemployed twice as frequently as white ones. A person unwise enough to be young stood an additional chance of unemployment. In the middle of 1975, 20 percent of all teenagers were idle as were more than 40 percent of black teenagers, and practically everybody agreed that these horrifying numbers fell far short of the truth. Youths who lack legal opportunities are unlikely to become full members of American society. They are very likely indeed to enter a street life of crime and hustling.

Thus the curse of unemployment afflicts the employed as well as the unemployed. Although the crisis of the American city is a complicated affair, one of its important elements is a shortage of jobs. Because jobs are scarce, welfare costs soar and crime frightens the respectable into flight to the suburbs. City life becomes agreeable only to the rich in garrisoned enclaves, and metropolises like Manhattan, whose past glory was their diversity of class and condition, turn into polarized communities of the rich and the poor—the wealthy in luxury towers guarded by armed men, treble locks, and closed-circuit television, and the poor sentenced to grim subsistence in their expanding slums.

From Athens onward, great civilizations have focused upon the city as the locus of artistic, scientific, and commercial excitement. The quality of American life is inseparably entwined with the health of its cities. The amenities which make these cities livable and precious rest upon the foundation of human care and human labor. The foundation crumbles as cities increasingly cannot afford to clean and protect their parks, staff their libraries and museums, collect their citizen's refuse, and protect the peaceable from the ravages of a violent minority.

Unemployed people produce nothing. They cost the employed a lot even in an ungenerous period. Put to work, they will produce something and cost less.

Let us dream together. Imagine that the time is January 1977 and that Teddy Kennedy or Fred Harris has just been inaugurated as president of the United States. The depression is still with us and the new Congress like the new president is eager to do something about it. In its first hundred days, Congress reforms the tax code, reallocates a large hunk of the Pentagon budget to mass transit, public housing, and urban rehabilitation, and—approves a permanent public-sector job program on a large scale.

Before dreaming onward, I concede without argument that even these delightful acts are not to be confused with the millenium. The most massive of job guarantees will not convert entire our hordes of alcoholics, drug addicts, social psychopaths, and outright criminals. For them treatment, supervision, and occasional restraint will remain essential. For some, neither dangerous nor capable, money is the answer. Good, old, reliable transfer payments on a more generous scale than we have thus far accepted are the decent response to members of this group.

There remain millions of men and women who are officially counted as unemployed, other millions who are so discouraged that they have given up the hunt for nonexistent jobs, and still more people who are operating far below their skill levels or working fewer hours than they prefer.*

Of work to be done there is no end. On any day in any month, school boards are busily curtailing services, deferring maintenance, raising class size, and allowing educational quality to decline still further. A year or two ago in New York City the West Side Highway collapsed from lack of maintenance. Along the East River, the Franklin D. Roosevelt Drive shows signs of sympathetic imitation. In the suburbs hard-pressed homeowners reject school budgets. Mayors reproach governors and governors reproach Congress and the White House for financially starving their communities. In hospital emergency rooms, the acutely ill wait endless hours for hurried medical attention. As the need of the poor for skilled representation expands, the funds for legal service programs contract. The story could

---

* In April 1975 the officially unemployed numbered 8.2 million and the official rate of unemployment was 8.9 percent. But an additional million and a half people were uncounted because they were so "discouraged" that they had withdrawn from the job hunt. If they were counted as unemployed and if the partially unemployed were converted into full-time unemployment equivalents, unemployment would have measured, conservatively, 13 or 14 percent.

be repeated for all public services aside, inevitably, from the Pentagon.

In public as in personal affairs, it is seldom possible to resolve two major problems with a single sensible action. But public jobs promise at once to reduce unemployment and revitalize the public sector. The net costs of such action are reassuringly smaller than immediate expenditures. A $10-billion program which created a million new jobs would be partially offset by tax collections from the newly employed and diminished welfare payments. Net costs might be as little as two-thirds of total costs.

Thus far this national opportunity has almost entirely been foregone. In 1971, frightened by earlier Nixon vetoes of more generous legislation, Congress enacted to presidential specifications an Emergency Employment Act (EEA), a wretchedly puny response to lingering unemployment, which authorized a mere 100,000 new jobs so scattered around the country as to minimize still further this already inadequate response to local emergencies. In late 1971 and 1972 when the program was in full operation, it provided 2,503 positions for New York City's 204,000 unemployed and 569 for Boston's 90,000.

In timid deference to a White House Scrooge then at the peak of his power, Congress wrote a statute that unrealistically stressed the temporary and transitional nature of the problems it aimed to resolve. Neglecting the plain fact of high unemployment as a permanent American ailment, EEA addressed itself only to times of "high unemployment," promised that any new jobs would be no more than "transitional," and again and again stated a preference for private-sector activity. The recipe for failure could scarcely have been better concocted by the president himself. Jobs were few, financing skimpy, duration uncertain, and federal dedication tepid.

In the summer of 1974, even before the sharp descent of the economy into mini-depression in the final months of the year, but when both unemployment and inflation were accelerating, public-service jobs again drew political attention. Representing an impeccably conservative position, Federal Reserve Chairman Burns told the Joint Economic Committee of Congress that he favored a $4-billion public job program, designed to employ eight hundred thousand state and local government workers at something less than $5,000 each, only slightly higher than the federal minimum wage or the 1974 poverty line.

Nothing much came of Dr. Burns' suggestion. Liberals favored more money, more jobs, and higher pay scales. Municipal unions and civil-service associations predictably protested against job designs which stigmatized new employees, threatened contract protections, and revived WPA myths of leaf raking and hole filling.

Once again, however, this slow and inadequate national response to unemployment requires explanation. It is not difficult to identify. Job guarantees on an adequate scale require major shifts in public attitudes and political conduct. The guarantees promise or, according to taste, threaten diminished economic inequality, restructured labor markets, and conceivably the creation of something like a legal right to some kind of job. Conservatives, including most economists, are quite correct in resisting anything which goes further than Burnsian schemes. For their part, radicals ought to be clear about the direction in which they are moving.

Take the consequences of national guarantees of full employment one by one. The first is significant decline in income inequality for several reasons. Income gains would be most substantial for the young, black, or female where unemployment is now most pervasive and wage rates for even the employed are usually low. As unemployment shrank for members of these groups, many would seek training and advancement. The pool of casual, underemployed, and underpaid labor would dry up. That substantial proportion of poverty which is the consequence of unemployment, underemployment, and ill-rewarded employment, would at last disappear. Differentials among skill categories would narrow both because fewer men and women were unskilled and because competition for superior jobs would increase. The financing of full employment would also have egalitarian effects. The same political forces which could conceivably guarantee full employment would surely pay for it by terminating tax loopholes which now favor corporations and the rich, increasing the progression of the personal income tax, levying heavier inheritance and gift taxes, and, possibly, introducing new imposts on wealth.*

But work, as radicals and some nonradicals have been saying ever since the writings of Marx, is an alienating experience for most people. As David Ricardo and other nineteenth-century English classical economists taught, work is a pain borne only because the wages of alienated labor purchase life's necessities and comforts. But work also

---

* Sweden, Denmark, Norway, Netherlands, and Ireland all tax wealth directly. These are some of the world's most successful societies by any criterion.

gives structure and legitimacy to daily life and meaning to leisure. In the presence of guaranteed full employment (and an accompanying promise of a decent cash benefit for those who choose not to work) many men and women would still prefer to continue to labor in dull or unpleasant jobs rather than live in idleness. Nevertheless, turnover rates in bad jobs would rise and employer recruitment difficulties mount.

The labor markets of a full-employment economy would be much different from those Americans are familiar with, in at least three respects. One way to persuade people to do unpleasant work is to pay a great deal for it. Although as a series of physical motions, certain work may remain unpleasant, its status will rise with rates of remuneration. Nobody calls a New York City sanitation worker a garbageman, partly because a militant union protects him and partly because that union has secured him salary and benefits equal to 90 percent of those paid to policemen and firefighters. No really well-paid job, say the collective-bargaining experts, is a bad job. There are instances in which the job is so unpleasant that even the balm of cash attracts too few recruits. A second market response entails eliminating the job. Numerous middle-class couples have discovered that, at prevailing urban wages for domestic employees, they can do their own cooking and cleaning and convert, at best, menial labor into tokens of family solidarity. Mining, still a dangerous and unpleasant job, at least uses fewer human beings and more machines than ever before. Finally, guaranteed full employment imposes upon employers pressures to redesign jobs so as to eliminate or diminish their more unattractive features. In Sweden, group assembly has enjoyed substantial success. Dividing the tasks among themselves, Swedish auto workers put together cars instead of endlessly repeating a simple operation as the relentless assembly line flows by them.

By increasing the relative importance of the public sector, full-employment guarantees also enlarge the significance of services and diminish the statistical share of commodity production in the gross national product. By and large, public services use fewer resources, pollute the air and water less, and consume less energy than consumer goods and business equipment. It follows that a substantial shift of jobs from factories which fabricate weapons, appliances, automobiles, and processed foods to state and municipal services would ease the demand for oil and coal, and protect the environment of the Far West by diminishing the economic pressure to strip-mine coal and extract oil from shale. As the cities became safer, cleaner, and more convenient, population migration to suburbs and exurbs would slow, stop, and ultimately reverse itself. The role of the automobile at that happy moment would permanently decline. Cities are more than traditional centers of intellectual originality and aesthetic excitement: they are potentially the thriftiest institutional mechanism for supporting large numbers of people.

Finally, job guarantees for all extend the protections now enjoyed by the tenured faculty of universities, civil-service workers, and members of strong unions. A guaranteed job is translatable into a guaranteed income. Full employment, in short, is akin to creation of property in work for the entire working population. As our society is now organized, most people own little more than a heavily mortgaged house and a mass of consumer appliances purchased on the never-never. The stubborn resistance of craft unions to membership on equal terms is less deliberate evasion of civil-rights guarantees than recognition that a union book is a species of property, passed on if at all possible by father to son. Guaranteed full employment economically enfranchises all who benefit from the guarantee.

When the going was good and stock market bulls pawed the earth, the New York Stock Exchange was wont to tout share ownership as a mode of participating in American wealth. There never was much to be said for this vision of stockholder democracy. Not much of a democracy when the votes are weighted according to the number of shares owned and the value of the shares fluctuates in mysterious ways. Of the possible varieties of new property, a job per person is the most valuable.

I like the prospect *because* it leaps from unsatisfactory to more humanly rewarding conditions of work and reward. I judge that the radical changes required are "good," not "bad." But who am I or anyone else to insert my own valuations into the competitive hubbub of the market?

Is this really none of an economist's business? So much the worse, possibly, for economics if our business is elsewhere.

———

Though an economist, let me be brave. I shall muse on the road to be traveled toward a fully employed economy. The place to begin is with a historical reminder. As World War II drew to its close, economists and politicians began to worry about the shape of the peace. Americans and Europeans shared the scars of the Great Depression. Americans in particular could hardly forget that on the eve of World War II unemployment was 14 percent. It had taken a war which at its peak consumed half the gross national product to create full or even overfull employment. The fear was naturally general that mass unemployment would soon be back.

Liberals, among them economists who had absorbed Keynes' message that unemployment was curable by spending more and taxing less,* agitated for legislative institutionalization of Keynesian fiscal teachings. The congressional quest for a suitable law shortly focused upon the Full Employment Bill of 1945 (as it started its journey through House and Senate) and the Employment Act of 1946 (as it ended that journey). The Full Employment Bill asserted that "all Americans able to work and seeking work have the right to useful, remunerative, regular and full-time employment, and it is the policy of the United States to assure the existence at all times of sufficient employment opportunities to enable all Americans who have finished schooling and who do not have full-time housekeeping responsibilities freely to exercise that right."[12]

The legislative story began on January 22, 1945 when victory in Europe and Asia was still months away. On that day Senator James E. Murray introduced the employment bill on his own behalf and that of Senators Robert Wagner of New York, Elbert Thomas of Utah, and Joseph O'Mahoney of Wyoming. These were four of the Senate's most effective liberal voices. Among them they had sponsored much of the New Deal. Their political task was to attract support from a wider spectrum of opinion than liberal journals like *The Nation* and *The New Republic* and other parts of the liberal establishment. Stephen K. Bailey, the historian of

---

* Keynes' *The General Theory of Employment, Interest and Money*, the most influential book by an economist thus far in the twentieth century, was published in 1936. Its author died ten years later.

the Employment Act,[13] analyzed the political task of the
bill's sponsors in this paragraph:

The proponents of S. 380 were from the beginning conscious
of the fact that they had an uphill fight on their hands. The
war was still on and public attention was riveted to military
news. Labor and liberal organizations, although interested in
full employment as a goal, were split on methods and divided
among themselves institutionally and power-politically. Opposition to S. 380 was to be expected from a large part of business, conservative farm organizations, to a lesser extent from
the old-line veterans' organizations, and strangely enough from
an influential left-wing group in the C. I. O. Strategically,
therefore, the proponents of the Full Employment Bill had
three major jobs on their hands outside of Congress: (1) to
arouse public interest, (2) to mobilize and unify the friends of
the Full Employment Bill, and (3) to split the opposition.

Congress in the end passed a law which surrendered much
of the original bill's substance. Was the victory more than
symbolic? Why was so little won? The liberals managed to
stay together, in defiance of their quarrelsome history and
nature. Even the AFL and the CIO, then separate and hostile, were persuaded to issue separate endorsements instead
of automatically choosing opposite sides of the issue. However, attempts to split the opposition were ineffective. The
smallest and most liberal farm organization, the National
Farmers' Union, did loudly support S. 380 but the National
Grange was tepid and the powerful American Farm Bureau
Federation from first to last stood adamant against employment guarantees.

Business, innocent of Keynes and eager to operate without
government interference, was still more hostile. Although
two small business groups, several individual businessmen,
and the moderate Committee for Economic Development

favored some sort of national legislation, they were exceptions. Their stronger brethren, led by the National Association of Manufacturers and the U.S. Chamber of Commerce, mounted a militant campaign directed in particular at members of the House of Representatives. The intellectual quality of their argument is revealed by the literary centerpiece of the NAM propaganda barrage, *A Compilation in Excerpt Form of Statements and Expressions of Views Exposing Inherent Fallacies and Contradictions of the So-called 'Full Employment Bill,' S. 380*. The eight main section heads approximated the standard set by this title:

SECTION 1   The Full Employment Bill . . . Means Government Controls.

SECTION 2   The Full Employment Bill . . . Destroys Private Enterprise.

SECTION 3   The Full Employment Bill . . . Will Increase the Powers of the Executive.

SECTION 4   'Full' Employment Guaranteed—Criticisms—Terms.

SECTION 5   The Full Employment Bill . . . Legalizes a Compensatory Fiscal Policy—Federal Spending and Pump Priming.

SECTION 6   The Full Employment Bill . . . Leads to Socialism.

SECTION 7   The Full Employment Bill . . . Items for Ridicule.

SECTION 8   The Full Employment Bill is Unworkable, Impractical and Promises too Much.[14]

A sample of the NAM sense of humor deserves exhumation:

RIDICULE AND LAUGH AT THEM

The Majority Report observes:
"Witnesses before the subcommittee and correspondents whose letters are in the Record emphasized that the present postwar outlook is *as unstable as our past experience*."

What! In the face of the abundant life brought in by the New Deal?

What! After fifteen years of super-efforts of the New Deal for 'recovery and reform'?

What! After spending $23 billions of government money in peacetime and over $250 billions in war?

Possibly because its opposition was less ludicrous and frenetic, the Chamber of Commerce was more effective. Its seventeen hundred local chapters represented a wider variety of business activity than the small number of huge indus-trialists banded together in the NAM crusade against the twentieth century.

Had it not been for lack of public interest, business oppo-sition alone might not have emasculated the Full Employ-ment Bill. Excitement over victory first in Europe and then in the Pacific took understandable precedence over any-thing that Congress was up to. At best, popular support for employment guarantees was wide but not intense. A 1944 *Fortune* poll did report that 67.7 percent of its respondents favored government action to take up the job slack during depression. In the 1944 presidential race Thomas E. Dewey and Franklin Roosevelt pledged, in rather general terms, national action to stimulate full employment.

It remained true that S. 380's advocates had failed to link these vague pronouncements to the specific legislation re-quired to fill them with meaning. In July 1945 an Illinois poll revealed that 69 percent of the voters had never heard of S. 380. Of those who could identify it, 19 percent lacked the remotest notion of its contents. A mere 8 percent were reasonably familiar with the bill's major provisions.

Two other circumstances conspired against strong legis-lation. The public reputation of the business community had been rehabilitated by the triumphs of war production which it had organized. Worse still, despite a profusion of gloomy forecasts, the economy remained embarrassingly buoyant. Civilian employers proved unexpectedly capable of absorbing hordes of returning veterans and legions of displaced war workers. Rejoicing in peace and prosperity, ordinary citizens were comprehensibly indifferent to the fate of a technical statute. In sum, the proponents of S. 380 were probably fortunate to shove any measure through Congress.

What emerged as the Employment Act of 1946 was a much tamer animal than the Full Employment Bill. The original legislation had proclaimed the fearful words *full employment* in an initial statement of purpose:

A BILL to establish a national policy and program for assuring continuing full employment in a free competitive economy, through the concerted efforts of industry, agriculture, State and local governments, and the Federal Government.

Although the bows to free enterprise were profuse, the initial Murray draft was in spiritual harmony with such serious foreign discussions of full-employment guarantees as English, Canadian, and Australian government white papers and Lord Beveridge's influential *Full Employment in a Free Society*. These were voices raised in favor of specific government spending and taxing policies addressed to full employment.

By depressing contrast, the 1946 Employment Act's turgid "Declaration of Policy" ran on like this:

The Congress hereby declares that it is the continuing policy and responsibility of the Federal Government to use all practicable means consistent with its needs and obligations and other essential considerations of national policy with the assistance and cooperation of industry, agriculture, labor, and State and local governments, to coordinate and utilize all its plans, functions, and resources for the purpose of creating and maintaining, in a manner calculated to foster and promote free competitive enterprise and the general welfare, conditions under which there will be afforded useful employment, for those able, willing, and seeking work, and to promote maximum employment, production, and purchasing power.[15]

If the nonstop sentence meant anything, it was no more than a weak assurance that, other things equal and nothing more important preventing, federal action really should assist the industrious poor to find jobs. *Full employment*, two words of semantic charm and ideological acrimony, vanished entirely. Sunk without trace was the notion of a general entitlement to work.

Original aspiration and glum reality contrasted still more drastically in the legislation's substantive clauses. In early form, S. 380 required federal spending and other policies to "stimulate and encourage the highest feasible levels of employment," preferably in the private sector but, if necessary, in public activities. Moreover, early drafts prescribed concrete procedures and imposed specific responsibilities upon presidents and congressmen. The president was required each year to submit a national production and employment budget which featured detailed forecasts of consumer expenditure, business investment, government spending, and resulting levels of activity and employment. Should less than full employment be the likely event, then the president was required to "transmit a general program for such Federal investment and expenditure as will be sufficient to bring . . . a full employment level of production."

Although the sober language was unlikely to stimulate

rioting in the streets, the bill meant business. Whenever the president's national production and employment budget registered an employment deficit, Congress was instructed to take rapid remedial action. A brand-new Joint Committee on the National Production and Employment Budget was charged with prescribing, for the use of other congressional committees, legislative guidelines for stimulative legislation.

No one can say how well these mechanisms might have worked. In the light of greater error by forecasters during the 1970s, a touching confidence was reposed in short-run economic forecasting. With responsibility shared between the White House and Congress, no effective sanction would have applied if either failed to act or acted only halfheartedly. There was, nevertheless, a strong political point to the bill's schedules and requirements, which granted voters a new reason to hold their elected leaders responsible for unemployment, slow growth, and other economic malfunctions.

The fact that these issues are once more before the nation in the 1970s suggests that the 1946 Employment Act failed to accomplish its mission.* No wonder. That act cast overboard the national production and employment budget. The president was asked to do no more than favor Congress within sixty days of its convening with a report on current economic conditions. After surgery, all that remained of the powerful Joint Committee on the National Production and Employment Budget was a pale shadow—the Joint Committee on the Economic Report, charged with studying and assessing the economic report—and no more.

---

* The Hawkins-Humphrey-Reuss Equal Opportunity and Full Employment Bill (H.R. 50), to be discussed in the next section, draws upon the history of the 1945 bill. One of the original drafters of the earlier measure, Bert Gross, has worked on H.R. 50.

The act did establish a Council of Economic Advisers to advise the president on preparation of his economic report, collect statistics, appraise government employment policy, and prepare "national economic policies to foster and promote free competitive enterprise, to avoid economic fluctuations, or to diminish the effects thereof, and to maintain employment, production, and purchasing power." But ever so judiciously Congress had rendered the act politically harmless. The Chief Executive might prepare yet another report. Congress would study or ignore it. Nothing compelled anybody to raise or lower taxes and public spending.

Was the result worth the struggle? Were liberal energies fruitlessly dissipated? If the late Senator Robert A. Taft (the present Ohio senator's father), the intellectual leader of Senate conservatives, could vote for S. 380, was there anything in the measure to please liberals? Just possibly. Congress had, in the end, accepted responsibility not, it is true, for full employment, but at least for "high levels of employment." In the hands of a liberal president and Council of Economic Advisers, the act was capable of encouraging constructive employment policy, as John F. Kennedy, Walter Heller, and his Council of Economic Advisers colleagues demonstrated in the events which culminated in the massive tax reductions of February 1964.

There is a more vital benefit of the Employment Act. Each national administration since its passage has tacitly accepted the political premise that the public will not reelect presidents and legislators who allow unemployment to rise very high and last very long. The instinct of survival spurs into anxious activity even conservative presidents and congressmen nostalgic for old-fashioned balanced budgets.

Our decade is littered with memories of the aborted hopes and thwarted programs of yesterday. The "novel" initiatives now in vogue frequently recall their predecessors of the 1930s and 1940s. As early as 1935, Franklin Roosevelt considered including universal health care in the draft of his social security bill. Harry Truman urged Congress to actually take this action. During the Johnson era, Congress did extend free health care to the elderly (medicare) and the medically indigent (medicaid).

Without the full-employment guarantees originally sought, the employment record of the last three decades has been mixed. Repetition of the grim thirties has fortunately not occurred. On the other hand, aside from the Korean war and the later stages of the Vietnam conflict, unemployment has usually been substantially higher than any full-employment definition would accept. Major depressions have been avoided, but there were two recessions in the 1940s, three more in the 1950s, one during the first Nixon administration and another during Mr. Nixon's final shabby years in office. The 1974–75 episode was deep enough to revive memories of the 1930s.*

This mixed record has revived the movement for job guarantees. The leading effort by congressional liberals† to

---

* Studs Terkel's *Working* (New York: Pantheon Books, 1975), a set of sensitive interviews with veterans of the Great Depression, was a best seller.

† The public supporters of full employment include much the same line-up that vainly clamored for the red meat of the 1945 Full Employment Bill. The AFL-CIO and civil-rights groups have endorsed Hawkins-Humphrey. Murray Finley, president of the Amalgamated Clothing Workers, and Coretta Scott King of the Southern Christian Leadership Conference are chairpersons of a Full Employment Action Council which has enlisted other union leaders, academics, civil-rights activists, and politicians.

complete the unfinished business of the 1940s is H.R. 50, the Hawkins-Humphrey-Reuss Equal Opportunity and Full Employment Act of 1975. Restoring the surrendered commitment to full employment, the act guarantees jobs to *all* adult Americans "willing and able" to work—at fair rates of compensation. Mindful of difficulties of coordinating the clumsy machinery of government, the drafters require the federal government "to develop programs and policies, binding on all Federal agencies, including the Federal Reserve Board, to achieve full employment. Pursuit of other economic goals, such as price stability, shall not limit pursuit of full employment."* Echoing again the 1945 Bill, H.R. 50 orders the president to send Congress each year a Full Employment and National Purposes Budget, "stating goals and policies with respect to full employment, full production and full purchasing power." Full employment is defined as 3 percent or less unemployment.

Unabashed, the statute calls next for planning: "The Purposes Budget established a comprehensive national plan. . . . Such comprehensive plan shall set forth policies, programs and goals related to natural resources, housing, environment, medical care . . . liquidation of poverty, income transfer programs," and so on. Well aware from recent experience that the Federal Reserve can thwart the best intentions of presidents and Congresses by clamping down on money and credit, the act meets the money managers head on: "The Federal Reserve Board is required (1) to report its monetary policy intentions, (2) to state how these poli-

---

* Here and in the analysis of H.R. 50 which follows I quote or paraphrase a print issued by the House Committee on Education and Labor on March 20, 1975.

cies will be consistent with full employment and full production, and (3) to act consistently with the Full Employment and National Purposes budget...."

Although the priority set upon employment is firm, H.R.
50 implies willingness to restrain inflation by "other measures" than restriction of demand. The central job creation
mechanism is to be a retitled U.S. Employment Service,
hereafter the "United States Full Employment Service"
which is charged with "developing and creating, with the
assistance of local planning councils, job opportunities
through a reservoir of public and private employment projects" all over the country. Within this revitalized agency,
a new Job Guarantee Office will refer some of the unemployed to existing job vacancies, others to positions specially
created, and the remainder to a Stand-by Job Corps which
will perform useful community services.

H.R. 50 may be too ambitious. Possibly alternative designs are preferable. Still it is sad that so few economists
either support it in its present form or are urgently engaged
in developing better national policies for high employment.

Solutions to poverty are well within American resources.
Since 1961, taxes on corporations have become less progressive. Affluent individuals also bear lighter burdens than they
did a decade and a half ago. Tax cuts in 1961, 1964, 1969,
1971, and 1975 have cost the Treasury at least $70 billion
in lost receipts each year. These $70 billion would finance
a negative income tax, a set of children's allowances, a liberalized Family Assistance Plan, or any number of other
modes of winning that unconditional war against poverty
of which Lyndon Johnson once spoke.

For believers in the American dream of equality, full employment is the best of all policies. As William Raspberry,

one of the country's few syndicated black columnists, realistically observed, "The white majority can be nudged toward the notion of special opportunity for those who have been specially victimized when the special opportunity doesn't cost them anything."[16] Prosperity and low unemployment favor the poor and tend somewhat to enlarge their share of the nation's income.

An enlightened community offers decent employment to all who want work and are capable of working. Those unable to work deserve, without stigma or recrimination, a reasonable cash grant. If poverty is to be vanquished and full employment to be achieved, inflationary potentialities must decrease. As much as anything else, they are the consequence of the power concentrated in professional societies, health insurers, large corporations, and some unions. The shape of the problem dictates the appropriate response—permanent statutory controls over wages and prices in markets where competition is absent or limited.

The program is neither visionary nor radical. It draws upon the current experience of countries like Sweden, the Netherlands, Australia, and Germany,* organized around the same principles of market capitalism as those dominant in the United States.

---

* Here is how the Germans treat their unemployed: "The Cologne labor office resembles a well-run medical clinic. Visitors trickle in to exchange a few murmured words with a receptionist and then space themselves out in cushioned chairs clustered around the room. Some stare at the fresh, robin's-egg-blue walls. First timers hunch intently over forms they fill out before being summoned into adjoining rooms for private consultation." (*The Wall Street Journal*, May 28, 1975, p. 1). German benefits average 68 percent of normal pay. American benefits, at a national average of sixty-one dollars per week, are substantially below the current definition of poverty income.

One might expect that economists, professional specialists in efficient use of resources, would be concerned above all with unemployment since the American record is worse than that of any other important industrial society. One would be wrong. Anyone who attends the meetings of the American Economic Association can learn as much as he likes (or possibly even more) about what the specialists are up to in capital theory, monetary models, the new economic history, sources and uses of microdata, and so on. For instruction on the ethics of a capitalist society, he must depend on such visiting firemen as the philosopher John Rawls, who at the 1973 sessions offered a version of his by now famous *A Theory of Justice*. Dr. Alice Rivlin at the next year's convention explained why this was so:

> In a truly amazing act of self-denial, economists of the past generation have taken themselves out of the theoretical-philosophical discussion of how income ought to be distributed. Since they abandoned the notion that interpersonal comparisons of utility were possible and rejected the commonsense assertion that taking a dollar from a rich man and giving it to a poor man generally enhanced the total welfare, they have not only stayed out of the argument, but devoted some of their most ingenious intellectual efforts to explaining to each other why they had so little to say.[17]

How very strange! Here is a specialty whose traditional subject matter has featured income, wealth, and economic welfare, but its practitioners now deny that they have anything worth saying about the distribution of the first two or the measurement of the third. It was not always so. Keynes, without apology, was prepared to share his own conclusions with the public in words like these:

For my own part, I believe that there is social and psychological justification for significant inequalities of incomes and wealth, but not such large disparities as exist to-day. There are valuable human activities which require the motive of money-making and the environment of private wealth-ownership for their full fruition. Moreover, dangerous human proclivities can be canalised into comparatively harmless channels by the existence of opportunities for money-making and private wealth, which, if they cannot be satisfied in this way, may find their outlet in cruelty, the reckless pursuit of personal power and authority, and other forms of self-aggrandisement. It is better that a man should tyrannise over his bank balance than over his fellow-citizens; and whilst the former is sometimes denounced as being but a means to the latter, sometimes at least it is an alternative. But it is not necessary for the stimulation of these proclivities that the game should be played for such high stakes as at present. Much lower stakes will serve the purpose equally well, as soon as the players are accustomed to them.[18]

How economists got where they now are is a long story, indeed the theme of the next chapter.

3

the socialization of economists

An economist by training thinks of himself as the guardian of rationality, the ascriber of rationality to others, and the prescriber of rationality to the social world. It is this role that I will play.

—KENNETH J. ARROW
Nobel Laureate

I would add one word for any student beginning economic study who may be discouraged by the severity of the effort which the study ... seems to require of him. The complicated analyses which economists endeavor to carry through are not mere gymnastic. They are instruments for the bettering of human life. The misery and squalor that surround us, the injurious luxury of some wealthy families, the terrible uncertainty overshadowing many families of the poor—these are

*evils too plain to be ignored. By the knowledge that our science
seeks it is possible that they may be restrained. Out of the
darkness light! To search for it is the task, to find it perhaps
the prize, which the "dismal science of Political Economy"
offers to those who face its discipline.*

—ARTHUR CECIL PIGOU

Nineteen seventy-six is a Scottish bicentennial year, not just
an American extravaganza, the date of publication of a certain book by an absent-minded professor of moral philosophy, Adam Smith's *The Wealth of Nations*. The course
of economics in the nineteenth century was faithful to its
origins in ethical and political philosophy. Smith himself
favored free competition because it promoted economic
growth, but he favored economic growth because only
growth was likely to improve the condition of England's
poor. Malthus, Ricardo, James and John Stuart Mill may
have justified Thomas Carlyle's slur upon the political economy of his time as the "dismal science," a phrase which has
never ceased to be popular. Carlyle, no cheery soul himself,
had been reading Malthus, a thinker perfectly capable of
encouraging his audience with sentiments like these:

Famine seems to be the last, the most dreadful resource of nature. The power of population is so superior to the power of
the earth to produce subsistence for man, that premature death
must in some shape or other visit the human race. The vices of
mankind are active and able ministers of depopulation. They
are the precursors in the great army of destruction; and they
often finish the dreadful work themselves. But should they fail
in this war of extermination, sickly seasons, epidemics, pesti-
lence and plague, advance in terrific array, and sweep off their
thousands and ten thousands. Should success be still incom-

plete; gigantic, inevitable famine stalks in the rear, and with one mighty blow, levels the population with the food of the world.[1]

Yet Malthus had traveled to his celebrated ratios—geometric for population and merely arithmetic for food, from the starting place of William Godwin's utopian speculations upon the perfectibility of human nature. His and other schemes for human equality were, Malthus argued, bound to founder upon the rocks of an inexorable population problem. Malthus' grim analysis pointed to the solution of population control as the prerequisite to the diminution of poverty, a goal he sought as eagerly as the utopian socialists of his time.

Malthus' population doctrine was taken as a banner for social reform rather than a counsel of despair by the Benthamites, who swallowed it undiluted. In his *Autobiography*, John Stuart Mill recalled his early reactions to Malthus:

Malthus's population principle was quite as much a banner, and a point of union among us, as any opinion specially belonging to Bentham. This great doctrine originally brought forward as an argument against the indefinite improvability of human affairs, we took up with ardent zeal in the contrary sense as indicating the sole means of realizing that improvability by securing full employment at high wages to the whole labouring population through a voluntary restriction of their numbers.[2]

Mill is a convenient example of the classical blend of abstract analysis and reforming passion which characterized English economics in the century after *The Wealth of Nations*. Mill, in economics the Paul Samuelson of his time, published in 1848 as a text his *Principles of Political Economy*. For more than a generation, in edition after edition (including a shortened workingmen's edition), Mill was the standard authority, the conclusive reference to the truths of political economy.

As an analytical economist, Mill did not take himself as strikingly original. What he taught his readers was an amalgam of Smith, Ricardo, Bentham, and Malthus. Several of their generalizations are still cherished by today's economists. Competition was crucial, for "only through the principle of competition has political economy any pretension to the character of a science. So far as rents, profits, wages, prices, are determined by competition, laws may be assigned for them. Assume competition to be their exclusive regulator, and principles of broad generality and scientific precision may be laid down."[3]

The law of diminishing returns governed the physical universe and controlled the activities of entrepreneurs. Mill could scarcely have put its claims more strongly:

After a certain, and not very advanced stage in the progress of agriculture, it is the law of production from the land, that in any given state of agricultural skill and knowledge, by increasing the labour, the produce is not increased in equal degree; doubling the labour does not double the produce; or to express the same thing in other words, every increase of produce is obtained by a more than proportional increase in the application of labour to the land.

Since manufacturing required raw materials, this law also limited the productivity of the factory. In economics no proposition was more powerful:

This general law of agricultural industry is the most important proposition in political economy. Were the law different, nearly all the phenomena of the production and distribution of wealth would be other than they are.[4]

Malthus, as noted, was Mill's guide to population. Malthus had "made the truth, though by no means universally admitted . . . fully known." Mill dismissed one of the most frequently repeated anti-Malthusian criticisms in a few terse lines: "It is in vain to say, that all mouths which the increase of mankind calls into existence, bring with them hands. The new mouths require as much food as the old ones, and the hands do not produce as much."[5]

As Mill summarized it, the final pillar of the classical system of economic thought was Say's law. At the start of the nineteenth century, Jean Baptiste Say, a French translator and disciple of Adam Smith, had argued that a competitive economy automatically moved toward full employment of men and nonhuman resources, on the ground that all of the income generated by the economy tended to be spent either by the people who earned the income or the merchants and factory owners to whom they loaned their savings. It followed that supply created its own demand, at least if governments refrained from officious interference. David Ricardo's gloss upon Say put the argument in a form that Mill accepted:

M. Say has, however, most satisfactorily shown, that there is no amount of capital which may not be employed in a country, because demand is only limited by production. No man produces, but with a view to consume or sell, and he never sells, but with an intention to purchase some other commodity, which may be immediately useful to him, or which may contribute to future production. By producing, then, he necessarily becomes either the consumer of his own goods, or the purchaser and consumer of the goods of some other person. . . . There cannot, then, be accumulated in a country any amount of capital which cannot be employed productively, until wages rise so high in consequence of the rise of necessaries, and so little consequently remains for the profits of stock, that the motive for accumulation ceases.[6]

Taking this apparatus for granted, Mill set himself to presenting it in clearer and more accessible language than masters of gnarled prose like Bentham and Ricardo customarily employed. This was no doubt worth the trouble but, Mill made it clear, those laws of political economy which partook of the character of "physical truths" were a preliminary to social policy, to considerations of the quality of daily life and how the character of English men and women could be improved. There was scope for much advance, for in Mill's estimation, "as soon as any idea of equality enters the mind of an uneducated English working man, his head is turned by it. When he ceases to be servile, he becomes insolent."[7]

English society was no more attractive than the people who inhabited it. In words which echo in some of the writings of contemporary opponents of unlimited growth Mill eloquently declared his dislike of the scramble for pelf and place:

I cannot, therefore, regard the stationary state of capital and wealth with the unaffected aversion so generally manifested by political economists of the old school. I am inclined to believe that it would be, on the whole a very considerable improvement in our present condition. I confess that I am not charmed with the ideal of life held out by those who think that the normal state of human beings is that of struggling to get on; that the trampling, crushing, elbowing, and treading on each other's heels, which form the existing type of social life, are the most desirable lot of human beings.[8]

The Industrial Revolution was less than a blessing to those who minded its machines: "hitherto it is questionable if all the mechanical inventions yet made have lightened the day's toil of any human beings."[9] Nor was this quite the worst of the human condition in the middle of the nineteenth century. At the heart of the daily routine of the factory there was a spreading cancer afflicting the relationship between worker and employer and poisoning the intercourse between them. Employers coldly insisted upon the last possible ounce of effort from their wage slaves. The latter retaliated by conscientious malingering. The experience demeaned both groups.

Although Mill's diagnosis was bold, even radical, his remedies were comparatively mild. Not in the end socialism. Mill's flirtation with the utopians of his day, Robert Owen, Fourier, and Comte, was long, tentative, and disappointing. Successive editions of the *Principles* displayed growing sympathy with the aims of socialism, admiration for the personal qualities of socialist leaders, and even respect for the socialist diagnosis of the ills of capitalism. It all went for nothing, for at a critical juncture Mill boggled. His faith in competition remained too strong to allow him to become a socialist: "I agree ... with the Socialist writers in their conception of the form which industrial operations tend to assume in the advance of improvement. . . . I utterly dissent from the most conspicuous and vehement part of their teaching, their declamations against competition." A pity, he lamented, that socialists "forget that wherever competition is not, monopoly is; and that monopoly in all its forms is the taxation of the industrious for the support of indolence, if not of plunder."[10]

If socialism were excluded, what was the answer? Even under capitalism, Mill asserted, life would significantly improve and politics become more enlightened if only population growth were halted and education made universal. And more could still be done—above all the transformation of work relationships. Ideally the interests of workers ought to run parallel to those of their masters, not opposite to them. Mill laid considerable stress upon profit sharing as a helpful technique. In numerous illustrations from the industrial practice of the mid-nineteenth century, Mill argued that laborers in profit-sharing schemes worked harder, improved their habits, increased their incomes, and even raised the profits of capital. And because workers voluntarily maintained factory discipline and punished the malingerers who reduced everybody's income, the quality of finished products soared.

Mill looked even beyond profit sharing to worker ownership and control. His ideas about the management of factories under such control were as vague as most syndicalist doctrines. Though the details were vague, the vision was noble: "... the relation of masters and workpeople will be gradually superseded by partnership, in one of two forms: in some cases, associations of the labourers with the capitalists; in others, and perhaps finally in all, associations of labourers among themselves."[11]

On the role of the state in improving the life of the masses, Mill was not always consistent. In the spirit of Smith and Ricardo, he began with this general rule: *"Laisser-faire*... should be the general practice: every departure from it, unless required by some great good, is a certain evil."[12] His case against government intervention was powerful. According to the principle of the division of labor, government was certain to be inefficient, tyrannically disposed, and ineffective in registering the wishes of the governed. Even if government were not such a blunt instrument of social choice, individual action is superior because it develops individual character.

A good case no doubt, but one that left Mill uncomfortable. His reservations took the shape of a long list of exceptions to the general rule that government ought not to intervene. The state could legitimately compel school attendance even against parental opposition. Children were simply not yet rational beings, old enough to judge for themselves. As for the parents, the community had the responsibility of deciding when they were too ignorant themselves to judge correctly their children's best interests. Lunatics and idiots were in much the same condition. There was another set of circumstances which justified state action, instances in which community sentiment, nearly united in support of some policy, required governmental action to implement majority sentiment against the sabotage of a minority. In the case of factory legislation, unless Parliament acted, a minority of employers could prevent a majority from reducing the length of the work day and the work week by refusing to go along. A very broad exception to the rule of laisser faire indeed, this argument could well justify the bulk of social-welfare legislation enacted in the twentieth century.

Mill was a reluctant interventionist. Yet, if the greatest good of the greatest number, a Benthamite rule he never abandoned, required such intervention, Mill's passion to help the poor compelled him to advocate it. Within these limits of personal commitment, Mill advanced a program, parts of which are still radical in the 1970s. He urged the limitation of inheritance. Here was a nearly ideal method of promoting equality without damaging incentives. Quite consistently, he opposed progressive income taxation because it did impair the incentive to work, innovate, and invest.

Mill was willing to take land away from large private

owners for the public convenience, upon payment of course of fair compensation. Could a modern statist say more than this: "The claim of the landowners to the land is altogether subordinate to the general policy of the state. The principle of property gives them no right to the land, but only a right to compensation for whatever portion of their interest in the land it may be the policy of the state to deprive them of. To that, their claim is indefeasible."[13]

Mill was typical rather than unique in his almost unargued belief that the proper role of the political economist was to improve the condition of his fellow citizens. He was almost casual in his certainty that as vessels of pleasure and pain, one human being was much like another. He adhered with equal clarity to the judgment that the general welfare was always improved by transfers of cash from people who had a lot of it to people who had very little of it, so long at least as the transfers did not seriously damage the motives to work and invest.

Alfred Marshall, whose 1890 *Principles of Economics* succeeded Mill's *Principles* as the authoritative text for a third of a century, began his brilliant Cambridge career as a student of mathematics. He shifted to economics in response to the common Victorian wish to do good in particular by ending poverty and, more important still, encouraging the poor to live noble lives. "In my vacations," he recalled, "I visited the poorest quarters of several cities and walked through one street after another, looking at the faces of the poorest people. Next, I resolved to make as thorough a study as I could of Political Economy."[14]

Until very recently, economics in English-speaking countries preserved something of the flavor of its Scottish origins. As a branch of moral philosophy, economics shared in the ethical search for principles of personal improvement and individual virtue. Economists' emphasis upon the material context of moral action was justified primarily by the argument that that material context exerted a powerful influence upon the quality of daily conduct.

———

Contemporary economists sing a different tune. Here is one influential statement of what economics ought to do: "Positive economics . . . deals with 'what is,' not with 'what ought to be.' Its task is to provide a system of generalizations that can be used to make correct predictions about the consequences of any change in circumstances. Its performance is to be judged by the precision, scope and conformity with experience of the predictions it yields."[15] Friedman's definition expresses his profession's aspirations toward ethical neutrality and scientific accuracy. An older and still more popular formulation is Lionel Robbins' 1935 declaration that "Economics is the science which studies human behavior as a relationship between ends and scarce means which have alternative uses."*

Robbins' words commanded general approbation and the

———

* Lionel Robbins (now Lord Robbins), *An Essay on the Nature and Significance of Economic Science*, 2nd ed. (London: Macmillan & Co., 1935), p. 16.

Historically by no means all observers of economics have been friendly. The medieval schoolman Nicole Oresme warned that "There are some occupations which cannot be carried on without sin; for there are menial tasks which soil the body, such as cleaning sewers or chimneys, and others which stain the soul, like those now in question." He meant trade and finance. Veblen stigmatized much economic activity as sabotage of human instincts of workmanship. Contemporary radicals view mainstream economics as apologetics for market capitalism. I have considerable sympathy for the last judgment.

sincere flattery of frequent plagiarism because they concisely summarized in a sentence a manageable set of technical issues, an intellectual approach to their solution, and an appropriate professional attitude for working economists. The technical challenges resemble those familiar to engineers and efficiency experts. How does a small, medium-sized, or large business enterprise, hedged by limited access to cash and credit, and facing a set of rational customers eager to buy at the lowest available price, so manipulate its affairs as to minimize its expenditures on labor, raw materials, and overhead items, and thus maximize its profit? How can ordinary families possessed of finite incomes so divide their cash and credit in supermarkets, auto showrooms, appliance stores, travel agencies, dentists' and doctors' offices, and so on, as to enable them to reflect in tranquility after all funds are spent that they bought wisely and well? If there are no decisions to regret, then, say the economists, these wise consumers have truly maximized their satisfactions. Between them producer and consumer choices determine who earns the large incomes and who, perforce, endures the small ones. Such are the standard topics of price and distribution theory, the heart of economic analysis, and the core of graduate programs in major departments of economics.*

Economists handle choice most comfortably where markets are competitive. Then and only then commodity prices

---

* Modern macroeconomics, the study of economic aggregates, was an invention of John Maynard Keynes in the 1930s. Although its contents look different from micro theory, macroeconomics on closer inspection is simply allocation writ large. The central issue concerns the division of finite resources between public and private uses through the mechanisms of central banking and federal budget choices.

as well as wages, salaries, rents, and profits can plausibly be interpreted as evolving "automatically" from rivalry among businessmen and free choices by hordes of buyers. The beneficial consequences of competition are describable in English and mathematics of infinite subtlety. With the aid of plane geometry and supply-and-demand curves college sophomores learn that equilibrium in a given market occurs at the gratifying intersection of a descending demand and a rising supply curve. Best of all, their teachers inform them, should a market be out of equilibrium, then forces are set in motion which shove buyers and sellers toward that blessed state. For when sellers try to hustle too much merchandise at too high prices, their inventories pile up, their stores become unprofitable havens of peace and quiet, and they reduce both prices and unwanted stocks of goods. If the customers clamor so eagerly for merchandise that merchants run out of stock, they promptly raise their prices and increase orders to their suppliers.*

If for some reason a college undergraduate decides to specialize in economics, he soon progresses to the suitably elegant techniques of indifference curves and isoquants, differential and integral calculus, linear and matrix algebra. It's the same old story but told now in ways inaccessible to the laity. Indeed, two centuries ago Adam Smith had a quite fair notion of how competitive markets worked. Here is his summary:

---

* If this apparatus does not completely destroy his common sense, the college student is likely to reflect sourly on how little General Motors, Ford, and Chrysler appeared to heed these immutable laws of the market in 1974 and 1975, when, in the face of fleeing customers, they stubbornly pushed their prices ever higher. Of their behavior, more in a later chapter.

When the quantity of any commodity which is brought to market falls short of the effectual demand, all those who are willing to pay the whole value of the rent, wages, and profit, which must be paid in order to bring it thither, cannot be supplied with the quantity which they want. Rather than want it altogether, some of them will be willing to give more. A competition will immediately begin among them, and the market price will rise more or less above the natural price, according either to the greatness of the deficiency, or the wealth and wanton luxury of the competitors. . . . When the quantity brought to market exceeds the effectual demand, it cannot be all sold to those who are willing to pay the whole value of the rent, wages, and profit, which must be paid to bring it thither. Some part must be sold to those who are willing to pay less, and the low price which they give for it must reduce the price of the whole.[16]

When supply is short, the lure of profit attracts capital and labor and shoves supply toward an equilibrium level. When demand is inadequate and supply excessive, employers, as soon as they are able, shift their capital to greener pastures and their employees shift to better jobs in expanding occupations.

Entirely self-propelled, as though by an "invisible hand," the mechanism of supply and demand is energized by the egotism of all the actors. Buyers cast about for low prices. Employers seek maximum profit. Their employees restlessly hunt high wages and steady work. Thus it is that though the human actors are selfish, the pursuit of individual advantages harmonizes with public good. Living standards rise because competition stimulates business efficiency. Ordinary men and women work harder and endure the pains of dull or dangerous jobs in order to derive incomes which yield them pleasure or utility. All these economic actors: sellers, buyers, landlords, lenders, borrowers, and savers emit a steady stream of signals to the market. Produce more or less. Cut prices and attract customers. Go north. Go south. Shift jobs. Change product lines. And so on and on.

Everybody in this prosaic universe is rational. When sellers behave rationally, they try to make as much profit as they can. For their part, the customers seek the maximum gratification or utility they can derive from the money available to them. What is rational is in the mind of the individual. All that the doctrine requires is movement toward a chosen objective by technically valid means. Thus, for example, someone's firm resolution to get drunk might appear irrational, but the person who harbors this aspiration acts rationally, all the same, when he purchases 100-proof bourbon instead of fruit juice. For sellers the guides to rational conduct are the carrot of profit and the stick of bankruptcy. No doubt it is hard on merchants to go broke; but the public interest is well served when efficient businessmen prosper, reduce their costs and prices, and expand their operations, and their inefficient rivals are forced into other activities.

Before they are completely socialized, young economists are well aware that these notions idealize actual conduct. Their teachers may concede that rationality, maximization, and competition are heuristic devices rather than compelling portraits of either business or consumer behavior. That of course is the point of an effective graduate program: it enables its survivors to rise above the common sense with which no doubt they were endowed at birth. Here, for example, is George Stigler's celebration of the process:

He is drilled in the problems of *all* [emphasis in original] economic systems and in the methods by which a price system solves these problems. It becomes impossible for him to believe that men of good will can by their individual actions stem inflation, or that it is possible to impose changes in any one market or industry without causing problems in other markets or industries. . . . He cannot believe that a change in the *form* [emphasis in the original] of social organization will eliminate basic economic problems.[17]

The impact of this training, enthusiastically applauded by Dr. Stigler who is himself an eminent, conservative celebrant of free markets, is to transform apprentice economists *as social scientists* into conservatives. This is not to say that as amateur politicians and occasional campaign strategists, economists do not frequently but always *nonprofessionally* advocate all sorts of schemes for social change. Economists invented Senator McGovern's 1972 $1,000-per-person demogrant and others prescribed his redistributive tax program.

As scientific workers, economists perceive wherever they look human preferences among which they are *not* free to choose, complex relationships among the parts of their economic system, and unanticipated consequences in one part of the system because of changes in other parts. They fear that the best-intentioned tinkering will upset delicate equilibria all over the place. Accordingly economists distrust all human interferences in the "automatic" processes of markets. Wage and price controls, for instance, distort consumer and seller responses. From Diocletian onward, controls have failed to master human greed. I have no doubt that it was this lingering effect of their professional training which induced liberal Democratic economists to join their conservative colleagues in welcoming the termination of the Nixon experiment in wage and price controls.

For much the same reason, liberal economists can seldom

conceal in time of recession a sneaking preference for tax reduction over more generous public expenditure, as a mode of economic stimulation. Tax cuts expand the realm of private choice. By unfortunate contrast, government spending of any variety (who is to say "scientifically" which are the good programs?) diminishes consumer freedom to select goods in the marketplace and business capacity to purchase or hire materials and men.

When moved by the spectacle of poverty, the incidence of malnutrition, the squalor of slum housing, and the horrors of health care for all but the affluent, sympathetic economists are prone on principle to favor free-choice palliatives over government-directed initiatives. Direct transfers of cash allow recipients to choose their own combinations of food, shelter, medical attention, training, and recreation. Moreover, should such items be scarce in low-income districts, increased demand by the families which receive benefits in cash will infallibly attract the attention of entrepreneurs on the lookout for new opportunities to turn an honest dollar. New demand evokes new supply. A sound attachment to human equality, moreover, extends middle-class freedoms to choose as far downward in the income distribution as ingenuity makes possible.

On such reasoning, economists have been increasingly uneasy about Great Society reforms. Much as they may favor assaults upon poverty and racism, they are professionally suspicious of the quality of government action because market tests seldom apply. Where the customers are not free to choose, how can anyone be certain that urban renovation, manpower training, pre-school education, and compensatory schooling are really using resources thriftily or responding to the preferences of the individuals who supposedly benefit from government attentions?*

Preference for dollar signs, faith in markets, confidence in the force of human rationality, value neutrality, and attachment to the intricacies of "natural" equilibria, have encouraged economists to erect intellectual edifices of delightful complexity. They have also encouraged a widening gap between the economic view of the world and the realities of societies dominated by the politics of large private and public institutions.

No one operates without exercising judgments which derive from sets of valuations. Economists simply start from an attachment to efficiency and freedom of choice, and move to the conclusion that the two are inseparable. Their preferences shape the design of statistical inquiries and analyses of public issues, even when the numbers are most "scientific" and their manipulators honorably impartial.

Consider the great god gross national product, one of a family of national income concepts almost universally used to measure progress from one year to the next and to compare one country with another. When American politicians wish to comfort their constituents, they are likely to utter numerical incantations like President Nixon's 1972 message to the country:

---

* See for example *The Great Society: Lessons for the Future*, edited by Eli Ginzberg and Robert M. Solow (New York: Basic Books, 1974). The contributors, scholars of good will, wrestle mightily essentially with issues of measuring the good done by nonmarket devices.

Nineteen hundred and seventy-one was in many ways a good economic year. Total employment, total output, output per person, real hourly earnings, and real income after tax per person all reached new highs. The inflation which had plagued the country since 1965 began to subside.[18]

What is "total output"? Here is a standard definition: "There are many conceivable measures of the economic well-being of society. It is generally agreed, however, that the best available indicator of an economy's health is its annual total output of goods and services or . . . the economy's aggregate output. The basic social accounting measure of the total output of goods and services is called the gross national product or, simply, GNP. It is defined as *the total market value of all final goods and services produced in the economy in one year*." (Emphasis in original)[19]

In principle the national income statisticians in the Department of Commerce simply add up the price tags on consumer goods, the price of medical and legal consultation, new machines and structures, and changes in business inventories. As always, they nobly refrain from judgment on the biological or social merits of the items which enter into the grand total. Neither for this year nor for last year does the investigator ask inconvenient questions about how the new goods and services happen to be divided among the rich, poor, and middling. Benthamite memory traces might remind economists that improvement in the condition of the poor ought to improve total welfare rather more than similar dollar benefits to the wealthy.

The oddities of GNP include its recorders' disposition to lump together good things, bad things, and indifferent things. If Americans decide to smoke twice as many cigarettes, GNP rises because of their decision (unless of course they decide to spend less on something else). If their behavior enlarges medical expenditures upon the treatment of lung cancer, tuberculosis, heart disease, and emphysema, these outlays also will solemnly swell GNP. So it goes. If new pulp mills discharge chemical wastes into hitherto clean streams, GNP will certainly expand both because of the mills' increased output and because other enterprises and municipalities downstream from the polluters' headquarters are compelled to invest in cleaning devices designed to restore the water to usable condition. GNP rises with both automobile sales and larger consumer outlays upon cleaning furniture, clothes, lungs, curtains, and bodies. Should marijuana be legalized (or, as occasionally it now is, decriminalized), market values for this unmeasured (because illegal) product will register in the GNP. So also will any additions to the sums now spent on antipot measures.

Paradoxes abound. If the country turns prohibitionist, GNP will decline both because the distilleries go broke and because the medical costs of alcoholism shrink toward invisibility. An end of smoking will carry in its train equally sharp GNP consequences. The myths of consumer sovereignty disguise the role of producers, merchandisers, and advertisers in hustling the customers. These black arts leave the customers unsatisfied. They create the undivine discontent which the purveyors of still newer goods and services turn to additional commercial profit.

The economists who most strenuously celebrate the virtues of free markets achieve their triumphs of allocation and maximization only within the context of given distributions of income and wealth. Inequitable distributions distort the pattern of GNP by producing more goods at high prices for the wealthy and fewer items at lower prices for the poor. The mechanisms of consumer choice are so defective that daily most people are compelled against their own wishes to consume items (not necessarily selected by themselves) and deprived of the chance to choose others they might prefer. When the archetypal American motorist acquires a car powered by a conventional internal-combustion engine, he purchases individual transportation, pleasure, and the enjoyable contemplation of his neighbors' envy. Inevitably he also endows himself with some additional air pollution from the emissions of his engine. Nobody offers him a choice between a vehicle (at a premium price) which traps and dissipates noxious vapors and a cheaper chariot which poisons the atmosphere in its wake. He is limited to the product as it is: pleasure plus pollution, or none at all.

In the absence of congressional legislation, why doesn't the market sort out consumer preferences? Some consumers like cheap, dirty cars. Others will pay more for cleaner vehicles. If the automobile industry were genuinely competitive, all tastes would be gratified. As matters stand, the three giants who jointly decide these things take care to produce essentially similar products, at essentially similar prices. Which is to say that where competition is limited or absent, the sacred "market" may do no better than government agencies in responding to consumer preferences.

One should avoid exaggeration. Consumers do retain some choice, if only to buy a car or to refrain from the purchase. But unless the eastern urban motorist migrates to Nevada, Montana, or Wyoming (where strip-mining and oil shale extraction pose new environmental hazards), he has no choice of air quality, for whether or not his own activities and possessions add minutely to the fouling of the atmosphere, he cannot escape inhaling the air which his fellow citizens have adulterated. As statisticians still measure the world, air, as a free good (or ill), need not be counted. Economics is about scarcity. As a result, if the output of cars and air pollution grows in tandem, GNP will swell both by the value of the extra cars *and* the amounts expended upon dry cleaners, doctors, lawyers, and insurance adjusters.

It is the inescapable truth that a great many business enterprises and a number of new industries have flourished because they have escaped some of the ecological costs of their own growth.* Nothing is really free. The prices of other products and the general level of taxes are higher, and the public sector is smaller because a favored few have been allowed to escape a portion of the costs of their own activities.

Externalities are a familiar topic among economists. A rather less congenial theme, forced upon the profession by the pressures of the women's movement, concerns the national income treatment of household activity. The full extent of error by (male) statisticians can possibly be indicated by an extended analogy to military activity. Until a few years ago, generals and admirals (and their congressional allies) agreed that conscription was the only way to collect a sufficient number of reluctant youths to be dragooned into two years of tedium, petty harassment, and advanced training in the use and abuse of drugs and alcohol. That unlucky minority who fought in front-line Vietnam

---

* In economic lingo, these are externalities: fouled streams, dirty air, ear-splitting racket, and so on. Historically the enterprises which generate the externalities have been able to shift their costs to the communities and individuals who suffer their adverse effects.

units encountered into the bargain serious threats to physical survival. In ways obvious to all, the military draft was an unfair, class- and income-biased mechanism from which many of the educated, affluent, and influential routinely escaped. The military services and especially the army, were peopled by the country's traditional losers—high-school dropouts, scions of urban and rural poverty, blacks and Hispanics, and that cohort of the male college population who were too honest, too maladroit, or, save the mark, too patriotic to evade their country's call to the colors.

One of the rare innovations of the Nixon era, aside from its celebrated advances in the arts of burglary, electronic surveillance, and character assassination, was substitution of an all-volunteer army, navy, and air force for the military draft, presumably as a device to diminish middle-class opposition to interminable war in Southeast Asia. In order to attract its human prizes, the Pentagon has been compelled to offer salaries comparable to the rewards of alternative civilian jobs. Thus it occurred that in 1975 the military novice earned (or at least received) something like $4,000 each year, in addition to free food, shelter, clothing, training, and medical attention.

For national income statisticians, the end of conscription meant the inflation of the gross national product which rose by the difference between the financial rewards of draftees and volunteers. Save on the implausible assumption that volunteers are more "productive" than draftees, the Pentagon extracted, man for man, a product no larger under new arrangements than under old ones. By the test of the market it was now clear that draftees had been compelled to labor at wages well below the value of their efforts in uncoerced markets. Or, to restate the proposition, draftees had been forced to subsidize national defense by the monetary difference between their payments under new and old arrangements.

Any economist will gladly explain (without invitation) that the misleading cheapness of conscripted military labor encouraged wasteful use of this underpriced resource. Despite Defense Secretary James Schlesinger's occasional anguish over congressional reluctance to appropriate every last dollar the military seeks, the army now plans to form two additional divisions out of its supply-and-support echelons. Such is normal entrepreneurial reaction to the handling of any suddenly expensive element of the productive process. Good managers economize as best they can and substitute machines for personnel.

Up to a point, the situation of women in the national income statistics is analogous to that of military conscripts. In January 1973 a British magistrate sentenced a certain Peter Giles to clean an old-age pensioner's flat as punishment for a minor misdemeanor. His colleagues on the bench rapidly emulated his tactic. On this practice a female reporter on the London *Evening Standard* commented with these winged words:

It may come as a surprise to the magistrate that thousands of women in this country are interned for varying periods of time, week in and week out, performing the new ultimate deterrent known as "housework." Many are finding it increasingly difficult to remember what offense they committed in the first place.[20]

If, as folk wisdom teaches, housework expands to fill the time available for its performance, the explanation (for economists) must be located in the circumstance that in market-oriented economies very few activities are genuinely esteemed unless they are validated by the sort of transaction which establishes a seller's merit by a buyer's eagerness to surrender cash for the service or product which is offered.* As an inferior substitute for commercial accolade, women compete for the praise of family and friends by experiments in gardening, couture, gourmet cookery, child manipulation, and interior decoration. The ambiguity of their devices is underlined by the extremely successful campaigns mounted by food processors, advertisers, and supermarket chains to substitute factory meals for home cooking, on the scarcely disguised premise that food chemists, industrial dieticians, advertising technicians, and corporate moguls know more than mere housewives about nutrition, food preparation, and the pleasures of the palate.

National income accounts, a male invention, have from their contemporary inception in the 1920s excluded household labor from the social product. As the author (male) of a recent introductory text explained this statistical convention:

> ...it is necessary for practical reasons to omit certain types of final product from gross national product. In particular, some nonmarketed goods and services, such as the services performed by housewives, are excluded from the gross national product. This is not because economists fail to appreciate these services, but because it would be extremely difficult to get reasonably reliable estimates of the money value of a housewife's services.

No reason to fret, our guide hastens to reassure us:

---

* As will later emerge, there are some interesting exceptions to this glum proposition.

At first glance, this may seem to be a very important weakness in our measure of total output . . . [however] so long as the value of these services does not change much (in relation to total output), the variation in gross national product will provide a reasonably accurate picture of the variation in total output. . . .[21]

Ah, the complacency of the dominant male. How on earth can the most erudite national income estimator tell whether the value of household services and products has altered over time unless he devotes as much attention to what goes on in the kitchens of his society as his colleagues in the Bureau of Labor Statistics dedicate to the collation of the sample family budgets upon which the consumer price index is based? A moment's search of childhood memories by any middle-aged person suffices to identify how much work which a generation or so ago was located in homes is now, for better or worse, the province of commercial laundries, bakeries, food processors, fast-food emporiums, and garment factories. If, all the same, women devote nearly as many hours to domestic tasks as their mothers and grandmothers before them, they obviously are doing something different and, in all probability, either more or less valuable. It must follow that unless home baking, cooking, and sewing are commercially worthless, the statisticians (overwhelmingly male) have steadily exaggerated historical improvement in living standards by the differences between the values of home and market products and services. It is impossible to guess at the magnitude of this numerical distortion until serious attention is paid to the labors which occupy much of women's time and lesser proportions of male energies.

The sexist bias of the experts is compounded by the fixation upon market measurement which eventuates in the misrepresentation of households as noneconomic units, presumably regulated by the higher human impulses of altruism and affection. One can hope and believe that these attractive emotions are pervasive in American homes without excluding the family's economic role, and skewing fatally the measurement of economic activity. As an economic unit, the household is a small business enterprise in which husbands, and, frequently, wives invest cash (their earnings) and labor (mostly female) in order to generate a predictable flow of meals, clean clothes in good repair, comfortable and attractive surroundings, transportation, and entertainment, not to mention minor medical treatment, instruction, and the pastoral services of advice, comfort, and reassurance. Each of these activities is matched by one or several commercial analogues, ranging from psychiatric treatment, through restaurant meals, to sugared breakfast cereal and TV dinners. The market is distinguishable from the home as an economic phenomenon by the tendency of the household partners to consume rather than sell the output of their enterprise.

The statistical implication of defining homes as economic units and their administrators as unpaid managers is startling. By durable national-income-accounting convention, rents are imputed to owner-occupied houses as a portion of national income. If a weekly salary were imputed even though not actually paid to the home managers, she (or he) would become eligible, *inter alia*, for social security coverage, workmen's compensation,* and, most important,

---

* As working environments, homes are more dangerous than offices and many, if not most, factories.

full tax credit for the business expenses of running the home. The sum of these imputed salaries would add some hundreds of billions of dollars to the gross national product.

Our national income measures suffer from other defects. Bound by the vows of neutrality their profession imposes, the experts treat one distribution of national income as if it is as commendable as any other. Consequently no judgment can be made on whether an increase in GNP which flows mostly to the top 5 percent of income recipients is better (or worse) than a similar dollar benefit which enlarges incomes among the bottom 5 percent of the population. Formally an extra million dollars for J. Paul Getty adds just as much to the nation's economic welfare as the same sum divided among ten thousand welfare families in New York's South Bronx. Indeed if welfare benefits *drop* by half a million and Mr. Getty's rewards *rise* by a similar amount, neither net loss nor net gain is recorded in the national income estimates.

The political naïveté of the technique is illustrated by the English situation in 1974 and 1975. English GNP scarcely increased and English per capita income probably shrank. Inflation sped along at rates which by mid-1975 had soared to 3 percent a month. Why in the midst of these troubles did the British electorate in February 1975 retain in office Harold Wilson and slightly increase his parliamentary majority? Why for that matter did they a few months later follow his advice and vote overwhelmingly in favor of continued British membership in the European Common Market? The simple answer is supplied by another statistic: wages and salaries were rising at 30 percent rates during the time that prices were soaring at approximately two-thirds that pace. The ordinary British worker was better off than he had been. As his real income improved, the rewards of stockholders, landlords, and other affluent types fell. Since there were more Britons in the first category than in the second, Harold Wilson remained in power. A democratic election registers popular sentiments about personal welfare. People do have opinions about good and bad distributions of income and wealth, even if the experts remain determinedly agnostic.

In sum, the national income measures, crown jewels of economic statistics, are almost trivial indicators of anything worth measuring. Are we suffering more than we used to from such negative externalities as fouled streams, dirty air, ear-splitting noise, and crowded highways? No way to tell from the official numbers. Is our distribution of income and wealth "better" or "worse" this year than last? What, responds the expert, do you mean by "better" and "worse"?

At best, GNP is an index of that portion of human effort which is registered by market sales and purchases or permits of easy imputation of market prices (as household activity does not). GNP abstracts from consideration of who gets how much. It lumps together goods and evils, so long as price tags happen to be attached to the items in each assortment. Our method of keeping the national accounts ignores the costs, psychic and financial, of crowding, pollution, urban disorder, and the sheer pressures of humans upon each other.

Americans are told that they are rich. Most of them feel poor. No wonder. The conventional measures of affluence cover smaller and smaller proportions of the elements of everyday pleasure and pain. One day possibly statisticians will deflate the gross national product by a plausible index of amenity, an approximation of the context within which daily acts of consumption, work, personal movement, and recreation occur. Such an index will no doubt heed public safety, quality of mass transportation, the state of parks and public places, the wholesomeness of air and water, and other urban and rural necessities.*

In the relentless search for ever more rationality, economists have pioneered in the evaluation of public activity, when they have been compelled to accept the necessity of that activity. Who better than an economist, after all, can evaluate resource allocation and use? Let us, then, cast our minds back to 1964 and 1965. In those days Robert McNamara was secretary of defense. Former teacher at the Harvard Business School, one of that famous group of "whiz kids" who rescued the Ford Motor Company after World War II, Mr. McNamara was a famed exponent of systems analysis, that combination of mathematics, statistical control, and engineering expertise practically guaranteed to maximize the profit of any enterprise.

The Pentagon does not sell its products, or at least not most of them. The easy criterion of the profit-and-loss statement accordingly was not applicable to its activities. But Mr. McNamara and his helpers substituted the notion of cost effectiveness as an almost equally rational measure of military efficiency. The Vietnam war was an exceedingly

---

* Some economists are working on the problem. At Yale, William Nordhaus and James Tobin have initiated a "pioneering study" (the words are those of Paul Samuelson) designed to measure the disamenities of economic growth and subtract them from GNP.

handy field of research and experiment. Investigators were able to seek answers to hosts of concrete questions: How much did it cost to kill one Vietcong by (*a*) bombing, (*b*) infantry action, (*c*) naval shellfire, (*d*) defoliation of forests and exposure of concealed enemy units, (*e*) concentration on the Ho Chi Minh trail? In the best tradition of economic inquiry, one tactfully avoided questions about what Americans were doing in Vietnam in the first place and whether any of the possible tactics might be said to offend against international law or morality. As usual, values and objectives came from elsewhere. Economists do best when they can concentrate upon technique.

By 1966 Secretary McNamara's star was very high indeed in the Washington firmament. In particular President Johnson was so impressed with Mr. McNamara's managerial triumphs that he ordered every cabinet agency to adopt as a new form of decision making and budget construction, a planning-programming-budgeting system (PPBS). The promulgated objectives of the system were deceptively straightforward. If Congress appropriated funds for adult basic education, then the Office of Education could reasonably be expected to say something sensible about which of the available pedagogical techniques taught the largest number of men and women to read and write. Before Head Start was enlarged, reduced, or transformed, someone could pair the effects of various instructional designs with their respective costs.

Examples were legion. Which of the assorted health activities of the Public Health Service were most effective (per dollar) in controlling infectious disease, prolonging life, and reducing the incidence of automative accidents? One of the chronic problems of efficient bureaucracy is use of what is available to maximum effect. PPBS was intended to compel public officials to identify program objectives, chart paths to their accomplishment, compare costs and benefits of the alternative paths, evaluate continuously their own performance, and shuffle resources according to the signals emitted by the evaluating process. Applying the approach to automobile accidents, experts in the Department of Health, Education and Welfare identified eight possible approaches to diminished highway slaughter:

(1) tougher licensing of drivers through a medical screening program;

(2) reduction of driver drinking through education about the hazards of driving while drunk;

(3) reduction of injuries to pedestrians via public instruction in the art of crossing streets safely;

(4) increased use of seat belts;

(5) additional safety restraint devices;

(6) reduction of motorcycle injuries by increased use of helmets and eye shields;

(7) improvement of driver skill through a national driver training program;

(8) enlarged emergency medical services.[22]

Making the best guesses it could, HEW concluded that the seat-belt approach promised the highest ratio of benefits to costs. If a mere $2 million were expended, $2,728,000,000 might be saved in property damage, lost earnings, and medical charges. The death toll would be reduced by 22,930 each year at a cost per life saved of a mere $87. The benefit-cost ratio was a majestic 1,351:4. In their enthusiasm, the analysts neglected to examine public attitudes toward the use of seat belts. When Congress, in pursuit of auto safety,

mandated seat belts in new cars and insisted on nasty buzz-
ing devices, key interlocks, and other restrictions upon the
freedom of Americans to injure others and themselves, the
public responded by disconnecting the safeguards, refusing
to wear the belts, and complaining vociferously enough to
force Congress in some embarrassment to repeal the more
annoying coercive features.

All the same the logic of cost-benefit analysis in a complicated society seems compelling. How else can even a
rich community decide among a host of worthy objectives
—control of which diseases, education how long of which
children, improved public health, fewer accidents at work
and elsewhere? Funds are always limited. The taxpayers
invariably want their money's worth. Why not choose rationally, neutrally, and impartially by application of a cer-
tified analytical technique? Even if all of us can't have all
that we want, it ought to be reassuring that our deprivation
is scientifically legitimized.

Nevertheless, performance-and-program budgeting turned
out to be an idea whose time had not yet come. In plural-
istic societies, technocratic dreams are invariably blighted.
As Aaron Wildavsky, an astute political scientist, observed
a decade ago, "cost-benefit analysis, useful as it unquestion-
ably is, is shot through with political and social value
choices and surrounded by uncertainties and difficulties of
computation. It is clear that we have come a long way since
our first fleeting glimpse of pure efficiency."[23]

As a substitute for the normal haggling of the political
process, cost-benefit devices started with the handicap of a
very serious bias in favor of the readily quantifiable. In
selecting highway routes, engineers can compute construction costs per mile over alternative routes far more readily

than they can assess the comparative scale of aesthetic and scenic damage. At the Storm King site along the Hudson River, Consolidated Edison was better able to calculate financial savings from a new installation than the impact upon scenery, marine life, and the Hudson River. Conscientious analysts take pains to *mention* what they cannot quantify. In tones of varying urgency, they advise their political and commercial employers to *evaluate* the unmeasured or the unmeasurable. However, since they don't (and can't) tell their masters how to turn this trick, the political and the corporate temptation is powerful to assign low or zero weights to what the computers are not programmed to figure into costs.

Quite aside from touchy matters of amenity and aesthetics, problem-solving techniques are dangerously open to the covert influences of individual and agency ideologies. Invariably the technique is far more subjective in application and conclusion than its "scientific" apparatus of computer programs and mathematical procedures superficially appears to be. Even the testimony of astute, friendly witnesses makes the point. Hear, for example, William Gorham of the Urban Institute, once an assistant secretary of HEW in charge of program analysis:

The problems of benefits measurement, however are not just technical; they are conceptual. It is far from obvious how the benefit of most health, education, and welfare programs should be defined. For example, Title I of the Elementary and Secondary Education Act provided special funds to local school districts for the education of deprived children. What is it that we want to measure? Should we test the children to see whether their reading comprehension, or their arithmetic achievement, has improved faster than would have been expected? Should we ask them whether they liked school any better or felt more confident of their abilities? Shall we wait and see whether they drop out of school less frequently, commit fewer crimes as teenagers, or go in greater proportions to colleges? Or shall we wait a decade or two and see how much they earn as adults, and whether, in fact, the cycle of poverty has been broken?

Discouraging? Gorham proceeded to issue still sterner warnings:

Even if we could conceptualize and measure the benefits of particular programs, there is the fact that benefits of different programs go to different people. Shall equal benefits to different individuals in the population be weighted equally? Is it equally important to raise the educational attainment of a suburban child and a slum child? Should an additional hundred dollars in welfare payments going to a mother with six children in Mississippi be weighted the same as an additional hundred dollars in Social Security payments going to an old man in Chicago? If the weights should not be equal, what should they be? Finally, even if benefits of different programs can be identified and measured and weighted, they cannot always be measured in the same units. Educational benefits may be measurable in terms of achievement test scores, and health benefits in terms of lives saved or days of sickness averted, and welfare benefits in terms of families rescued from poverty. When these benefits are forced into monetary terms, a great deal of violence is inevitably done to their heterogeneity, and useful information is suppressed.[24]

A series of excellent questions. After hearing them, one is hard-pressed to avoid the conclusion that cost-benefit analysis is as inescapably imprecise, when responsibly applied, as the openly unscientific program choices made by untutored congressmen or overweening presidents according to the calculus of political advantage. Gorham's own expectations are only moderately more cheerful: "While the big choices may not be greatly illuminated by cost-benefit analysis, the narrower ones can be. It is possible to group programs and potential programs which have the same objective and to examine the effectiveness (relative to cost) of each in reaching the objective."[25]

The expert's writ does not run very far or very fast. Of course, sensible folk will estimate the costs of various social initiatives according to whatever quantitative accounting techniques are in fashion. If cost-benefit analysis "forces people to think about the objectives of government programs and how they can be measured," well, splendid. What were they doing before Robert McNamara used the technique to conduct a disastrous war?

This is only to say what sensible men and women, unbefuddled by graduate training in economics, knew all the time. In the conduct of public affairs all the issues worth fretting about are intractably bound up with group interest, social prejudice, and class ideology. Any one of Gorham's queries readily illustrates the situation. "Shall," he asked, "equal benefits to different individuals in the population be weighted equally?" Yes, said Congress in 1965, when it enacted Title I of the Elementary and Secondary Education Act. By channeling funds to low-income school districts, the statute explicitly registered a political preference for more rapid improvement in the education of poor youngsters than of middle-class and affluent children. Title I gave legislative voice to a brief popular inclination to redeem long neglected promises of racial equality. Extra money for inner-city black and Spanish-speaking slums was Congress' way of compensating for decades of neglect of the children of the poor and decades of preference for the needs of the white middle class.

No doubt once Congress makes up its mind and appropriates some money for something, the funds ought to be wisely spent. Review and evaluation ought to be routine. But this is the ancient wisdom of everybody from Aristotle onward who ever wrote about public finance and the responsibilities of the sovereign. Little that occurred throughout the short summer of social ferment during the Kennedy-Johnson years or the conservative Nixon reaction which followed, was free from the usual trappings of politics, interest-group haggling, or pecuniary pressure from the rich and mighty. New Frontiersmen, Great Societarians, and New American Revolutionaries* all professed attachment to nonideological problem-solving techniques. All acted fairly predictably in response to the preferences and pressures of their respective constituencies.

Thus, as an intellectual style, problem solving is hobbled by the disabling assumption of general agreement within the political community upon basic goals and values. The actual existence of such agreement in the private sector explains the comparative success of rational planning and allocation within large corporations animated by the single but powerful aspiration to maximum profit. When victory is a military objective, the generals and admirals enjoy comparable success in focusing materials, men, and women in the right factories and on the right battlefields.

But in the ordinary politics of democratic communities, problem solving is efficacious only when there is general agreement that it is wrong to try to solve many problems. During the Eisenhower years when the natives were calm

---

* Who remembers Nixon's New American Revolution—born January 1971, buried about two months later?

and most citizens, exhausted by World War II and then the Korean conflict, were content to find jobs, buy homes, worry about their children's schools, and allow the government to fight communism and restrain inflation, it was easy for a quietist administration to agree on the desirability of more automobiles and better highways to accommodate them. Practically the only domestic initiative taken by the Eisenhower administration was a massive highway construction program that to this day continues to pave the country long after the consensus upon which it was premised dissolved.

Sputnik spurred a race to the moon. Americans, a few sour dissenters excepted, briefly joined hands in national refusal to lose the big game with the Red Machine. In the mid-1960s, a considerably feebler majority favored more rapid economic growth and accepted tax reduction as the way to get the growth. Moral: When agreement is general, problem solving, old- or new-style, works, especially if a wholesome dose of anticommunist ideology acts as a binding social agent.

The common experience of political conflict involves inherently unquantifiable values. In abortion debates, the right-to-life side of the argument is certain to be unmoved by statistical demonstrations of population pressure, food shortage, or the costs of damage inflicted by clandestine abortionists. Several generations of historical study have demonstrated the failure of capital punishment to deter murderers, rapists, or traitors. In eighteenth-century England pickpockets plied their trades as their colleagues awaited execution on the Newgate gallows. Crime and punishment stir deep personal emotions. The satisfactions of vengeance are for some strong enough to overcome any variety of argument of a pecuniary cast. Dr. James Coleman's massive study of American schools revealed that lower-class pupils (of any color) significantly improve their academic performance if they are taught in classrooms whose majorities are middle class. Although Coleman's findings stimulated a good many attempts in urban environments to bus youngsters so as to increase the chances of the poorer children, middle-class parents resisted and when their resistance failed, moved to the suburbs even though Coleman also proved that the performance of the middle-class students did not suffer after a *minority* of lower-class boys and girls joined them.*

Ideology is invariably buried in techniques of analysis, however neutral they appear to be. For its partisans, community control of government functions is far more than a mere technique of alternative administrative style. It is the shared value that precedes and legitimizes each practical policy choice. The ideology of local control emphasizes the folk wisdom of local residents and the untrustworthiness of mandarins, mercenary experts, and those crafty beasts, professional politicians. For their part, the experts deploy their own ideology; fostering exaggerated confidence in techniques which equip them to generalize beyond specific neighborhoods, they draw strength from modes of data collection and manipulation inscrutable to the laity, and, in the end, achieve results that are often incomprehensible to their alleged beneficiaries. The experts can't help them-

---

* Urban schools are now lower in average class and blacker in color than they were before integration efforts began. This fact has led Coleman to oppose further busing efforts as likely to aggravate rather than diminish racial discrimination.

selves: with the best will in the world, their mystery converts them into wire-pullers, practitioners of court politics, manipulators of popular opinion, and secret rulers.

But too often they operate with something less than the best will in the world. City-planning officials and their expert advisers in fact implement the wishes of the mayors at whose pleasure they serve. The attorneys in the civil-rights and antitrust divisions of the Department of Justice interpreted the civil-rights statutes and the antitrust laws quite differently in the Johnson and the Nixon administrations. John Mitchell was an attorney general quite distinguishable from Ramsey Clark. The difference was not lost upon their subordinates who best protected their own positions, reputations, and future opportunities by serving the prejudices, opinions, and political welfare of their masters.

The reality from which economists flee is the arena of power and pelf. In that arena milk producers increase their profits not by squeezing more milk out of each cow or persuading the customers to eat more ice cream, but by heavy contributions to the campaign funds of influential politicians of both major parties. Money is bipartisan. Over the years Harold Geneen did more for the profits of International Telephone and Telegraph by lobbying at presidential and cabinet level for favorable antitrust treatment and generous indemnity for Chilean confiscation of ITT properties than by any miracles of corporate management. Dita Beard, ITT's indiscreet Washington lobbyist, understood how these matters were arranged only too well. Her famous July 1971 memo featuring a direct connection between an ITT financial contribution to the 1972 Republican convention and a favorable resolution of pending antitrust action was a blunt document indeed:

Other than permitting John Mitchell ... Bob Haldeman, and Nixon, no one has known from whom that $400,000 had come. I am convinced ... our noble committment has gone a long way toward our negotiations on the mergers coming out as Hal wants them. Certainly the President has told Mitchell to see that things are worked out fairly. It is still only McLaren's Mickey Mouse we are suffering. ... Please destroy this, huh?[26]

By happy coincidence, a few weeks later, the Department of Justice, though insistent until then on bringing ITT to court and testing the impact of conglomerate operations upon competition, now suddenly agreed to a settlement which allowed ITT to retain the Hartford Fire Insurance Company.

Where pecuniary calculation rules, no holds are barred. For nine years Reserve Mining, a wholly owned subsidiary of Republic and Armco, has been dumping taconite tailings into Lake Superior. The sixty-seven thousand tons daily added have been converting the world's largest body of unpolluted fresh water into a garbage dump. Far worse, the asbestos fibers embedded in the refuse contain carcinogens capable of damaging human larynges, lungs, and gastro-intestinal tracts. During nearly a decade, Reserve has lobbied against Minnesota attempts to get it to construct on-land disposal facilities. It has threatened Silver Bay, a town of three thousand which harbors the existing plant, with shutting down and throwing a third of the local residents out of work. In 1974 a Federal District Judge, Miles Lord, after a nine-month trial, ordered Reserve to halt its dumping and expressed a certain lack of admiration for Reserve's behavior:

In 1969 you made a decision. You came to a fork in the road and you headed down the fork that said you would spend your money on attorneys' fees, on public relations and politics, rather than to spend your money on trying to do the engineering and actually moving out of the lake. . . . It was your choice whether to make the investment or abandon your employees and the state of Minnesota.*

Economists' ideas of how property is created are as naïve as their conceptions of how profits are best maximized. In standard texts, property is so taken for granted as to merit no separate discussion. Property in land, personal possessions, cash, securities, or other forms is aseptically taken as the fruits of the efforts and ingenuity of employees and entrepreneurs now alive or as inheritance from ancestors similarly engaged. By heavy implication, the existing pattern of ownership is accepted as at least tolerable if not equitable. As the *International Encyclopedia of the Social Sciences* gravely commented, "Few thinkers in the social sciences have written works that are primarily devoted to the elucidation of the institution of property."[27] It is no accident that the minority who have paused over the origins and effects of property have included radicals like Karl Marx and Thorstein Veblen.

No reason to be astonished then that in our own time a radical law professor has been more illuminating than conventional economists on the operations of property in America. In *The Greening of America,* a best seller of the

---

* See "Setback for Polluters," *Progressive,* June 1974, pp. 9–10. The setback was only temporary. On appeal, first the circuit court and then the Supreme Court reversed the lower-court decision. At present writing, Reserve is still dumping taconite tailings into Lake Superior. Cancer comes later. In Veblen's words, "the officials of a railway commonly prefer to avoid wrecks and manslaughter, even if there is no pecuniary advantage in choosing the more humane course," but, he hastened to add, "the captains of the first class are necessarily relatively exempt from these unbusinesslike scruples." American corporations are full of captains of the first class.

turbulent 1960s, Charles Reich of Yale focused under the rubric of the New Property,[28] on the role of government "largess" as creator of new forms of property and reinterpreter of old varieties of ownership. The largess in question includes a host of benefits. Welfare, social security, and veterans' pensions add to the incomes of their recipients. Protected by social security, as well as civil service, government jobs are a species of property. So also are occupational licenses, bus, truck, airline, and taxi franchises, subsidies to farmers, shipbuilders, and defense contractors. Property arises when the Department of the Interior grants access on indulgent terms to miners, lumberers, and graziers on public lands. Still other types of largess include subsidized business-mail delivery, free technical information for farmers and businessmen, and restricted entry into banking and insurance.

Politicians and administrators like to define largess as acts of grace. Those who vie with each other for it tend understandably to view hard-won benefits and privileges like older varieties of property.* There is, nevertheless, a distinction emphasized by Reich between government largess and more conventional kinds of property. The money made by athletes and firemen, farmers and businessmen, singers and writers, landlords and lenders, all derives from

---

* Many of the reprisals taken or contemplated by the Nixon administration involved the loss of property by "enemies." In the wake of Watergate, White House staff stirred up challenges to license renewals for profitable Florida TV channels owned by *The Washington Post*. Although these challenges were unsuccessful, the *Post* incurred heavy legal expenses and thus partially suffered the property damage contemplated by the president. The audit attentions of the Internal Revenue Service cost afflicted taxpayers time and the fees of expert advisers at least. At worst additional taxes are assessed.

the sale of a service or a commodity in markets for the most part privately operated. By contrast, largess reflects and reinforces the existing distribution of economic and political power. Respectable newspapers secure and renew radio and television licenses far more readily than do Black Panthers, drug reformers, or revolutionaries. By and large government largess further enriches the wealthy and enlarges the power of the already powerful. Large commercial farmers and agribusinesses collar most agricultural subsidies. Federal Housing Administration loan guarantees facilitated the middle-class exodus to the suburbs and thus exacerbated racial conflict. In the deserted cities, urban renewal has shrunk the inventory of low-cost dwellings which have been exchanged for convention halls and luxury flats. The tax and fee structure of California's state universities and colleges combine to generate subsidies for the middle-class youngsters admitted to Berkeley and UCLA at the expense of white- and blue-collar families whose children in larger proportions attend two-year colleges much less expensively administered. The first law of public largess reads that great social need accompanies slight political power. The second is its converse.

When the customers stray, businessmen lose money and their employees lose jobs. Still, alert businessmen act before too many customers depart, and in any event, their good or bad fortune is the consequence of nobody's arbitrary intervention. Much government largess can be capriciously conferred or suspended at the pleasure of administrators armed with considerable discretionary power either by actual congressional intent, presidential delegation, or their own statutory interpretations. These powers tend to expand. With no sign of popular dissent, Congress decreed that "any person shown by evidence satisfactory to the Administrator to be guilty of mutiny, treason, sabotage, or rendering assistance to any enemy of the United States or of its allies shall forfeit all accrued or future benefits under law administered by the Veterans' Administration." Veterans' benefits, related to past honorable military service, might appear to possess no logical relation to future conduct, but Congress thought otherwise.

The tendency of government is to insist where its citizens are weak that rights are surrendered in return for benefits. Few groups are weaker than welfare families. Accordingly the rights sought in return for assistance are more numerous. Until a series of liberal Supreme Court decisions during the 1960s, Alabama and other southern states could terminate aid to a woman and her children if she cohabited with a man even on a very occasional basis outside of her own home. By creative legal fiction, her sexual partner was deemed a substitute parent. In California's Alameda County, midnight raids in search of men were a feature of welfare administration. Several states, including New York, tried to restrict welfare grants to individuals and families who had been in the state a year or more. In the years just before Mr. Nixon assumed office, the Supreme Court appeared to be moving toward the definition of welfare as a right protected by the due-process safeguards of the Fifth and Fourteenth Amendments. Four Nixon appointees to the Court have reversed that trend.

The present position of the Court emerges from Justice Blackmun's majority decision in the case of *James* v. *Wyman*. Mrs. James refused to allow her caseworker to make a home visit. The welfare department threatened to terminate aid unless she relented. Her lawyers argued that a coerced visit was a violation of Fourth Amendment guarantees against unreasonable searches. Mr. Justice Blackmun denied that a home visit was a search within the meaning of the Constitution, because what was involved was not a right but a gift from the state. As he phrased the situation,

> One who dispenses purely private charity naturally has an interest in and expects to know how his charitable funds are utilized and put to work. The public, when it is the provider, rightly expects the same.[29]

As Justice Douglas, dissenting, commented:

> If the welfare recipient was not Barbara James but a prominent, affluent cotton or wheat farmer receiving benefit payments for not growing crops, would not the approach be different? Welfare in aid of dependent children, like social security and unemployment benefits, has an aura of suspicion. ... But constitutional rights—here the privacy of the *home*—are obviously not dependent on the poverty or on the affluence of the beneficiary.[30]

Perhaps Justice Douglas would more accurately have written that constitutional rights ought not be dependent on wealth or poverty. Frequently they actually are.

To make the point it is only necessary to contrast the rigors of welfare administration with the courtesy and understanding which surround sporadic efforts at antitrust enforcement. Americans have traditionally opposed corporate sin as well as individual sin. The antitrust laws are a monument to the national expectation that businessmen comport themselves according to the competitive ethics of *The Wealth of Nations*. Enacted in 1890, the Sherman Act preaches in two articles of legal language the old-time faith:

SECTION 1 Every contract, combination in the form of trust or otherwise, or conspiracy in restraint of trade or commerce among the several States, or with foreign nations, is hereby declared to be illegal. . . .

SECTION 2 Every person who shall monopolize, or attempt to monopolize, or combine or conspire with any other person or persons, to monopolize any part of the trade or commerce among the several States, or with a foreign nation, shall be deemed guilty of a misdemeanor.[31]

The monitory language was almost too powerful for the anticlimax of the small crime of misdemeanor.

In 1914 Congress underlined its horror of monopoly, price fixing, and restraints upon competition, by passage of two statutes. The Clayton Act asserted the illegality of four restrictive practices popular at the time: price discrimination, exclusive dealing and tying contracts, acquisition of rivals, and interlocking directorates. Congress, in its second law, created the Federal Trade Commission the better to extirpate "Unfair methods of competition in commerce and unfair or deceptive acts or practices in commerce."[32] Subsequently, however, the courts, various presidents, and the legal departments of large corporations so disposed of the various prohibitions and injunctions to good behavior in these laws that by 1967 four automobile companies controlled 99 percent of the market, four aluminum companies 96 percent, four cigarette companies 80 percent, four soap companies 72 percent, four aircraft companies 59 percent, and four steel companies 50 percent.[33]

Without undue cynicism, it might be said that the mild, seldom imposed penalties allowed by the antitrust laws exert approximately the same impact on actual conduct as the New Testament did upon the conspirators of Watergate. Exceptions test rules. In 1962 a certain maverick Philadelphia federal judge actually had the temerity to sentence a group of General Electric, Westinghouse, and Allis Chalmers executives to short jail terms because of their role in an extensive and intricate price-fixing conspiracy. Of the thirty days imposed in each instance, only twenty-one were served: nine days were remitted for good behavior.

Although the companies had collected tens of millions of dollars in illegal overcharges some part of which their aggrieved customers recovered by suing, the responsible company officials were punished far less severely than run-of-the-mill embezzlers, check forgers, or other minor-league white-collar criminals. The lesson to the small fry, as usual, seems to have been, when you steal, steal big. In business circles the felonious executives were hailed as martyrs. For their peers who just possibly realized that there but for the grace of the Department of Justice went themselves, their worst transgression was poor business judgment and inefficient conduct of their conspiracy. Corporate criminals have little reason to fear imprisonment. Over the decades the Department of Justice has rarely brought criminal charges against respectable businessmen. Attorneys general have preferred amicable negotiation with antitrust offenders, terminating in consent decrees which protect corporations from damage suits brought by customers or competitors, and spare them the embarrassment of revelation in open court of conduct offensive to the law. On occasion, corporations are ordered to spin off one of their divisions or dispose of one or two of their acquisitions. More frequently they are instructed to stop their more blatant anticompetitive practices.

In 1911 the Department of Justice won a famous victory against Standard Oil, the tyrant of its industry. In 1973 and 1974 the Seven Sisters, the dominant multinational oil firms, administered OPEC's oil boycott and its subsequent quadrupling of petroleum prices. The seven oil giants were partners in a shared monopoly. Was anyone better off after the 1911 court victory? Well, yes. The lawyers on both sides. In 1974, sixty years after the Clayton Act prohibited tie-in sales, the Department of Justice was pursuing the major oil companies which during a fuel shortage made gasoline deliveries to service stations conditional on purchase from them of unwanted supplies and appliances.

Is antitrust a fake? Was Thurman Arnold a generation ago correct in concluding that "the actual result of the antitrust laws was to promote the growth of great industrial organizations by deflecting the attack on them into purely moral and ceremonial channels?"[34] The late Richard Hofstadter, a noted historian of the Progressive Era, described antitrust as a "faded passion of American reform." These astute students of American mores recorded the truth that a good blast against monopoly entertains the voters who enjoy a good fight while doing no harm to corporate activity. A genuine attempt to break up giant corporations,* is just about as popular as school busing in South Boston or scatter-site housing in Queens.

Antitrust legislation is much better economics than politics. Economists who believe in the efficacy of competitive market mechanisms ought to be leading the agitation for radical antitrust and genuine fragmentation of huge cor-

---

* Senator Philip Hart (D.-Mich.) has introduced a measure aimed at fragmentation. Neither he nor anyone else expects that Congress will in the visible future enact it.

porations in concentrated industries. A few of them are. Most pay scant attention to the topic. Writers of introductory texts typically devote three to five pages to the contents, administration, and effects of the three major antitrust statutes.

This is odd. For generations economists have been boring their students with geometric demonstrations that markets operate with maximum efficiency, respond most efficiently to the tastes of their customers, and shift resources most quickly when those tastes change in the presence of genuine price competition. It is this rivalry which maximizes pressure upon costs, encourages innovation, and compels producers to give the customers what they want when they want it.

For economists, of all people, the very existence of General Motors, Exxon, ITT, and their gigantic peers ought to be condemned as a high crime against the ideal of market competition. If GM were fragmented into a hundred or more pieces, competition might again flower. Efficiency and economies of scale neither justify nor explain the size of the larger corporations. If engineering economy increased in step with size, GM would assemble its cars and trucks in a single plant instead of the hundreds that operate globally. The savings that size affords in raising money, and in the costs of advertising and marketing, are largely or completely offset by the bureaucratic inefficiencies of any large organization. The rivers of memoranda and computer printouts which clog the channels of communication do a lot to explain why the American auto industry resisted until just yesterday the manifest desire of American motorists to shift to smaller and thriftier vehicles. During the years that elapsed before the idea penetrated executive skulls, foreign auto producers collared over a fifth of the

American market.* In the absence of foreign competition, it is entirely likely that Detroit would still be concentrating on the huge gas-guzzlers.

One ought to grant the large corporation pride of place in a catalog of departures from the economist's competitive dream world. I shall in fairness devote the next chapter to this institution. But while acknowledging the extent of corporate responsibility for stifling competition, the host of shelters erected by individuals, groups, enterprises, and governmental allies against the fierce blast of actual or potential rivals must at least be mentioned. Tariffs, quotas, and subsidies to shipbuilders, farmers, oil speculators, building developers, deficient entrepreneurs in railroads, airlines, cattle raising, and poultry breeding, to note a few recent objects of congressional solicitude, all impinge malignantly upon competition. When homeowners and buyers are subsidized and renters are not, the market is artificially skewed away from downtown department stores, urban housing construction, and inner-city athletic stadiums, and toward single-family housing tracts and suburban shopping centers close at hand. Because of marine subsidies, approximately five hundred vessels sail under the American flag. Possibly the hundred most efficient would survive without subsidy. If the businessmen who plunder the public treasury ran their enterprises as efficiently as they lobby in Washington and state capitols, they would need no government largess and America would be a land of milk and honey.

It is not only businessmen who play the protection game.

---

* Emma Rothschild's *Paradise Lost* (New York: Vintage, 1974) is an excellent critique of the American automobile industry. She likens it to the dinosaur, famous for immense body and tiny brain. The dinosaur is now extinct.

The public insists upon licensing doctors, dentists, and lawyers because in matters of life, health, and money it is nice to know that one has employed a medical-school graduate instead of a meat cutter and a law-school graduate instead of a high-school dropout. What begins as public protection turns readily into mutual benefit societies for club members and exclusionary schemes against potential competitors. At the time of licensing, nearly all doctors and lawyers are probably at least minimally competent. If in the course of time, they become addicted to drugs or alcohol, afflicted by Parkinson's disease or multiple sclerosis, or simply stop reading the medical literature, seldom indeed will their professional brethren seek to remove them from practice on unfortunate patients. Customers, clients, and pupils are rarely capable of evaluating the quality of credentials issued years or decades ago.

Exaggeration ought to be avoided. Competition is not everywhere dead. There is an unplanned sector—retail trade, a few manufacturing industries, and a dwindling band of family farms—which operates more or less according to the rules of price theory textbooks. But the planned sector —the largest part of manufacturing, finance, and insurance, and much professional activity—is manifestly more important and steadily growing in size relative to the economy at large. Conglomerates have resumed swallowing up independent enterprises on the same principle as sharks eat large fish and large fish their smaller brethren.*

---

* Book publishing, once a quirky sort of business in which strikingly independent spirits occasionally fared well, has increasingly fallen into conglomerate hands. RCA owns Random House. CBS operates Holt, Rinehart, and Winston. Crowell-Collier long ago acquired the Free Press. Harper & Row, a large publisher, has swallowed Basic Books, a small but distinguished publisher of serious nonfiction. And so on.

Does anybody but economists really love competition and free markets? Perhaps the country will be safe for competition on the day when the National Association of Manufacturers concedes that corporate giantism is bad, farmers cry out against Department of Agriculture subsidies; the American Medical Association insists that doctors be periodically examined for reaccreditation by boards that include public members; the American Bar Association sues to purge its roster of incompetent and dishonest members and ceases, after public apology for past misfeasance, to circulate minimum fee schedules; the American Association of University Professors, after careful scholarly evaluation, reveals that tenure damages faculty quality; politicians spontaneously agree to finance campaigns for *all* offices (not just presidential races) out of the small contributions of grateful constituents; defense contractors proudly proclaim that bankruptcy in the service of freedom is no shame; and the American public, no fools, conclude that there is now a genuine chance to make headway against the formidable conspiracies of the rich, powerful, and successful.

The problem-solving style is deficient not only because economists usually justify it upon the premise of a degree of competition and a type of market organization which simply are not present in the American economy or that of any other advanced nation. It suffers from a tendency to reduce other impulses to the rational maximization upon which economic reasoning has long been based. If market imperatives extended their imperial sway as effectively and efficiently as economists usually argue, then the rules of business competition would confer upon our senior citizens the best available nursing-home care at the lowest possible prices. Instead, as sporadic inquiries over the last twenty years have each time concluded, the elderly are cheated, poorly fed and cared for, and substantially overcharged. Andrew Stein, the ambitious New York City assemblyman who in 1974 conducted an extended investigation of his state's nursing homes, is seeking to halt the licensing of additional commercial nursing homes and to encourage nonprofit alternatives.

That altruism, the precepts of economics to the contrary notwithstanding, is sometimes a more efficient principle of organization than profit maximization, can be inferred from the contrasting methods of blood collection in England and the United States. American hospitals buy their blood mostly from the poor and frequently the drug addicted. In England blood is given, seldom if ever sold. Any economist inspired by the gospel according to Milton Friedman, Ayn Rand, and her disciple Alan Greenspan, would instantly predict that blood would be in scarce English supply and abundant American supply. After all, did not Alfred Marshall, eager for ethical advance as he was, advise his pupils to place their trust in man's strongest motives, notably avarice, rather than in such more benign motives as altruism?

But, as the late Richard Titmuss[35] demonstrated in vivid detail, the facts in both countries contradicted the economists. In the United States blood is desperately scarce, routinely maldistributed, and frequently an avenue of infection. In England blood is usually available as needed. It is also much less likely to transmit infectious hepatitis than in this country. In short, altruism here is not only good for the character of the altruists, it is also a more efficient way to transfer resources from the less to the more needy.

Given half a chance, economists will convert all activity into market opportunity. It is worth examining at some length how economists infatuated by markets have approached the problems of public education. In this country public education has been a major encouragement to social mobility, the institutional embodiment of parental aspirations for their children, and the conveyor of such elements of the American civic religion as the hagiography of great presidents, the role of the United States in teaching democracy to the world, and the primacy of this country in everything from baseball to basic medical research. The storm clouds which in recent years have gathered around the public schools have been the consequence of protracted warfare over racial integration, spreading doubt that the schools are preparing their clients for prosperous futures,* challenges to traditional roles of school boards, teachers, and principals, and intense disagreements among parents over permissible and desirable curricular materials. These are matters which go to the heart of a society.

There are many who believe that the public schools have "failed" in some important way. Conservative blue-collar parents in West Virginia and elsewhere resent the "permissiveness" of their children's teachers and the "pornography" of the readings they assign. They are angered by the schools' inability to inculcate old-fashioned loyalties to the president (whoever he happens to be), the police, official sexual morality, hard work, and the country right or wrong.

---

* See such serious challenges to the commercial value of educational credentials as Ivar Berg's *The Great Training Robbery* (New York: Praeger, 1970) and Caroline Bird's *The Case Against College* (New York: David McKay Co., 1975).

Equipped with ample evidence, many black parents perceive public schools as tainted with white, middle-class elitism. In their bitter judgment, the agents of the educational establishment socialize black children into the acceptance of low estimates of their intellectual capacity and pessimistic predictions of their vocational prospects. For some black and Hispanic parents, community control of local schools represents a last, desperate opportunity to improve the life chances of their youngsters.

Although the complaints of middle-class suburbanites are predictably more varied, what afflicts them most acutely is the status race. When they moved out of the central cities, their choice of new homes was heavily influenced by the reputation of the local schools. On the secondary level, these schools are thought to be doing their job only when the alumni get into the best colleges. What counts then is not whether a school is really "good," assuming parents could tell, but its superiority over other schools as measured by the admission selections of a very short list of elite colleges. Since the Harvards and Yales cannot possibly accommodate all the middle-class youngsters who apply (and if they did, many of the reasons for going to Yale and Harvard would vanish), there exists an inchoate majority of middle-class parents whose opinion of their local schools is likely to be sour.

That fact has registered itself in the rising tide of school bond proposals rejected in suburban schools. Although the negative votes since 1973 have been powerfully influenced by inflation and unemployment, the tide had begun to turn by 1969 when 44 percent of new proposals were approved. A few years earlier 80 percent or more won support. Parents who fled the cities to escape black neighbors, high crime rates, soaring taxes and other urban afflictions began to discover suburban schools which permitted their children to major in drugs, sex, and assault upon teachers and each other. Why raise property taxes to finance these dubious curricula? Support for public schools has always been weakest, naturally enough, among those Catholic, Lutheran, and Jewish parents who enroll their children in parochial or day schools.

Who admires the public schools, apart from Albert Shanker and the New York City superintendent of schools? Critics on the left who deplore oppression and seek liberation and critics on the right who yearn for clean literature, the McGuffey Readers, and ancient skills of penmanship, spelling, computation, and literacy, join the customers, the children themselves, in judging schools even more harshly than the parents.

When communal values conflict, healthy societies debate them until a reasonable range of institutional compromises evolves from the contest of ideologies and interests. Less healthy societies do their best to evade discussion, preferably by the invention of some apparently neutral technical device. Here, as we have learned to expect, we find the social scientists at work. Their favorite resolution of the public-school crisis is the voucher device for the transformation of elementary and secondary education.

Vouchers come in two basic styles, conservative and liberal, each displaying different advantages and defects. As an application of free-market principle, the conservative case owes an intellectual debt to Adam Smith who claimed that "were there no public institutions for education, no system, no science would be taught for which there was not some demand"—an outcome he believed entirely desirable. For Smith, the children of the poor presented special problems. It was in the public interest that they learn to read, write, and count but it was also important that the schoolmasters of the poor be kept in a state of wholesome security, lest they wax fat and lazy like Smith's own Oxford tutors. The public would best assist the poor "by establishing in every parish or district a little school, where children may be taught for a reward so moderate, that even a common laborer may afford it; the master being partly, but not wholly paid by the public; because, if he was wholly, or even principally paid by it, he would soon learn to neglect his business."[35]

In 1962, Milton Friedman, the modern prophet of the free market, brought Adam Smith up to date. In *Capitalism and Freedom*, he started from an ideological preference for universal freedom of consumer choice, and a number of crucial factual assumptions. The latter are the familiar conclusions that public education has lamentably failed either to integrate the races or democratize the experience of rich, middle-income, and low-income children; that de facto racial segregation in northern cities is paralleled by sedulously stratified income segregation in the suburbs; and that those who fear that vouchers will convert urban public schools into dumping grounds for unwanted pupils fail to note that this event has already occurred.

In the presence of these "facts," Friedman argued that the risks of doing something different were minimal and the possible gains enormous. He offered a proposal of dazzling simplicity, the transfer to parents of the funds now devoted out of tax revenues to run the public schools. Parents would be issued a voucher for each school-age child. They would then assign the voucher to the school of their choice—public, private, parochial, profit-making, or altruistic in organization. Schools would proceed to cash in their vouchers at rates publicly established by government agencies. The parents would be placed in a position to shop freely for the school they believed suited their child best, and, nearly as important, alert entrepreneurs would rapidly widen the available choices by founding new schools better adapted to the tastes of prospective customers.

To be sure, this plan departed in one significant respect from a complete free-market model, the public treasury rather than parents financed education, public and private. Friedman justified this erosion of pure principle by citing what economists term neighborhood effects. The argument for imposing taxes to support schools upon spinsters, bachelors, the superannuated, the childless, and the invincibly ignorant, is, at its crassest, their interest in protecting their persons and property from the violent and the criminal. Everybody has an interest in a civilized society.

The glories of vouchers are several. They promise not only to stimulate experiment and diversity and match available supply to parental demand, they may even rescue the public school. Under the spur of increased competition, public-school administrators will acquire reason to take a new lease on life and improve their performance to the degree that induces parents to enroll their children in public rather than private schools. As it does elsewhere, competition will enhance educational efficiency in all the schools.

Liberal proponents of vouchers endeavor to combine the virtues of diversity and free choice with progress toward objectives high on standard liberal shopping lists. The liberal variant has been most powerfully espoused by Christopher Jencks who at the instance of the Office of Economic

Opportunity undertook a major study of possible voucher schemes. *Education Vouchers: A Report on Financing Elementary Education by Grants to Parents*, published in late 1970, surveyed no fewer than eleven different voucher designs, ranging from unregulated free markets in educational services, through an egalitarian model, to Jencks' preferred candidate, a regulated compensatory plan.

Milton Friedman's simple device had grown quite complicated, but for good reason. Jencks was concerned with five major questions raised by liberals and radicals who objected to vouchers in their pristine, free-market, conservative garb: Would vouchers increase de facto racial segregation? Would the separation of church and state be endangered? Would an unregulated market for education increase expenditure upon rich children more than upon poor ones? Do the public schools stand in danger of becoming schools of last resort, semipenal institutions for boys and girls nobody else wants around? Finally, is it really a good idea to give such rank educational amateurs as most parents are what amounts to a veto over the actions of the experts? Five tough issues.

Jencks, a man of the left, defined his challenge to be the development of a voucher system that confronted these valid questions while preserving the merits of free educational choice. He believed that he had succeeded in designing a voucher plan which "regulates the educational marketplace more than most conservatives would like, and contains far more safeguards for the interests of disadvantaged children." For, he continued, "an unregulated voucher system would be the most serious setback for the education of disadvantaged children in the history of the United States," just as "a properly regulated system . . . could inaugurate a new era of innovation and reform in American schools."

Before examining Jencks' paragon, the regulated compensatory model, it is worth looking at the alternatives which he rejected. He flatly rejected totally free-market vouchers because they were certain to aggravate existing misallocations of resources between the children of the rich and poor. Although such plans granted parents of all incomes vouchers of equal value, poor parents could afford to enroll their progeny only in schools whose tuition charges did not exceed the cash value of the voucher. By contrast, starting with the voucher as a base, more affluent parents could supplement it with additional fees designed to purchase superior education for their offspring. Because the public schools would end up in such circumstances even more income-segregated than they already are, Jencks evaluated conservative vouchers as even worse than existing, deplorable arrangements.

At first glance, egalitarian vouchers seem more attractive. They would put all parents on an equal basis as far as voucher values go, and the schools would be prohibited from charging tuition fees higher than the stated voucher value. In theory at least, poor parents might fare as well as rich ones in the hunt for superior educational opportunity. Closely examined, however, this arrangement seems likely to produce less satisfactory consequences. If the schools retain control over admissions, their administrators will try to make their own lives easier and their results more impressive by admitting intelligent, well-behaved, appropriately motivated pupils instead of the slow learners, emotionally disturbed, and potentially disruptive. The rejects will land in the public schools. Since they are by definition harder to teach and control than their luckier agemates, the equal resources available to the public schools will prove inadequate even though the same sums expended on students of superior intelligence might be larger than are really needed. In short, like the free-market model, the egalitarian model threatens to operate to the disadvantage of poor, black, handicapped, retarded, and difficult children.

Still another way of operating a voucher plan has been dubbed "achievement vouchers," a notion which features accountability. The amounts received by the school for each voucher would depend upon the progress made by each child during the school year. All these schemes, however designed, seem likely to deteriorate into versions of the unregulated free-market approach, largely because every school would feel that its resources are inadequate. Predictably schools would decide to use their scant resources most efficiently by excluding students who are troublesome or difficult to teach and concentrating admission on upper-class, middle-class, and exceptionally talented lower-class candidates. Here the achievement model suffers a special defect.

How then is it possible at once to preserve free parental choice and advance the fortunes of poor, black, and difficult children? The regulated compensatory voucher, Jencks' chosen instrument, is, with one crucial difference, a variant of the egalitarian voucher. As with egalitarian vouchers, Jencks' voucher would be of equal value for all comers and schools which experimented with either variant would be forbidden to set tuition charges higher than the voucher's declared value. However, public payments to the school would increase in step with the proportion of disadvantaged youngsters it taught. The clue to ensuring that good schools work hard on difficult cases is in the admissions process. Jencks relies partly upon financial rewards to schools which admit difficult boys and girls and partly on a mandated lottery covering 50 percent of new admissions. In this way average and below-average pupils, black or white, poor or rich, would get a shot at the schools which their parents (or they themselves) prefer. Any lottery would thwart the sturdy determination of middle-class parents to get their youngsters, by fair means or foul, into the best nursery schools, kindergartens, primary schools, high schools, and universities.

Education administered according to Jencks' prescription would grant its major benefits to poor parents and children. The schools would increase their responsiveness to children's needs. Parents' views would raise the quality of education for all, but particularly for the offspring of low-income parents.

Thus conservative vouchers conform to the economists' dream of free-market resolution of ethical as well as financial controversies. Of course the markets are no more free here than they are in autos, petroleum, or medical and legal services. Unregulated free markets in education would retard integration efforts in the few places where they are still being made. They would enlarge existing disparities between resources devoted to rich and poor children by, in effect, subsidizing parents who prefer color-, class-, or religion-segregated schools. In cities where the public schools are not already last resorts for unwanted youngsters, schools would rapidly gallop toward that unpleasant condition.

Liberal, Jencks-style vouchers are on initial impression substantially preferable. Far from pretending to separate themselves from specific social objectives, they profess attachment to egalitarian goals and endeavor to combine progress toward the goals with dismantling of swollen educational bureaucracies and commensurate enlargement of parental participation in the selection and management of schools. Of course, the Educational Voucher Authority, Jencks' chosen instrument of administration, might well swell into a bureaucracy of its own. It would be charged with disseminating meaningful information to parents about the quality of different schools, a responsibility which inevitably entails school inspection and evaluation. EVA would supervise admission lotteries and protect children from unfair suspension or expulsion.

Even if the perils of old bureaucracy in new administrative bottles could somehow be averted, liberal vouchers founder on the utopian premise that some consensus on crucial educational values already exists. Aside from social scientists infatuated with rational-market techniques, the supporters of vouchers tend to favor them for reasons quite distinguishable from Jencks' (and my) aspirations toward racial and economic equality. They perceive American life, far from inaccurately, as meritocracy. As Jencks himself said of middle-class parents, "They want to send their children to school with other middle- or upper-middle-class children, and they see vouchers as an easy and apparently legitimate way to do this."

In the present climate of opinion, a generalized voucher plan would lack the ghost of a chance to win politically if it remained faithful to Jencks' criteria: tuition ceilings, rewards for schools that educate difficult children, 50 percent lotteries, and effective supervision over publicity, admissions, suspension, and expulsion. If by some major miracle, liberal vouchers were inaugurated, middle-class parents would place enormous pressure upon voucher authorities to influence the operation in favor of their own children. EVAs would either cave in or find their tasks radically redefined by legislatures responding to middle-class pressures.

Even if for a year to two, voucher authorities refused to buckle and legislatures failed to act, EVAs would need to devote so many of their resources to ferreting out evasions of their criteria that they would be able to do very little else.

Thus liberal vouchers in short order would deteriorate into the essentially unregulated free-market style favored by Dr. Friedman and his followers. Just as no one should expect to do good by stealth, no one should anticipate that an institutional novelty will convert conservative and elitest impulses into integrationist and egalitarian virtue, or, for that matter, suspend within the political arena the usual play of ideology and interest. If in 1975 or 1976 pressures toward income redistribution and racial integration were powerful, there would be ample evidence of their influence upon public education. White as well as black parents would be insisting that new schools be constructed in racially mixed areas or on the boundaries dividing whites and blacks. Rich as well as poor voters would be urging municipal authorities to experiment with educational parks and school pairing. Suburbanities would be agitating to get black, low-income pupils bused into their schools and insisting that their own children get the opportunity to experience education in inner-city public schools.

The argument over vouchers illustrates yet again the truism that when resources are unequally divided, the principle that prevails is never one man one vote. All votes are dollar-weighted. Insofar as the dollar weighting is mitigated, it is because of the presence of public mechanisms which are to a degree influenced by one-man-one-vote practices. A clear vision of politics in a plutocracy compels the judgment that nonplutocrats are least well off in ostensibly free markets and somewhat better off when goods and services flow their way through the political process.

For the majority in capitalist democracies it is preferable to expand rights rather than widen markets. What has cushioned many Americans in modest financial circumstances against the full force of the worst depression since the 1930s has been the existence of a set of entitlements which were a political consequence of the horrors of the Great Depression: retirement on increasingly liberal social security pensions; unemployment compensation benefits; food stamps; and even, despite its humiliations, public welfare.

As I shall subsequently argue at greater length, past progress implies a strategy for new gains such as guarantees of jobs and adequate income maintenance for those unable or unqualified to work. This is to say that economists and other social scientists who surrender their neutrality to pursue explicit goals of social equity are far more likely to enjoy a measure of success by pursuing legal and political tactics than by indulging fantasies of universal free markets, particularly when, as the next chapter argues, there are so few free markets visible to the untrained eye.

4

economists
and
corporations

*The international corporation has no country to which it owes
more loyalty than any other, nor any country where it feels
completely at home.*

—CHARLES P. KINDLEBERGER

*The rise of the planetary enterprise is producing an organiza-
tional revolution as profound in its implications for modern
man as the Industrial Revolution and the rise of the nation-
state itself.*

—RICHARD J. BARNET AND RONALD E. MÜLLER

The large multinational corporation is without serious competition the most powerful and the fastest growing of
twentieth-century institutional forms. It is a challenge to

orthodox political sovereignty, it is also an intellectual burden upon economists who by now should have charted the anatomy and the physiology of these monstrous creatures thrashing about in the business jungle.

In 1974 this country's five hundred largest industrial corporations sold goods and services whose price tags totaled no less than $844 billion, considerably more than half the gross national product and 25 percent more than in the preceding year. After taxes, profits were $44 billion, a 12.8 percent improvement over 1973. These economic goliaths employed over fifteen million men and women. According to *Fortune*, the mighty five hundred accounted for 66 percent of all manufacturing sales, and gave jobs to three-quarters of the men and women who held jobs in American manufacturing. Although 1974 was a poor year for auto sales, General Motors, titan of titans, disposed of close to $32 billion of its merchandise, considerably more than the gross national products of most members of the United Nations. Three-quarters of a million people labored in General Motors plants and offices.

Two hundred and three corporations sold at least $1 billion of their wares, twenty-four sold at least $5 billion, and eleven at least $10 billion. Those eleven accounted for 27 percent of the sales of the entire five hundred. Even the smallest of the five hundred, Tyler, a Dallas pipe-maker, rang up $286 million on its cash registers and listed 6,450 men and women on its payrolls.*

---

* I have drawn the items in this statistical feast from *Fortune*, which each May celebrates the accomplishments of the corporations it most admires. See pp. 208 ff. of the May 1975 issue.

Other parts of the economy are equally dominated by majestic corporate leaders. The Bank of America, First National City, Chase Manhattan, Morgan Guaranty, and their few peers exercise powerful influence upon their smaller colleagues and upon the governance of American cities. Their refusal in 1974 to market additional New York City securities caused a crisis which by the middle of that year had resulted in additional state supervision of the city, the creation of Big MAC (the Municipal Assistance Corporation) to police city policies, and the layoff of thousands of policemen, firemen, sanitationmen, and teachers. Metropolitan Life, Equitable, and Prudential write billions of dollars in policies each year, control vast assets, and, next to the banks, exert the strongest influence upon the location, type, and quantity of investment in housing and real estate. A relatively small and little-known member of the fraternity, Argonaut, precipitated job actions by doctors in California and New York when it decided initially to treble rates on malpractice protection and subsequently to withdraw entirely from the field. Farming, guardian of the myth of the family enterprise as a national character-builder, has come increasingly under the sway of agribusinesses which own farms, feedlots, meatpacking plants, canneries, and supermarket chains.

The corporation has extended its influence to book publishing, advertising, law, and medicine, trades or professions historically practiced by lone operators or partnerships. Corporate logic is accounting logic, as recorded by bottom lines in profit-and-loss statements. Alert corporate managers are as ready to make a dollar in contraceptives as corn flakes, nursing homes, fast food, deodorants, or pornographic films.

Large corporations, with rare exceptions, are conglomerates which offer many products and services located in an assortment of industries. They tend to locate in countries where labor is cheap and grateful and governments refrain from untactful regulation and taxation. They hawk their merchandise in the markets of the world. Their managers and admirers speak and write reverentially of the global corporation's sacred mission. George Ball, a former undersecretary of state, now an investment banker, claimed that "working through great corporations that straddle the earth, men are able for the first time to utilize world resources with an efficiency dictated by the objective logic of profit."* Aurelio Peccei of Fiat envisages global corporations as "the most powerful agent for the internationalization of human society." The veteran business consultant and philosopher Peter Drucker exults at the emergence of a "global shopping center."

Even corporate executives dream, though perhaps not as you and I. Here is the vision of Carl A. Gerstacker, Dow Chemical's Chairman:

I have long dreamed of buying an island owned by no nation, and of establishing the World Headquarters [caps in original] of the Dow Company on the truly neutral ground of such an island, beholden to no nation or society. If we were located on such truly neutral ground we could then really operate in the United States as U.S. citizens, in Japan as Japanese citizens, and in Brazil as Brazilians rather than being governed in prime by the laws of the United States. . . . We could even pay any natives handsomely to move elsewhere.[1]

---

* This is one of a garland of quotations celebrating corporate aspirations gathered by Richard Barnet and Ronald Müller in *Global Reach* (New York: Simon & Schuster, 1974). See pp. 13–14.

We know less than we should know about the machina-
tions around the world of the global managers, partly because only a relatively small number of economists have
devoted themselves to the laborious job of untangling the
complex multinational operations and partly because the
corporations have taken pains to cover their tracks. What
we do know is the combined product of congressional inquiry and the enterprise of a small band of journalists and
scholars.*

International Telephone and Telegraph (ITT) is a convenient example of a multinational about which quite a bit
has become public information. In 1974 it ranked tenth
among *Fortune*'s five hundred. That year its sales exceeded
$11 billion, its profits were close to half a billion dollars,
and its employees numbered more than four hundred thousand.[2] By 1969, the end of a decade of Harold Geneen's
solitary domination, ITT operated factories in twenty-
seven countries and facilities in seventy more. Sixty percent
of its sales were North American and it had long since
ceased to resemble its original loosely coordinated collection
of foreign telephone companies. By virtuoso stock manipulation, Mr. Geneen and his helpers had acquired Sheraton
Hotels, Avis, Levitt home building, Bobbs-Merrill, Penn-
sylvania Glass & Sand (the biggest American producer of
silica and clay for glass and ceramics), Rayonier (a major
processor of chemical cellulose), Continental Baking (largest in the United States), and had been thwarted in its attempt to acquire the American Broadcasting Company.

---

* Senator Frank Church's subcommittee on multinationals has evolved
interesting testimony. Barnet and Müller's *Global Reach* and Sampson's
The Sovereign State of ITT are excellent explorations of the multinational world.

As the British journalist Anthony Sampson, ITT's un-loving chronicler, summarized the record, Harold Geneen

built up an astonishing ragbag of companies whose only com-mon factor was profits. Some were huge, some were tiny; they included Bramwell Business College, for $40,000, and the Nancy Taylor Secretarial Finishing School of Chicago, for $50,000. Geneen bought insurance companies, mutual funds, pump companies, lamp-makers. . . . In 1966 he bought Apcoa, the car-parking company . . . which fitted well with Avis; and the next year he bought Cleveland Motels, for $7.5 million, which provided somewhere for the cars to go.[3]

If potential profitability directs acquisitions, the transla-tion of potential into actual profit requires a set of tight accounting controls under which local managers succeed and fail. The modern conglomerate proceeds from the premise that universally applicable managerial and financial techniques (available at the Harvard Business School and lesser institutions) can master the most heterogeneous col-lection of industrial, commercial, and financial activities.

In pursuit of profit, conglomerates sell abroad pharma-ceutical preparations that the Food and Drug Administra-tion bans in the United States. U.S. drug companies have charged Colombian subsidiaries prices for Valium eighty-two times higher than international market prices.[4] In the same country Container Corporation of America and the B. F. Goodrich Company have used prison workers at sub-stantially less than prevailing wage rates. Although the minimum wage for free labor is only $1.33 *per day*, the prisoners are still cheaper.[5] The United States outlawed corporate use of prison labor early in this century. Bribery of public officials, illegal in this country, is a way of life in many parts of the globe. Conglomerates who conform to such local mores can deduct their expenditures as "ordinary and necessary business expense," in the unemotional language of the Internal Revenue Code.

The almost unfettered mobility of the conglomerates allows their managers to hire South Koreans at fourteen cents an hour to assemble television components in place of Americans at four dollars an hour or Japanese at two dollars and fifty cents. The rules of resource allocation are sedulously obeyed. Labor is cheap in South Korea, Taiwan, and Hong Kong because unions are weak, public authorities are eager to attract international investors, and multitudes of men and women are willing to work for exceedingly small rewards. Labor, for precisely opposite reasons, is expensive in Western Europe, Japan, and our own country.

Economists are likely at this juncture to advise patience. If markets are allowed to operate properly, advanced countries in time will cease to lose jobs and poorer countries stop gaining them. As the demand for Asian workers absorbs the supply of potential recruits, wage rates will surely rise. Where labor now is expensive, wages will rise more slowly or not at all. Accordingly, as wage differentials narrow, so also will the financial incentive to shift production facilities out of the developed into the developing lands. Japan, once a low-wage haven for businessmen, is now one of the higher-wage industrial powers. Given time, South Korea and Taiwan will achieve the same successful condition.

Even from the economist's standpoint, complacency is probably a mistake, for the conglomerates play mysterious pricing games which cast into serious doubt the technical efficiency of their operations. The financial object of the game is to shift as much profit as possible away from high-tax jurisdictions toward low-tax countries. Here the wonders of transfer pricing, the amount charged by one tentacle of the global corporation to another, come into play. Plainly the thing to do is to sell products and services fabricated in the high-tax country at artificially low prices to the subsidiary in a market whose tax climate is balmy. Profits will be reduced in the exporting country and raised in the importing country. In other words, the location of productive facilities and the character of pricing policy around the world have quite possibly as much or more to do with the politics and tax policies of assorted governments than the asserted "real" economies of operation in one place rather than another.

Even if this process of global maneuver were as efficient as the conglomerateurs assert, its consequences for specific groups of workers are exceedingly painful. It is slim consolation for middle-aged garment workers to be told that relocation of their industry in Asia is a rational response to the signals emitted by competitive world markets, even if they believed the story. Laid-off members of the United Auto Workers are more likely to demand tariffs and quotas on Italian, French, German, and Japanese cars than to accept the logic of resource utilization which directs them to seek employment in other industries. Cash floats smoothly from place to place, adjusting itself without strain to the character of profitable opportunity. Human beings unfortunately cannot quite so readily shift from auto assembly lines to computer programming or public accounting.

Operating between the cracks among the legal codes of many lands, the global corporations escape much of the regulation and control which purely domestic rivals experience. Often they are even capable of thwarting domestic economic policy. When, as in 1969–70, the Federal Reserve sought to restrain inflation by tightening credit and raising interest rates, it was child's play for the multinational operators to finance their American expansion from the proceeds of loans floated abroad. In much the same way the dominant money-market banks headquartered in New York and Los Angeles were able to enlarge their reserves and expand their lending by tapping vast accumulations of Eurodollars on deposit in European financial centers.

It is a safe bet that the multinationals will react to American efforts to protect the environment by threatening to divert expansion to less fussy countries and to shut down domestic facilities which cannot be inexpensively altered to conform to antipollution standards. There are more forms of competition than those hailed by economists, and the multinationals are adept players in political games among the fifty states of the nation and the hundreds of separate polities of the world.

It is illuminating to take a closer look at a single specimen, the world's most celebrated global corporation, Harold Geneen's ITT. The story of ITT's activities in Chile is a good example of how the giant corporation behaves in the real world.[6] It begins in May 1970 when Harold Geneen and John McCone, former CIA director but now an ITT consultant, started to worry about the possibility that a Marxist government, headed by Salvatore Allende, might win the approaching September national election. McCone communicated his concern to Richard Helms, his successor as the head of the CIA. One meeting led to another in June at which Helms promised to send a CIA representative to see Geneen.

On July 16 the promised meeting took place in Washington at the Sheraton-Carlton hotel. Geneen offered William Broe, a CIA operative, a "substantial sum" to stop Allende. In August, McCone and Helms had a telephone conversation still on the topic of Chile. A little later in the month ITT's Jack Neal discussed Chile at the State Department and Ned Gerrity informed his ITT colleague, Timothy Dunleavy, that "I am instructing Hendrix to make a 50% commitment." To what remains a mystery.

Whatever was actually done among the CIA, ITT, and the State Department to stop him, on September 4 Allende came in first of the three major candidates. Nothing daunted, at an ITT board meeting September 9 and 10, Geneen and McCone agreed to make a second effort to prevent Allende's inauguration. McCone explained the new ITT plan to Henry Kissinger and Helms without delay on September 11 and 12. Attuned to the uses of social gaiety, ITT threw a party on September 13 in honor of Secretary of State William Rogers. In attendance were the Geneens and Attorney General John Mitchell.

The plot thickened. On September 14 Jack Neal communicated to the White House ITT readiness to contribute $1 million toward overthrowing Allende. At the end of the month, the CIA's Broe clued ITT's Gerrity into the details of a plan to create economic chaos in Chile. McCone and Geneen decided that the plan would not work. On October 7 Broe warned ITT that the outlook in Chile was bad and getting worse. On October 15, Neal discussed the desirability of a hard American line with Edward Korry, the ambassador to Chile. Six days later Secretary Rogers conferred with ITT and representatives of other large corporations with Chilean interests. He assured all present that President Nixon was running a "business administration."

Meanwhile, Allende's winning streak continued. On October 24 his party won the congressional elections. As though in response, in November, Anaconda Copper proposed an ad hoc committee of corporations against Allende and Kissinger thanked ITT for a hard-line memo. Anxious consultation among corporate and government officials continued. During January 1971 occurred the first of several meetings of company officials in ITT offices attended by officers of Anaconda, ITT, Kennecott, and other major operators.

On February 5 ITT conferred with Arnold Nachmanoff of Kissinger's national security staff. Nachmanoff recommended "quiet pressure" on Allende. Four days later ITT urged that Kissinger be the one to apply the quiet pressure. Two days later, in a demonstration of honor among corporations, Gerrity advised Geneen to deal separately with Allende, ditching the other American companies. Thus it occurred that on March 10 Dunleavy and his ITT retinue enjoyed an amiable meeting with Allende, the devil himself, to work out a possible joint venture between ITT and the Chilean government. During the rest of the month and continuing in April, ITT negotiated with Allende on this project as well as the compensation that Chile might offer in the event that Allende decided to nationalize ITT properties.

Allende chose nationalization. On May 26 ITT was told that its telephone company would quickly be taken into government hands. ITT proceeded on two fronts. On July 18 it sought compensation from the Overseas Private Investment Corporation (OPIC), a federal agency empowered by Congress to reimburse American companies whose overseas properties had been nationalized without compensation. On September 14 Geneen lunched with

Peter Peterson of the White House staff and General Alexander Haig, Kissinger's deputy. Still trying, William Merriam, head of ITT's Washington office, on October 1 transmitted to Peterson an eighteen-point plan to drive Allende out of office.

Allende survived longer than ITT and the White House intended. Still the narrative had a happy ending: a military dictatorship far friendlier to American capital took bloody charge of the country.

Children and economists may think that the men at the head of our great corporations spend their time thinking about new ways to please the customers or improve the efficiency of their factories and offices. What they actually concentrate on is enlisting their government to protect their foreign and domestic interests. During 1970 and 1971 Chile was not the only thing on the indefatigable Harold Geneen's mind. There was the troublesome meddling of the antitrust division of the Department of Justice into ITT acquisition plans, a matter which has already concerned us. An additional word is perhaps in order, again as emphasis upon the intimate ties between government and business. Early in 1970 Geneen conferred with Secretary of Commerce Maurice Stans (of eventual Watergate celebrity) and Ned Gerrity spoke to Richard McLaren, the assistant attorney general in charge of antitrust. Taking a hard line, McLaren insisted that ITT divest itself of the Hartford Fire Insurance Group, a key acquisition.

The pattern of pressure repeated itself. Geneen met Attorney General Mitchell at a White House dinner. Gerrity discussed antitrust with Vice President Agnew who worked on Deputy Attorney General Richard Kleindienst. Geneen and Merriam met with Charles Colson and John Ehrlichman. Gerrity alerted ITT lobbyists to mount an anti-McLaren campaign. A memo from John Ryan, Merriam's deputy, to Merriam expressed hope that Agnew could operate effectively upon McLaren: "This," he commented, "may be the break." Toward the end of 1970 ITT suggested a settlement to the Department of Justice which featured retention of Hartford. Undefeated (as yet), McLaren rejected the offer.

Patience and pressure brought their reward, all the same, in 1971. In January Geneen enlisted among his confidants in high office Peter Flanigan, an influential White House aide, and Treasury Secretary David Kennedy. Conservative congressman and Nixon intimate Bob Wilson led an attack on McLaren. As the cherry blossoms bloomed, ITT's John Ryan persuaded Kleindienst at a party to talk with ITT representatives about the antitrust case. Early in April Geneen asked Felix Rohatyn, a merger expert associated with Lazard Frères, to whip up an economic brief in support of ITT's retention of Hartford. At the end of April Rohatyn, after seeing Attorney General Mitchell, made his presentation to Kleindienst and McLaren.

May enlarged the cast of characters with the name of John Connally, the new secretary of the treasury, who advocated restructuring of the antitrust laws presumably in a manner indulgent to ITT interests. Finally on June 17, McLaren agreed to let ITT retain Hartford. On July 31 the government settled its suit against ITT and the Department of Justice surrendered an opportunity to test in the courts the legality of conglomerate expansion. Soon afterward President Nixon appointed McLaren a federal judge.

No mystery surrounds ITT's triumph of lobbying and

political pressure. What opened the White House doors was the power of money. Among the varied horrors of Watergate, one of the more sickening was disclosure of the extent to which the fundraisers of the Committee for the Reelection of the President traded prospective favors for campaign contributions. As the ITT chronicle reaffirms, all major corporations are intricately involved with the Internal Revenue Service, the Department of Justice, the Federal Communications Commission, the Food and Drug Administration, the Federal Trade Commission, the Civil Aeronautics Board, the cabinet agencies, Congress, and the White House itself. It is business truism that the path to profitable opportunity, such as a new airline route, a TV license, endorsement by the antitrust folk of a proposed merger, IRS approval of a dubious accounting innovation, FDA licensing of sketchily tested new drugs, advance information from the Department of Agriculture about crop yields, sympathetic interpretation of statutes which govern environmental protection and occupational health and safety, and so on and on, is smoothest for White House friends and full of potholes for individuals and corporations on an enemies list. As far as ITT was concerned, it was the president of the United States himself who in the end directed Deputy Attorney General Richard Kleindienst, with many expletives deleted, to lay off ITT and drop the government's antitrust action.

Concentration of political influence parallels concentration of market power. In their respective industries, the four largest corporations dominate the market. In economic lingo, these industries are oligopolies. They watch each other closely and pay heed to the voice and actions of their leader, usually the largest of their number. As economists have long argued, the consequences of oligopoly are higher prices, smaller outputs, larger expenditures for advertising, and more trivial style changes and miscellaneous product differentiation than would occur in more competitive industries. Almost all the stars of *Fortune*'s roster of corporate celebrity are more profitable than smaller firms in more competitive industries.

By common consent price competition among the giants is discouraged as ungentlemanly. The late Senator Estes Kefauver, a noted harrier of monopolists and oligopolists, once at a hearing of his Subcommittee on Economic Concentration pressed a Ford vice president, himself an economist of repute, to explain how his company could possibly be competing under the circumstances which had been revealed by corporate testimony. The whole thing was an embarrassment. Ford had happened to introduce its new models a bit earlier than General Motors, the industry's price leader. When a little later General Motors revealed its new chariots to a breathless world, it attached somewhat higher prices on comparable models in its line. A naïve soul might have thought it entirely to Ford's commercial advantage to keep its prices relatively low and enlarge its share of the market. Instead Ford hastily hiked its prices in line with its mighty rival. As the Ford vice president was unable to say in public, Ford was completely aware that if it started a price war, it was certain to lose against its larger, more efficient, and richer opponent. Better for all the oligopolists, then, to compete in their advertising and styling. Let the dealers haggle with the customers about prices at their own rather than the manufacturers' financial peril.

Economists have not done well with the phenomenon of the large corporation. It is not that they are unaware of its presence. It is not hard to find in any good introductory text a long analytical demonstration that perfect competition among large numbers of small producers or sellers, on the basis of price, for the custom of large numbers of purchasers, is certain to generate maximum efficiency in resource use, the closest congruence between the wishes of the customers and the actual composition of output, speedy response to alterations in consumer preferences, and the minimum level of profit consistent with efficient business conduct.

Economists have often reported an absence of technical benefit attributable to very large corporate scale. They deplore monopoly and oligopoly because they diminish the benefits to consumers and the community of competition. Although the specialists continue to argue about trends in market concentration, none seems to believe that oligopoly has become less significant in the course of the twentieth century. Multinational corporations are the fastest growing segment of global enterprise. They can hardly be described as boons to competition.

Professional awareness of these propositions might suggest concentration by many economists on the study of large corporations and, as a result of that study, a considerable advance in the theory of the business firm. One hungers for a general theory of oligopoly and an explanation, at a fashionably high level of intellectual abstraction, of how the multinationals work their wonders. What are the comparative advantages of conglomerates and producers of single products? How do marketing and advertising outlays differ as between concentrated and competitive industries?

What effect upon domestic employment and growth does the unprecedented geographical mobility of the global corporations impose? There are, in short, an endless series of issues, some analytical, some institutional, and others quantitative, which the looming presence of the giant corporation ought to be raising among economists. Does, for example, monopoly and oligopoly enlarge existing inequity of wealth and income distribution?

It exaggerates the situation to claim that such inquiries have been entirely neglected. Most economists are men and women of at least average sensitivity to matters of equity. Politically they probably average out somewhere to the left of the voters in a presidential election. Textbook writers take unusual care to cite heterodox souls like Paul Sweezy and the late Paul Baran, who criticize the corporation from an explicitly Marxist standpoint. Galbraith's views of the large corporation as a planned and increasingly important sector of the economy are almost invariably reported. Nevertheless, good textbooks faithfully represent the state of their art or science. Of current texts, Edwin Mansfield's *Economics* is one of the best recent entries. Mansfield's prose is superior, his analysis is lucid, his diagrams are correct, his distribution of space among major controversies fair, and his account of policy choices well-balanced.*

How does this exemplary writer handle the business firm and the market for goods? Let us see. The most elegant of the analytical chapters explain how consumers make their choices, business firms operate, and levels of gross national product are reached. In England and the United States,

---

* I have used Mansfield on occasion in my own introductory courses.

theories of consumer demand and profit maximization are likely to fit within a Marshallian context.* Although he carefully noted qualifications and exceptions in footnotes and appendixes, in the body of his text Marshall assumed a generous degree of competition throughout the economy. He imputed to consumers a capacity independent of the blandishments of sellers and advertisers to maximize their satisfaction within the constraints of their finite incomes.

Mansfield's version of these two basic assumptions is attentive to claims by Galbraith and others that advertisers manipulate the tastes of the customers who as a consequence choose under the influence of covert coercion. Alas, he does not incorporate such subversive arguments into the diagrams and prose which narrate standard theory. A student who masters the apparatus, no small feat, invests his time, energy, and tuition fees to acquire an explanation of behavior often at variance with the conduct of actual consumers and actual producers. If he or she is truly unlucky, he or she will be fascinated by the sheer elegance of economic theory, invest still more time, energy, and money, and become an economist. It is a tribute to the intelligent realism of most students that few of them take more than a single introductory course in economics.

Mansfield's is not entirely a dream world. He devotes three chapters, grouped in a section of their very own, to examining market structures, contrasting competition and monopoly, analyzing oligopoly and monopolistic competi-

---

* Alfred Marshall, a Cambridge teacher of John Maynard Keynes, wrote his enormously influential *Principles of Economics* in 1890. During his own lifetime it went through eight editions, the last issued in 1920, four years before his death.

tion, and reminding his readers that the Sherman and Clayton Acts still are the law of the land. It all goes for naught because nowhere in these chapters or elsewhere (including competing texts) is to be found a satisfactory theory of oligopoly. As Mansfield puts it, "there is no single unified model of oligopoly. Instead there are a number of models, each based on a somewhat different set of assumptions concerning the relationships among the firms that make up the oligopoly. Basically, no single model exists because economists have not yet been able to devise one that would cover all the relevant cases adequately."[7]

Embarrassing, one might expect, to be unable to explain the dominant institution in one's portion of society. Still more embarrassing to note the partial theories in vogue. The first reverts to something called the kinked demand curve, invented in 1939 by Paul Sweezy, then a young economist. His hypothesis, a work of imagination rather than of factual inquiry, sought to explain why oligopolistic prices tended to change less rapidly than prices in competitive markets. He suggested that it was a losing proposition for an oligopolist to cut his prices in hope of collaring a larger share of the market because his rivals would follow him downward and all parties would lose as a consequence of a price war. But it was equally ill-advised for a single monopolist to raise prices by himself. In such a circumstance, his fellow oligopolists would refuse to follow his lead, many of his customers would desert him, and the misguided oligopolist would be compelled to hastily withdraw his unilateral price maneuver. Prices in these concentrated markets, then, changed when the dominant corporation decided it was time for them to change and then they changed for everybody.

Mansfield summarizes as an alternative to Sweezy's explanation of price rigidity a 1944 comparison of oligopolistic pricing and strategy at cards. The late John von Neumann's and Oskar Morgentern's *Theory of Games and Economic Behavior*[8] held that oligopolistic pricing, like poker, involved for each participant or player an attempt to maximize individual profits or winnings. No participant by himself was in a position to determine the outcome of the contest. Successive moves or plays conformed to a fixed set of rules (poker) or an implicit set of understandings (oligopoly). Of course, as Mansfield adds, there is still a third available explanation of oligopoly: outright or covert collusion, illegal naturally under American law, but frequently both lawful and favored by the statutes of other countries.*

Little that Mansfield offers describes systematically the way that actual oligopolists operate and the literature in general seldom explores the messy details of concentrated industries. There are bland business histories by the gross, traditionally commissioned by executives who expect themselves and their activities to be canonized on the occasion of an important anniversary. From time to time, Congress makes revealing inquiries into such episodes as the 1972 grain sale to Russia, the response of the oil giants to the OPEC embargo, and the operations of ITT in Chile. An occasional free-lance exposé like Jerry Cohen's and Morton Mintz's *America, Inc.*[9] lifts the curtain an inch or two. Valuable individual studies like Anthony Sampson's dissection of ITT and Peter Drucker's sympathetic analysis of General Motors[10] offer some institutional understanding

---

* OPEC has administered a lesson to the rest of the world in just how efficacious a well-organized cartel can be.

based on solid factual detail. Nevertheless, these contributions are essentially random events rather than systematic empirical inquiry fostered by specific analytical hypotheses.

Because no adequate theory explains the large corporation, empirical inquiry is itself clumsier, less cumulative, and, consequently, less influential than it would be in the presence of a solid theory to be tested, explored, modified, accepted or rejected.

Thus, the large corporation, the key institution of contemporary market capitalism, is an apparition never fully materialized by conventional economics. It is an institution which, worse still, tends to be explained in excessively simple terms. No doubt the conventional doctrine of profit maximization adequately explains the behavior of small, competitive, business units, just as its companion, the maximizing consumer, may summarize customer behavior in really competitive markets. But huge corporations and militant unions are more than maximizing agencies, these are systems of power, free to choose as objectives growth, or larger market shares as objectives complementary to profit maximization.[11] Such has been the thrust of John Kenneth Galbraith's analysis in *The New Industrial State*[12] and subsequent writings.

There are good reasons why economists have been singularly unprepared to make sense of the major corporation as a private government which exercises sovereignty, legitimate or otherwise, over employees, suppliers, distributors, customers, and polities. Economists are not accustomed to exploring these matters or evaluating the countervailing roles of unions, occasionally aggressive government authorities, and rival corporations of commensurate potency. Whether or not the economists follow the trail of power, large corporations almost routinely take the sort of action which political theory assigns to legitimate public authority and democratically selected legislatures. During the oil embargo which followed the 1973 Yom Kippur war, the Seven Sisters, Exxon and its six best friends, reallocated oil from non-Arab sources to the Netherlands. The companies acted, it is reasonable to suspect, less out of empathy with the pro-Israeli sentiments of the Dutch who had angered the Arabs than out of the calculation that Rotterdam is the refining center for much of Western Europe. By striking at the Dutch, OPEC struck also at important markets for the major oil companies. It was the Seven Sisters, not the governments of Western Europe or the United States, who acted to alleviate Dutch shortages. One must hasten to add that in this action, the oil companies were acting benignly.

The foreign policies of the global corporation are not always altruistic. When General Motors and Ford shift assembly operations out of the United States to places where wages are lower, labor more docile, and politicians more hospitable, their decisions depress the United States economy and stimulate the economies of the countries where they relocate their facilities. In effect the corporations administer a deflationary American fiscal policy which may well contradict the official posture of their own government. When, as in the case of Reserve Mining, a corporation evades enforcement of environmental statutes and threatens to relocate when evasion fails, its officers are acting as legislators: they are seeking to repeal an inconvenient law.

Corporate executives are in the best position to explain the political sociology and political science of corporate management. Unfortunately, active executives also have the least interest in rendering honest accounts of their stewardship. To do so would almost certainly be fatal for the indiscreet author. Occasionally a corporate maverick blows his whistle but very rarely indeed.* Telling the truth is perceived as disloyalty to associates and friends, as a fouling of one's own nest.

Economists rarely attain high corporate office. Accountants like Harold Geneen and lawyers like Dupont's Irving Shapiro offer computing and verbal skills of evidently larger utility. By the time an economist does in a rare instance scale the pinnacle of corporate power, he has been sufficiently socialized by his experience and pleasantly enough rewarded for his contributions as to be rendered no more prone to inconvenient disclosure than any other corporate executive. For the most part, of course, economists are staff personnel, several levels at least below the corporate boardrooms, private clubs, isolated hunting lodges, and executive yachts which are the locales of important decisions. What we know about any closed, quasi-authoritarian society—CIA, FBI, army, navy, or large corporation—is dependent upon the luck of defection by sufficiently knowledgeable and eloquent former employees. We know something of the CIA from such of its sometime servants as Victor Marchetti, Philip Agee, and Sam Adams. Possibly because corporations pay better than government agencies, few of its

---

* The late T. K. Quinn drew heavily upon his own experience as a General Electric vice president in *Giant Business: Threat to Democracy* (New York: Exposition Press, 1954) and *Giant Corporations: Challenge to Freedom* (New York: Exposition Press, 1956). His revelations of corporate betrayal of consumer interest, now two decades old, have few parallels.

alumni write other than glowing accounts of their recent employers.

Economists in the employ of corporations have excellent personal reasons to restrain curiosity about awkward topics and particularly to avoid publication of serious criticism. As flourishing members of Galbraith's technostructure, the assortment of experts of many stripes who actually operate day-to-day affairs, they soon realize that their future prosperity and status among peers and neighbors correlate with successful analysis, forecasting, and operations control. After all, why not? In their graduate training, apprentice economists struggle to master esoteric techniques of linear programming, systems analysis, and operations research. Corporations do them a favor by paying them to apply such investments of time and intellectual capital to real problems with quantitative outcomes.

David Blank, a Columbia Ph.D. in economics, exemplifies the successful industrial economist. He is chief economist and a vice president of the Columbia Broadcasting System, responsible for all the social-science research which might involve CBS interests in records, books, and periodicals, as well as radio and television. A man who enjoys his work, Blank was quoted as saying happily, "You can get the most refined, detailed view of the broadcasting industry because there is such a volume of data available. It's a gold mine— you can spend all your life studying it."[13] On condition, that is to say, that you refrain from controversies which damage your employer's interest. And this is easiest done, for men and women of conscience, by coming to accept your employer's view of the world. It is not cynicism which turns social-science critics and intellectuals into useful technicians: it is the human process which over time assimilates self-interest to larger social purposes.

Economists are members of the American meritocracy. Traditionally, advanced degrees have opened doors to professional status, financial reward, and upward class mobility to hordes of lower-middle-class Jews, Irish, Italians, and, in the last decade, blacks, women, and Hispanics. For these ambitious strivers, the more quickly the appropriate credential can be wrested from the graduate department the better. Here is a difficulty. A twenty-four-year-old degree candidate in economics at a good university has been well-trained in a cluster of fashionable mathematical and econometric techniques. Unfortunately youth and training conspire to render him ignorant of the central economic institutions of his society. At best he has picked up a few scraps of information about the misdeeds of corporations, a distorted view of unions, and a vague feeling that government regulation distorts some of the markets upon which he has been taught to theorize.

Now to write a dissertation about an industry or a regulatory agency is exceedingly time-consuming for graduate students who start with little empirical information. The danger is real that needed data will be treated as corporate secrets and that months and years will be wasted on vain attempts to piece together an adequate statistical picture. In the meanwhile, craftier classmates are forging forward in races for publication and tenure by choosing topics susceptible to fewer uncertainties and speedier conclusions. The trick is to apply an arcane mathematical method to a small problem or available body of data, manipulate the information elegantly in a computer, and defend the results to an approving dissertation committee whose members are also eager to speed their students on paths of professional glory. Under these conditions, few dissertations are likely to add to the stock of useful information. Almost none do.

Ignorance of the real world is more than bliss: it is very nearly a prerequisite to a successful career in conventional economics. No wonder then that economic textbooks are so abstract and that graduate schools continue to teach the rarefied, contentless versions of business behavior and consumer choice which their faculties are most comfortable with. Thus it is in the intellectual self-interest of the profession to chat about Pareto-optimality and to content themselves with scraps of old explanations of the behavior and influence of the great corporations which bestride the planet.

The real world constantly astonishes the adept economist. Unemployment rises but inflation persists. Cartels refuse to disintegrate. Unions behave differently at different times in different places. Fiscal and monetary policies sometimes work, other times don't. Whole industries are puzzlingly sluggish in their responses to the clear signals from the market. Even altruism on occasion is a device more efficient than the market. But so long as business audiences will pay economic stars $3,000 a lecture to repeat the analyses which past events have invalidated, there is little reason for them or their less affluent colleagues to accept such reproofs as Galbraith's:

Power being so comprehensively deployed in a very large part of the total economy, there can no longer, except for reasons of game-playing or more deliberate intellectual evasion, be any separation between economics and politics. When the modern corporation acquires power over markets, power in the community, power over the state, power over belief, it is a political instrument, different in form and degree but not in kind from the state itself.[14]

5

trade unions: theoretical nuisances

I last met with a room full of economists in Boston at the Industrial Relations Research Association annual meeting of 1963 —and there discussed the relationships between Labor and Intellectuals.

Preparing for that meeting, I remember feeling that I would be facing an impenetrable wall of prejudice—the more difficult to cope with because it was erected by people whose assurance regarding their lack of prejudice was total. Now, having distanced myself from the union movement by retirement, after decades of activity and service inside it, I cannot say that my views have changed much.

I believe that prejudice against unions and workers in American society is pervasive and profound. . . .

—Brendan Sexton, a long-time
United Auto Workers Officer

For nearly two centuries unionism has annoyed economists. As economic organizations, unions frequently (as in the building trades) do their best to raise wages by restricting the number of new apprentices they will accept. If they are strong enough, unions will interfere with employer discretion over the introduction of labor-saving devices. By insisting on grievance procedures and due-process hearings, unions threaten factory discipline and handcuff foremen and supervisors. Because unions traditionally prescribe a single hourly or weekly rate for each job, employers are precluded from rewarding their more adept and conscientious employees. Although they rarely succeed, unions endeavor to secure monopoly power over job rewards and job definitions.

In the last decade economists who rely on the ill-fated Phillips curve have assigned major responsibility for inflation to union negotiators who push wages up far faster than productivity rises. In self-defense their employers are compelled to adjust prices, these higher prices justify new wage demands, and off the economy goes to the inflationary races. Economists have had little good to say about unions as economic institutions. There is widespread agreement that unions damage productivity, interfere with individual incentives, and promote inflation.

Nor does this indictment by any means complete the charges against unions. It is difficult, for one thing, to explain their behavior by consistent theory. As I write in mid-1975, some unions have indicated to their employers that they prefer that younger members be laid off rather than that everybody share the work or accept reduced benefits. Such was the choice of New York City's policemen, firemen, and sanitation workers. But other unions, among them garment workers and airline pilots, have preferred to protect jobs and postpone contractually promised pay increases. In the United States wage increases have for three years lagged behind rising consumer prices. In England by contrast, unions have steadily extracted additional wages at rates higher than movements in the English cost of living.

As economic institutions, unions are harmful to the fantasies of pure competition cherished by economists; as political organizations they are perceived as disruptive of the established order. Conservative Britons of advancing age frighten themselves with recollections of England's 1925 General Strike. In the 1930s American workers menaced the rights of property by refusing to leave factories until their employers agreed to recognize their unions and initiate collective bargaining. Respectable men and women of affairs muttered of revolution. Current events supply more up-to-date examples of misbehavior. Well-disciplined German unions have secured representation on corporate boards of directors, codetermination of management in legal form if not in operating practice. English shop stewards call wildcat strikes at the drop of a grievance. Unionized Portuguese printers set themselves up as guides to the editorial line taken by *Republica*, the socialist newspaper which hired them.

Economists have been no better able to cope with unions which mingle aspirations for income redistribution, worker control, and proletarian brotherhood with conventional demands for high wages, shorter hours, and new fringe benefits than they are equipped to grapple with large corporations as impure mixtures of avarice and political power.

Samuelson's handling of unions is an example of his profession's somewhat gingerly treatment of institutions which show no sign of disappearing of their own accord but which serve (for economists) ambiguous functions. The eighth edition of his text devotes a single chapter to "Labor and Industrial Relations." In fourteen pages, Samuelson says something about union structure; the history of the American labor movement; communism, corruption, and democracy as influences upon union behavior; labor legislation; and current issues in collective bargaining. Unions reappear twenty-two chapters onward. At this point three pages on wage determination explain the four methods by which unions seek to enlarge the compensation of their members. Appropriate diagrams garnish the exposition.

Samuelson, a veteran sympathizer with liberal Democrats from John F. Kennedy on, quickly surrenders the delicate task of evaluating the significance of unions to the economy to accredited experts. He quotes one of them, Princeton's Albert E. Rees, to the following effect:

We tend to overemphasize the role of unions, both in . . . their own industries and . . . the economy as a whole. . . . The other two-thirds may have their wages and salaries influenced by what the unions do, but I feel there are very strong independent forces on the demand side that govern their rates of pay. . . . Even in the . . . unionized (one-third) there are some very weak or almost impotent unions that have had very little to do with the wages of their members. . . .

In a series of rough guesses, I would say perhaps a third of the trade unions have raised the wages of their members by 15 percent to 20 percent above what they might be in a non-union situation; another third by perhaps 5 percent to 10 percent, and the remaining third not at all. . . . The high figures tend to be found, not in periods of inflation, but in periods of posperity combined with stable prices. . . . In an (inflationary) period like 1946–1948, for example, the union people may even lag behind simply because of the rigidities involved in the collective bargaining process.[1]

Rees, in other words, comforts himself with the conclusion that unions are on the whole too weak to do much harm.

Yale's Lloyd Reynolds, Samuelson's second expert witness, though possibly a trace warmer in his union sympathies, nevertheless approximates Rees' conclusions:

Summing up these diverse consequences of collective bargaining, one can make a strong case that unionism has at any rate not worsened the wage structure. We are inclined to be more venturesome than this, and to say that its net effect has been beneficial. This conclusion will doubtless strike many economists as surprising. . . .

Fears that complete unionization will bring seismic disruption of the wage structure do not seem to be well founded. . . . The countries with the strongest union movements appear to have a wage structure which is more orderly and defensible than the wage structure of countries where unionism has been weak.[2]

Let it be said again that neither Samuelson nor his two chosen authorities are hostile to unions, although Reynolds clearly intimates that a good many other economists tend to view unions without enthusiasm. For that matter, Samuelson himself discusses union wage-raising tactics in a section on market imperfections, no sign of favor to union behavior. A few economists, not many, have enjoyed relationships of trust and mutual respect with unions. Leon Keyserling and Robert Nathan, old New Dealers, have worked with and for unions. John Dunlop, the present secretary of labor, has over the years enjoyed close ties in particular with the construction unions. Even more startlingly he enjoys the friendship and admiration of the AFL-CIO's durable tyrant George Meany.

All honor to the exceptions, but for most academic economists unions rank low on their research agenda. Graduate departments seldom encourage their students to enter union employment as staff economists. In the opinion of a significant professional minority, by no means quarantined in Chicago and its East and West Coast outposts, unions are a seriously harmful form of market corruption, rising at worst to monopoly itself. As Milton Friedman has stated this position:

Unions have . . . not only harmed the public at large and workers as a whole by distorting the use of labor; they have also made the incomes of the working class more unequal by reducing the opportunities available to the most disadvantaged workers.[3]

In Chicago, evidently, unions have lost ground since Adam Smith, no admirer of unions, thought it wise to point out that "masters are always and every where in a sort of tacit, but constant and uniform combination, not to raise the wages of labour above their actual rate."[4] Even more warmly, he scolded "our merchants and manufacturers" who "complain much of the bad effects of high wages in raising the price, and thereby lessening the sale of their goods at home and abroad. They say nothing concerning the bad effects of high profits. They are silent with regard to the pernicious effects of their own gains. They complain only of those of other people."[5] In two hundred years, some things have changed very little.

The point is not that in some sense "unions are right" and economists wrong, it is again that American and English economists have by and large perceived unions incompletely and, therefore, inaccurately. From the union side, economics often appears irrelevant because its practitioners refuse to cope with unions as political organizations. Even oversimplification of union objectives to the single goal of wage bill maximization does not escape the political. Whose wage bill? Over what time period? By whose choice? A union's negotiating stance is the consequence of arguments over interest and ideology within unions and between unions. The shape of actual collective bargaining inevitably reflects membership moods, the political strength of union leaders, and union rivalries and relationships.

To say this much ought simply to repeat the banal. But it is less banal to claim that on serious issues of national importance the natural tendency of many economists, among them charter members of the profession's New Frontier–Great Society wing is to perceive the world at an angle quite distant from that of even conventional union officials. When President Nixon on August 15, 1971, for example, abruptly shifted his administration's economic policy, economists, businessmen, and unionists reacted quite differently to the initial ninety-day freeze on wages and prices.

Business economists are generally loyal to their corporate employers. It is reasonable then to take the reactions of the National Association of Business Economists as representative of business opinion. Soon after the freeze, NABE surveyed its members and evoked from them "a composite forecast of the economy in 1972 that sounded as if it were written by a White House speech writer; strong steady growth with declining inflation and unemployment and rising profits and stock prices."[6]

The ecstatic economists endorsed both the freeze itself and the more selective program promised by the president when the freeze ended. Under controls, they were convinced, GNP would soar 9 percent, consumer prices edge upward a mere 3.2 percent, and unemployment downward to a tolerable (for the employed) figure of 5.1 percent by the end of 1972. Best of all corporate profits were to grow at a 12 percent rate. Business sentiment in favor of controls had been rising in the months before the president took his bold action. Now that they had come to pass, the business community was pleased and relieved. Attention was being paid by the White House, at last, to the drift of the economy.

For liberals, radicals, and trade unionists a program which is wildly popular in the business sector becomes automatically a candidate for close inspection, and suspicious evaluation. Liberal economists did criticize some of the tax concessions to business that constituted part of the Nixon program. To a degree they were concerned that the controls treat equitably wage earners, stockholders, and other recipients of property income. Nevertheless, liberal economists halted quite early on a road that unionists were attracted by. Thus both Michigan's Gardner Ackley and Brookings' Arthur Okun (former chairman of the Council of Economic Advisers in the Johnson era) specifically opposed an excess-profits tax. In late August, testifying before the Joint Economic Committee, the former described himself as "firmly opposed" to "any limitation on profits." Profits "had been excessively low and should be allowed to rise." He dismissed excess-profits levies as a "lousy idea." Generally concurring in his colleague's judgments, Okun proposed a 5 percent standard for wage improvements during the controls period.[7]

The gap between unions and liberal allies ought not to be exaggerated. Both groups favored tax benefits to the poor, generalized income maintenance, public service jobs, and a

rich diet of federal expenditure upon social and environmental betterment. Nevertheless, the economists favored
these good things within important constraints which in the
end separated them from their occasional union allies.

The constraints in 1971 (and 1975) were of three kinds.
In the first place, liberal economists favor social progress as
one of several important objectives, among them rapid economic growth. In the attempt to jointly maximize several
desired goals, trade-offs are inevitable. It is perpetually
tempting for economists to include among the trade-offs
the sanctity of union contracts and the equity of income
distribution.* Moreover, liberal economists are, according
to their own lights, practical men and women who look
further into the future and identify wider consequences of
otherwise desirable policies than labor leaders can usually
afford to. Keeping an eye upon growth, inflation, and efficiency as well as justice, liberal economists are concerned
also with political possibility, and are prone to accept half-
loaves or thick slices in preference to no bread at all. Cau-
tious economists are likely to endorse defective proposals,
like Nixon's Family Assistance Plan, as first steps toward
genuine negative income taxes. Even though controls may
be less than fairly formulated and administered, they may
permit increased fiscal stimulus and enhanced economic
growth.

The third constraint is much the most important. It is the
reminder that economists are, after all, economists before

---

* Arthur Okun's 1974 Godkin Lectures at Harvard focused on the trade-
offs between equity and efficiency. See *Equity and Efficiency: the Big
Tradeoff* (Washington: Brookings Institution, 1975).

they are liberals, redistributionists, or mild radicals. Like their more conservative colleagues, liberal economists preserve faith in markets. With all their imperfections, markets, they like to believe, do allocate resources with reasonable efficiency. And with all its inequities, the existing structure of income distribution does roughly measure an impersonal market judgement upon the comparative contributions to salable merchandise of different human beings and assorted nonhuman resources. Excess-profits taxes are notoriously difficult to administer and easy to evade. It is hard to avoid thinking, however, that liberal economists justify their opposition to excess-profits taxation by their fear of dampening incentives; they appear to lack any sense of overpowering inequity in the existing distribution of income and wealth by size and function.

Their training, as George Stigler reminded us, has had a conservative influence upon them. They do not believe in free lunch. They are partial to theories of marginal change and competitive markets because only through the analysis of such markets under such assumptions can economics aspire to scientific status.

Unions live with the reality of supermarket prices, cost-of-living clauses in contracts, and the pressures upon their members of both inflation and unemployment. They are more often aware than most economists of the monopoly power exercised by the employer in both labor and product markets. Long before August 15, 1971, George Meany had signified his support for an "equitable" income policy, one which pressed with equal force upon labor and nonlabor forms of income. His assessment of the Nixon program was accordingly vehement:

Today's political cliché—"reordering national priorities"—has been applied with a vengeance by President Nixon. But he applied it in reverse.

Unprecedented and unhealthy tax relief to corporations would be the ultimate effect of the keystone of the President's new economic program. It would reverse progress in America. The government of compassion which many believed had come into being would be halted. Corporate profit-and-loss charts—not the public need—would have first priority. The poor, the cities and states, federal employees, wage and salary earners—all would foot the bill and the sole beneficiaries would be the wealthy and the corporation.[8]

Descending from these rhetorical heights, Meany proceeded to attack specific administration tax proposals as a "radical departure from the concept of a graduated income tax based on ability to pay." As Meany interpreted its impact, the investment tax credit (an important part of the Nixon program), promised little for employment, threatened a tax loss to the Treasury aggregating $70 billion the ensuing decade, and, most outrageous of all, shifted tax burdens from corporations and their stockholders to middle- and low-income taxpayers.

No doubt President Meany had his own schedule of trade-offs. But the unmistakable emphasis upon jobs and equity strongly implied a weighting system different from that in vogue among the economists. Although some fashionable critics on the left dismiss unions as burnt-out cases and deplore the hard-line anticommunist stance of the AFL-CIO, the embarrassing fact is that no other important interest group aside from the unions persistently stresses in its own media and the speeches of its leaders issues of economic justice, redistribution, enlargement of the public sector, universal health care, adequate public housing, and the close connections between these issues and jobs for members—any union's overriding priority.

In foreign policy the national AFL-CIO often seems locked into Cold War postures a generation outmoded. But on domestic issues the official literature of the trade union movement describes American society in terms long associated with the Old Left, the nonpotsmoking, Marx-reading radicals of the thirties and forties. The allegedly conservative AFL-CIO is far more concerned than any but an inconsequential fraction of economists with concentration of economic power, monopoly, and maldistribution of income, wealth, and authority.

On a whole series of controversies which deeply concern trade unions, the standard academic position is, if not unwise, at least conservative. Nowhere is this conservatism more obvious than in the area of wage-price controls where economists suggest that the prior responsibility for inflation belongs with unions rather than corporate managers. When economists reluctantly come around to advocating controls, they invariably propose to regulate wages and prices. In England matters may be otherwise ordered, but in this country the formula distorts actual relationships of power. Corporations are frequently more powerful than the regulatory agencies which endeavor to restrain their actions. With rare exceptions they are much stronger than the unions with which they deal, if only because they can shift their operations out of one locality or one country much more easily than union members can uproot themselves and follow their fleeing employers. Employers are stronger than unions also because the media are on the whole unsympathetic to unions. Newspapers and national periodicals are owned by capitalists, not by unions. As the late A. J.

Liebling said, the way to enjoy a free press is to own one. Unions win few battles against powerful corporations. Their victories are against city governments, small contractors, and other relatively vulnerable opponents.

Battles over controls translate into issues of income distribution in which the union case is usually ignored or ill-heard. Thus guidelines of the Kennedy-Johnson variety, tied to estimates of national productivity trends, are recipes for the freezing of functional income shares and reaffirmations of economic growth as the drug of choice for the ills of the unemployed, black, female, and poor. These guidelines accept existing distribution of income and wealth as at least tolerable, and at most just.

It is enduringly difficult for a profession, which tends out of professional self-interest to exaggerate the role of competitive markets, not to believe in the broad equity of the decisions that these "impersonal" markets make about who is to get what, who is to live in Beverly Hills and who in Watts.

It was much of the burden of chapter 3 that economists have handicapped themselves with prohibitions against comparing the satisfactions of the rich and poor and by a preference for private over public activity because the market allegedly disciplines private but not public providers of goods and services. Accordingly, conventional specialists are likely to be tempted by the virtues of tax reductions which leave unchanged the relative situations of the economic actors and at the same time enlarge the scope of those private markets in which competition putatively reigns.

Those economists deserve praise who have bent their energies to enlargement of the public sector and resistance to the attempts of the unneedy to further widen the gaping loopholes through which inordinate quantities of new wealth flow to them. It is sad, all the same, how little economic wisdom is available in support of limitations of private advertising, genuinely redistributive taxation, and confiscatory inheritance levies.

Aside from issues of growth and efficiency, economists as specialists and "scientists" (as distinguished from their roles as politicians, trade union aides, presidential appointees, speech writers, classroom teachers, and plain citizens) have amazingly little to say about the major social and economic issues that afflict their society. Long ago Keynes expressed hope that "if economists could manage to get themselves thought of as humble competent people on a level with dentists, that would be splendid." Few of his contemporaries confused Keynes with the model dentist. The pity is that economists are in a fair way to approximating Keynes' dream and supplying technical analyses, like dentures, to anyone who happens to want them.

Of all social scientists economists are happiest with evidence that class considerations are of diminishing importance, for the steady bias of conventional economics is in the direction of registering events as the consequence of the atomistic decisions of independent actors, performing their calculations of utility and profit in splendid isolation from group, class, and ethnic influences. Economists have been happy with the current cliché which holds that unions have become increasingly conservative as their members have risen into the middle class and secured for their families the standard American package of consumer goods: car, color TV, air-conditioning, barbecue pit, vacation cottage, and boat. But as books like Sar Levitan's collection *Blue-Collar Workers*[9] and Andrew Levison's *The Working Class Majority*[10] sharply demonstrate, not very many union members are in the middle class, at least if this status is defined by job security, educational credentials, and community standing. Large numbers of blue- and white-collar workers have precariously acquired middle-class incomes by dint of moonlighting, the full-time labor of their wives, and the contributions of adolescent children. A recession like the 1969–70 episode, small by business-cycle historical precedents, is enough to remind "affluent" unionists just how precarious their status is. In the current 1973–75 deep recession or small depression, unemployment among building trade workers, archetypes of conservative, middle-class unionism, has been close to 25 percent. It is simply not middle class to be unemployed for long periods. Nor is it middle class to realize that your financial security is utterly out of your own control.

The public image of George Meany appears to be founded on his lifelong, hard anticommunism and his undeviating support of American policy in Vietnam. But it is a grave error to translate these attitudes into domestic conservatism. In 1975, the "conservative" head of the "establishment" AFL-CIO, by distant craft origin a plumber, comes on remarkably radical by comparison with most liberal economists. His plea for full employment and tax reform, for example, is in the first instance implicitly and in the second explicitly redistributive. Full employment, which many liberal economists have been reluctant to press seriously because of fancied inflation trade-offs, does most for the most vulnerable portions of the labor force: blacks, Hispanics, teenagers, and women. As the last chapter indicated, it is no accident that the Ford administration, the most conservative in recent history, plainly welcomes high rates of unemployment for the next few years. By themselves, such rates increase existing inequalities of income, wealth, and power and diminish union influence on Congress and their own members. In bad times, even a George Meany lives on the edge of the class struggle.

Union experience dictates ideological stances. At the plant level, local officials struggle hard over job definitions, work rules, new processes, retiming, and the minutiae of rest breaks, locker-room facilities, vacation schedules, and sick leaves. At the professional level, it is amazing how quickly workers like schoolteachers and college teachers come to appreciate the importance of these small matters when boards of education propose to increase class size, limit sabbatical leaves, or add to the number of courses to be taught. At contract time, union negotiators fight hard over the division of the sales or tax dollar. When the settlements are national in scope, time and again, friendly or hostile presidents pleasantly or painfully influence the shape of ultimate agreements. An armory of federal statutes awaits the selective enforcement of secretaries of labor and attorneys general. Congress has been known to intervene. And as the external battle is waged, private intraunion fights between old and young, blacks and whites, newcomers and veterans, men and women, and skilled and less-skilled operatives, must somehow be adjusted.

Perhaps in the end, just as economists assert, union gains are closely correlated with per capita productivity. But rank-and-file unionists and even their leaders should be pardoned if they interpret the negotiating process as an exercise in the uses of power. In many and possibly in most of the industries in which unions operate successfully, large corporate units sufficiently manage their markets so that they pass on to their customers the larger wages they agree to pay their employees. Wage restraint on the part of unions is at least as likely to swell corporate profits as to moderate corporate prices.

The union model of reality focuses upon politics and power rather than free markets and marginal productivity. In their struggles with employers and politicians, unions generally perceive themselves as weaker than their adversaries. In this country at least they are usually correct. Unions are nearer the root of the matter than the economists in assuming that in the American economy income and wealth are generated by private and public power as well as by the more conventional economic processes featured in the price theory treatises.

None of the foregoing is to be taken as enrolling George Meany in the senior auxiliary of Charles Reich's Consciousness III. However, unions, unlike conventional economists, have long and sensibly taken it for granted that private power and political influence are important sources of income and wealth. One guesses that few alert members of unions would be startled by the items which appeared in Reich's catalog of public largess.

Macroeconomic monetary and fiscal policy is an inevitable exercise in the creation of new property and the alteration of existing property. When in the holy war against inflation, the Federal Reserve System feels compelled to raise interest rates, banks impose these rates on borrowers, bank earnings rise, and bank stockholders, few of them poor widows and orphans, benefit. If to stimulate economic growth, encourage energy exploration, or prevent future bottlenecks, Congress and the president give tax incentives hitched to increased corporate purchases of machines, tools, and factory facilities, the politicians may or may not accomplish their explicit objective, but they will certainly enlarge the size of deductible business expense, raise profits, and please another (or the same) assortment of predominantly wealthy stockholders.

Unions have every reason to struggle ferociously over the formulation of controls legislation and the membership of control agencies. After their experience of Nixon controls, it is plain to unions that controls as administered by conservative national administrations, whatever their surface even-handedness, will press most heavily upon wages and most lightly upon profits and other forms of property income.

By comparison with other countries, American unions are both conservative in their goals and tactics, and weak in their confrontations with the larger corporations. In England where unions are more militant, Marxist, responsive to rank-and-file opinion, and powerful, unions in the first half of this decade have not only pushed wages up far more rapidly than the efficiency of the British economy warranted (and thus contributed to an inflation which by mid-1975 was running at an annual 36 percent rate), they have also succeeded in these five years in keeping ahead of the cost of living. Since English growth has been negligible, the result has been a substantial redistribution of income away from the rich and the middle class toward blue-collar workers.

The state of England does not suggest that American redistributionists would be well advised to emulate the British model. The economy stays afloat because much Arab money is on deposit in the City of London and North Sea oil has at last begun to flow. British economists, however, are unlikely to share the complacency of their American brethren about the neutral consequences of union activity. The AFL-CIO may be as relatively weak and relatively nonideological as I have suggested, but there is no doubt that in its absence the pressures by corporations and affluent individuals to widen tax privileges still further, extract government subsidies, and assist the unneedy, would be entirely successful, instead of only mostly successful.

Old Leftists and new radicals are prone to despair of union attitudes on military budgets and environmental protections. One of the numerous reasons why Senator McGovern fared badly among blue-collar workers in 1972 was his advocacy of a one-third reduction in the Pentagon share of the federal pie. According to the pollsters, blue-collar workers during the Vietnam conflict were just about as hawkish as the population in general. They were alarmed by the prospect of the war ending, even if lukewarm or opposed to the war, because jobs were threatened. The situation is similar when environmental regulations appear to threaten employment. Unionists are no more eager than members of the Sierra Club to breathe polluted air or drink carcinogenic water. Almost surely larger proportions of factory workers enjoy hunting, fishing, boating, and expeditions to the national parks than do urban Friends of the Earth. But theirs is the exceedingly unpleasant trade-off between next week's paycheck and other, usually more-distant, diffused, and abstract benefits. No wonder that so many union members and even more of their wives voted for the Hero of Watergate.

Something is ignored, however, when these attitudes are

understood as matters of choice. It is just because unions are weak, American politicians mostly conservative, and unemployment endemic that unions are constrained to protect jobs in inefficient industries by tariffs and quotas, in harmful activities by opposing environmental protection, and in useless arms production by resisting cuts in the Pentagon budget. Where are the alternatives to these jobs that conscious planning in a less conservative community would surely provide?

Some unions are corrupt. Others operate out of a concept of their members' interests too narrow even for the good of their members. Nevertheless, the union view of the American economy is considerably more realistic and substantially more radical than that of the economic profession.

6

four visionaries

When I laid down the last volume of the Traité, I had become a different being. The "principle of utility" understood as Bentham understood it, and applied in the manner in which he applied it through these three volumes, fell exactly into its place as the keystone which held together the detached and fragmentary component parts of my knowledge and beliefs. It gave unity to my conceptions of things. I now had opinions, a creed, a doctrine, a religion; the inculcation and diffusion of which could be made the principal outward purpose of a life. And I had a grand conception laid before me of changes to be effected in the condition of mankind through that doctrine.

—JOHN STUART MILL
AUTOBIOGRAPHY

206

In his magisterial *History of Economic Analysis,* Joseph Schumpeter generalized that economists of originality invariably began with a vision of their field of inquiry, an outline both of the contours of reality and of the strategies, moral and intellectual, necessary to widen the understanding of their subject. According to Schumpeter, "Analytic effort starts when we have conceived our vision of the set of phenomena that caught our interest, no matter whether this set lies in virgin soil or in land that has been cultivated before." Once this crucial choice is made, "we assemble further facts in addition to those perceived already, and learn to distrust others that figured in the original vision." This process is anything but "scientific," neutral, or free from value judgment. To the contrary, "it should be perfectly clear that there is a wide gate for ideology to enter this process. In fact, it enters on the very ground floor, into the preanalytic, cognitive act of which we have been speaking. Analytic work begins with material provided by our vision of things, and this vision is ideological almost by definition."[1]

It has been the theme of this book that standard economics in either its neo-Keynesian or its neoclassical, Chicago variant, starts from a vision which, whatever once may have been its congruence to the realities of capitalism, now is outmoded by changes in behavior, economic institutions, and power relationships within domestic boundaries and among nations. Only in calm periods and places do establishment economists act as reliable analysts of the present and acute forecasters of future change.

In the last generation relations between developing and developed countries have significantly changed. The relative weight of the American economy in the "free world" has diminished and that of the more dynamic German and Japanese societies has increased. Food and energy are unlikely ever to be as cheap in the future as they were in the past. Ominous signs multiply that neo-Malthusian disparities between population and resource growth pose problems potentially as alarming as the prospect of nuclear war. OPEC embargoes, dramatic crop failures, and unexpected depletion of American food reserves are the sort of events which cause the curves on graphs to shoot agitatedly up or down.

As the events of 1974 and 1975 ought demonstrate to even the slowest economist, minor adjustments in tax, monetary, and budgetary policy—just about the entire armory of modern macroeconomics, are incapable of resolving intertwined dilemmas of inflation, unemployment, and energy supply. For mainstream practitioners to accept 5.5–6.0 percent unemployment as a permanent anti-inflation barrier is to confess intellectual bankruptcy. To call such figures full employment is to indulge in Newspeak.

In the 1970s, economics is beginning to seem nearly as irrelevant to a skeptical public as it did in the 1930s, and for similar reasons. The standard agenda drifts farther and farther from the anxieties of men and women in ordinary jobs. Economists ought to be thinking about full employment, democratic planning, equitable distribution of income and wealth, taming of oligopolies, domesticating global corporations, increasing worker participation in management, and organizing universal health care. There are, it is only fair to concede, *some* economists so engaged, but the professional prizes continue to go to virtuosos of economic theory that is comprehensible by few and useful to none.

There was a time, not that distant in the past, when economists of the first rank were endowed with moral vision, a feeling for institutional complexity, and a sense of history. To recall when the going was good for economics is more than a sentimental journey to the tombs of giants. As we shall shortly see, Smith, Marx, Veblen, and Keynes are, dare one say, more relevant to the comprehension of our baffling world than any economist now living whom one would care to nominate.

More than the piety which legitimately attends the bicentennial celebration of *The Wealth of Nations* justifies that attention be paid to the historical Adam Smith, who, of course, was a radical not a reactionary. His leisurely eighteenth-century prose emitted a perfume of compassion for the poor and the oppressed, at a time when the conventional wisdom of mercantilism actually favored poverty as an aid to national greatness. Although since 1776, the ignorant and the tendentious have enlisted Smith as an apologist for a rising capitalist class, his own heart went out to laborers on farms and in workshops. Smith, as earlier noted, deplored the unfairness of criticizing incipient trade unions and ignoring the far more serious malfeasances of employers. Smith's suspicion of business morality very nearly approximated the medieval, Catholic distaste for the pursuit of gain as a threat to individual virtue and ultimate hope of salvation. "People of the same trade," he complained, "seldom meet together, even for merriment and diversion, but the conversation ends in a conspiracy against the public, or in some contrivance to raise prices."[2] He praised "country gentlemen and farmers" because they "are to their great honor, of all people, the least subject to the wretched spirit of monopoly."[3] In favor of consumers Smith uttered probably the first good words in the record of economic commentary: "Consumption is the sole end and purpose of all production; and the interest of the producer ought to be attended to, only so far as it may be necessary for promoting that of the consumer. The maxim is so perfectly self-evident, that it would be absurd to attempt to prove it."[4] Words which have long been less than "perfectly self-evident" to the commissioners of regulatory agencies now operated in producer interests.

A child of the Scottish enlightenment, Smith believed in the probability of human progress. It was a hard-headed confidence, no woolly utopian fantasy, for Smith premised his optimism not on altruism but upon the innate selfishness of the human species and the natural harmony of interests among competing egotisms which laissez-faire societies at peace with their neighbors were certain to enjoy. Human beings were certainly no angels: "Every individual is continually exerting himself to find out the most advantageous employment for whatever capital he can command. It is his own advantage, indeed, and not that of the society, which he has in view. But the study of his own advantage naturally . . . leads him to prefer that employment which is most advantageous to the society."[5] Or in an even sturdier version of the same doctrine, "The uniform, constant, and uninterrupted effort of every man to better his own condition, the principle from which public and national, as well as private opulence is originally derived, is frequently powerful enough to maintain the natural progress of things toward improvement, in spite both of the extravagance of government, and of the greatest errors of administration."[6]

The final elements of the vision with which Smith started

his exploration of the economic universe were a principle of technical efficiency and a view of human ability. The division of labor was at the center of Smith's theory of economic development. Like so many other aspects of social behavior, "this division of labour, from which so many advantages are derived, is not originally the effect of any human wisdom, which foresees and intends that general opulence to which it gives occasion." No, "it is the necessary, though very slow and gradual, consequence of a certain propensity in human nature which has in view no such extensive utility; the propensity to truck, barter, and exchange one thing for another."[7] As Walter Bagehot aptly put it, Smith was convinced that each infant was born with a tiny Scotsman implanted in his bosom.

Smith's conception of human talent and achievement was egalitarian. Heredity counted for little and environment for nearly everything. True to John Locke, Smith asserted that "the difference between the most dissimilar characters, between a philosopher and a common street porter, for example, seems to arise not so much from nature, as from habit, custom, and education." For, "when they come into the world, and for the first six or eight years of their existence, they were, perhaps, very much alike, and neither their parents nor playfellows could perceive any remarkable difference."[8]

There was, according to Smith, no dodging the feckless tendencies of humankind. We are none of us born anything really special. It is our good luck that God or nature implants in each baby certain instincts, among them that powerful drive to "truck" and "barter." This instinct, allied to each person's "uniform" and "uninterrupted" effort to get rich and rise in the world, drives each of us to work harder, save money, produce the things the customers are willing to buy, and, as a providential side effect, enrich the community as well. No use complaining. Men and women were naturally selfish.

Two centuries ago such a vision of human affairs was quite enough to make its owner a radical critic of the way his government acted and the economy operated. This natural order of free competition which a benign but indolent deity had arranged, required good human behavior and intelligent political institutions. Among much else, natural liberty depended upon an absence of monopoly, unhampered movement of workers from lesser- to better-paid jobs, unimpeded flow of capital from low- to high-profit business opportunities, and, above all, freedom from government intervention.

In the eighteenth century, this was heresy. The rulers of England, like those of other respectable European states, were mercantilists. They knew that the first task of the king's ministers was central direction of the economy for the monarch's greater glory, and not at all incidentally, the more rapid accumulation of gold and silver in the royal exchequer. Gold and glory were in the mercantilist universe inseparable allies. This doctrine had less pernicious effects in England than in France only because English public administration was weak, the English Channel allowed Britain to dispense with standing armies, and, in consequence, little armed force was available to enforce bad policies. Nevertheless, English officials from time to time did make sporadic and partially successful attempts to interfere with the normal operations of natural liberty, particularly in the area of foreign trade. Navigation acts preferred English vessels and excluded foreign carriers. An intricate collection of tariffs, quotas, and rebates to exporters checked the normal flow of trade and turned smuggling into a major growth industry.

The landscape was cluttered with obstacles to the pursuit of self-interest. Anachronistic guilds imposed long apprenticeships and limited entry into the mysteries of their crafts. Laws of settlement demanded financial guarantees from men and women who had moved from one parish to another because they had no money and hoped to make some. Henry Fielding's Squire Western spent much of his time as a justice of the peace ordering indigent migrants shipped back to the sources of their poverty. England gained because these cruel and inefficient regulations were more frequently evaded than obeyed. Better still to repeal these foolish laws.

Smith inveighed against such practices in literally hundreds of pages of eloquent and angry polemic. Insofar as they were effective, they were barriers to the free play of self-interest, which, if given its way, would infallibly redound to public advantage, as though an "invisible hand" were at work. Smith demolished one mercantilist argument after another. Were gold and silver necessary to defend the realm? Not at all: "Fleets and armies are maintained not with gold and silver, but with consumable goods."[9] Does England need French brandy, Spanish sherry, Indian cotton, Portuguese madeira and port, maize from the American colonies? Then free trade is the way to purchase these and anything else made in foreign parts: "We trust with perfect security," averred Smith, "that the freedom of trade, without any attention of government, will always supply us with the wine which we have occasion for: and we may trust with equal security that it will always supply us with all the gold and silver which we can afford to employ, either in circulating our commodities, or in other uses."[10] In international commerce, countries bartered merchandise with each other, using money as a convenient intermediary. All the trading partners gained from these transactions.

Hence bounties, drawbacks, exclusive trade treaties, and sumptuary laws which attempted to restrict English importation and consumption of sugar, tea, cotton fabrics, and so on, restricted attainable gain from international trade. Although "defence . . . is of much more importance than opulence"[11] and, on that premise, Smith advised continued protection of the English merchant marine as a nursery of seamen for the Royal Navy, he also argued that universal acceptance of the principles of natural liberty would in time to come eliminate the causes of armed conflict among nations and leave them all the advantages of uninterrupted commerce. The world would be richer when free trade was general because men and women everywhere would direct their energy and their capital into channels which would enrich both them and a trading community as extensive as the globe itself.

The pretensions of government in Smith's day were overweening. The appropriate role for government was minimal. Smith assigned just three tasks to intelligent rulers guided by his advice. There was a case for public construction of roads and harbor installations on the ground that, although they were essential aids to wider markets, they were too unprofitable to attract private investment. Government's second duty was the maintenance of justice. Justice is a natural human aspiration, but it is also a necessity of business activity. Some accepted authority has to settle disputes among merchants, punish fraud, and enforce legitimate contracts. Finally, only government can defend the nation against foreign adversaries. If universal peace replaced war, as Smith hoped, then this function would atrophy, and so much the better.

For Smith economic liberty promised, in our terms, steady growth of gross national product, and rising per capita real income. More than that, only the natural system of liberty could more nearly fulfill each individual's aspirations. Smith did not anticipate anything like equality of results if each contestant in the economic races started on equal terms. He plainly did expect that the enormous gap between rich and poor which disgraced his own society would distinctly narrow. For better or worse, Smith combined a vision of progress which substituted hosts of small entrepreneurs and independent artisans for a meddling government.

In 1976, the natural heirs of Adam Smith are not the presidents of giant corporations who speak on public occasions in favor of the competition which they have done their best to suppress. Nor conservative politicians who do their best to weaken antitrust enforcement and increase corporate tax advantages. Nor yet free-market economists who attack big government daily and big unions weekly but somehow slide hastily past big business.

The English Established Church . . . will more readily pardon an attack on 38 of its 39 articles than on $\frac{1}{39}$ of its income.

—Karl Marx

The conditions under which men produce and exchange vary from country to country, and within each country from generation to generation. Political economy, therefore, cannot be the same for all countries and for all historical epochs.

—Friedrich Engels

A while back *Ramparts* magazine asked on its cover, "Capitalism in One Country?" The United States of course is not the world's only capitalist society but by the criteria of population and land area, more of the world is Marxist than capitalist. The United States is probably the most conservative of industrial societies, and its economists predictably the least susceptible to Marxist doctrine. Even here the signs of change are visible. The Union for Radical Political Economy (URPE) enrolls several thousand, mostly younger, economists. Although the ideology of URPE is diffuse, its members tend to concentrate upon class, power, and imperialism frequently in explicitly Marxist terms. It is another sign of rising interest in Marxism that the latest edition of Paul Samuelson's *Economics* devotes seventeen pages to Marxist theory, considerably more than in earlier editions, including a remarkable appendix which in nine pages anatomizes the pure theory of Marxist economics.

The relation between conventional and Marxist economics in this country has usually been less a matter of hostility than of pursuit of contrasting interests. Marxists concern themselves with capitalist evolution, the anatomy of crisis, the state of class warfare, the distribution of income, wealth, and power, and the shape of economic concentration. Non-Marxists consider that such matters, save for aspects of the final pair, are the concern of historians and sociologists. They, for their part, prefer to concentrate upon price and income theory, where the profession speaks with unique authority.

Generations of intellectuals have been attracted to Marxism by the majestic breadth of its basic vision, even when they have rejected some Marxist premises and prophecies. Marxism is at once philosophy, sociology, history, and economics. Among economists, Old Leftists rely upon the labor theory of value and the tendencies predicated upon its categories. New Leftists have rediscovered the young, humanistic, prescientific Marx who notably in *The Economic and Philosophic Manuscripts of 1844* powerfully analyzed the disastrous effects of factories upon the human beings herded inside them.

Alienation has been the focus of neo-Marxists like Herbert Marcuse and Erich Fromm. Marx stressed the separation of workers from their products, daily labors, and fellow laborers. In Marx's words,

... labor is *external* [italics in original] to the worker, i.e., it does not belong to his essential being ... his work, therefore, ... does not affirm himself but denies himself, does not make him feel content but unhappy, does not develop freely his physical and mental energy but mortifies his body and ruins his mind.... He is at home when he is not working, and when he is working, he is not at home.... As a result, therefore, man ... only feels himself freely active in his animal functions—eating, drinking, procreating.... What is animal becomes human and what is human becomes animal.[12]

Alienation deprived the worker of the artisan's mastery of his production, the symbiosis between tools and objects. The objects now exerted power over workers, not the reverse. As a consequence, factory operatives were alienated from their own efforts: "This relation is the relation of the worker to his own activity as an alien activity not belonging to him."[13] Finally, the fragmentation into meaningless bits of factory operations separated an individual from his species. Division of labor prevented the artisan from participating in cooperation with other men and women in the creation of a universe of objects friendly to human aspirations.

Modern factories are less inhumane than their nineteenth-century predecessors. Hours are shorter, union grievance procedures afford a measure of protection against the arbitrary acts of foremen, vacations are now granted, and pensions are paid to the survivors of the factory. It is accordingly all the more remarkable that sensitive, novelistic accounts of life in the auto factory, like Harvey Swados' *On the Line* and numerous journalistic descriptions of the Lordstown revolt against General Motors' attempt to turn out one hundred Vegas per hour, all read like revisions of an original Marxist statement whose essential features have been proven accurate.

Karl Marx and his scarcely less original collaborator Friedrich Engels were scholars, polemicists, historians, journalists, refugees, and revolutionaries. Not the least of Marxism's durable influence is its blend of thought and action, theory and practice. Here, resisting other temptations, I shall focus upon Marx's economics. Since the economics are embedded in history and philosophy, something inevitably must first be said about dialectical materialism and the philosophy of Hegel.

As an economist, Marx owed and acknowledged a substantial debt to David Ricardo, Adam Smith's greatest and most pessimistic critic and disciple. Writing in the immediate aftermath of the Napoleonic wars, Ricardo was dismayed by inflation, currency disturbances, the size of the English national debt, the disarray of English international trade, and, above all, by the danger that population would grow far more swiftly than the supply of food to feed the new mouths. Ricardo had swallowed Malthus whole: people threatened to increase in number geometrically—2-4-8-16-32-64-128-256-512, and so on. The produce of the soil at best might enlarge itself arithmetically: 1-2-3-4-5-6-7-8, and so on. These were the famous ratios which depressed two generations of English classical economists.

Not expecting the national product to rise very rapidly, fearing that even if it did population pressure would preclude improvement in average living standards, Ricardo sketched a society in which distribution rather than growth was the crucial economic issue. Capitalists, wage earners, and landlords quarreled over the division of a social product inadequate to their needs and expectations. The only winners were the landowners. Land, a fixed resource, became increasingly scarce and valuable as population increased. Accordingly, rent was fated to rise as a share of national income, so long as it was left in the possession of private landlords. Wages could not fall below subsistence. Once they reached that level, the only way rents could continue to rise was for profits to drop. In this dour system, entrepreneurs, England's most dynamic class, were fated to be increasingly disheartened by ever-shrinking profits. Landlords, a completely useless set of monopolists, were rewarded more and more lavishly by the pure accident of inheritance. Workers were condemned to a marginal existence on scant wages. Nature and human sexual drives had constructed this trap. The only possible exit from it was voluntary limitation of population.

Although Marx rejected Malthusian population theories, he adopted and adapted Ricardian notions of class conflict. Merging landlords and capitalists, Marx reduced the contestants to two: proletarians and bourgeoisie—workers and capitalists. On Ricardian foundations, he erected a more complex and dogmatic theory of value. And, starting with Ricardo's burgeoning uneasiness about the harmful effects of machinery upon the laboring class, Marx developed a thundering indictment of technology's damage to its servants.

Ricardo possessed a powerful, but ill-educated intellect. He wrote as though English property relationships were permanent and universal and as though Benthamite philosophy completed the human exploration of behavior and motive. Ricardian socialists, but never Ricardo himself, favored public ownership of land or confiscatory taxes on rents. Ricardo sighed but left landowners in undisturbed possession of their property. Whatever he borrowed from Ricardo, Marx also extended and generalized.

Like Adam Smith, Marx was a trained philosopher. Smith's masters were Locke and Hume. The product of a German education, Marx, a student of Hegelian doctrine, developed in dialectical materialism a unified explanation of how changes in both human affairs and the physical universe occur. Change meant development and improvement, for, in his own fashion, Marx was as optimistic as Adam Smith or a French *philosophe* of the eighteenth century. History moved in stages, each higher and thus more complex than its predecessor. Any initial situation—historical, physical, mathematical, or conceptual—was a "thesis"; its successor was an "antithesis"; and a third term a "synthesis." Each synthesis was a new beginning, the initial term of a new triad, rather than a conclusion, for no historical form, social order, political arrangement, or intellectual doctrine was fixed for all time. Each contained within itself the seeds of change and transformation.

History was seen to operate through the mechanisms of class struggle. As capitalism succeeded feudalism and the bourgeoisie displaced lords and knights, so in due time socialism would supplant capitalism, and proletarians would eject property owners. In their day even the feudal lords were agents of progress, of liberation from slavery. So it has been with the bourgeoisie. As Marx and Engels freely concluded *The Communist Manifesto*, in the nineteenth century, the capitalists invented "revolutionary instruments of production." They created world markets and "more massive and more colossal productive forces than have all preceding generations together."

Three rules firmly governed the process of dialectical change. The unity of opposites pointed to the necessary coexistence of disparate and hostile elements within social structures and systems of thought. In the capitalist order, bourgeoisie and proletarians temporarily cooperate as well as oppose each other. History is never static because social and economic forms of the utmost superficial stability actually are coalitions of unfriendly neighbors who are predestined to come into ultimate, open conflict. No society is monolithic. No political system is free from the tensions of internal contradiction.

A second rule, the negation of negation, put the conflicting forces into motion. Capitalism negated a feudalism which, in its centuries of hegemony, struck its subjects as indestructible—the Thousand Year Reich of the era. Capitalism may also appear eternal, but like the historical forms which preceded bourgeois domination, it is actually transitory. Phenomena are negated by their opposites. Often extraordinary subtlety of historical analysis is required to ascertain just what an opposite is. In 1917 Leon Trotsky theorized that Alexander Kerensky's bourgeois democratic revolution, an appropriate opposite, was as the next stage in Russia's evolution a negation of czarist tyranny. Lenin, arguing otherwise, led a second revolution premised upon the opposition between czarism and the small industrial working class then in Russia.

The third and last rule related quantity to quality. If heat were applied to water in a kettle, one of Engels' examples, at first the only noticeable result is hotter water. Eventually, however, when the water's temperature reaches 212 degrees Fahrenheit at sea level, a qualitative transformation occurs: water turns into steam. As in nature, so in society. Capitalism increases the oppression of wage earners. To paraphrase *The Communist Manifesto*, the triumphant bourgeoisie convert doctors, lawyers, poets, and men of science into wage laborers. They translate the love and affection of the precapitalist family into "mere money relations." Nevertheless, the victims are initially too weak and demoralized to resist. In time, as misery increases and class consciousness grows, the conditions of qualitative change begin to emerge. Revolution is at hand.

In Hegel the dialectical process was idealist: its sphere of activity was the human mind. The exterior world was subsidiary to mental activity. As Marx believed, he reversed the priority. Finding Hegel standing on his head, he thoughtfully upended him and stood him on his feet. For Marx all significant change took place in the world of material objects. The economic base was all-important and other phenomena reacted to the events which occurred in the base. All the same, development remained dialectical even while occurring in non-Hegelian locations. In sum, dialectical materialism postulated Hegelian triads of continuous change centered in the concrete phenomena of machines, equipment, materials, and human labor, as well as the legal relations of ownership with which they were entangled.

The Communist Manifesto, written in 1848—that year of failed revolution in France, Italy, Austria, and Poland— perceived the past as the history of class struggles: "Free-man and slave, patrician and plebian, lord and serf, guild-master and journeyman, in a word, oppressor and oppressed, stood in constant opposition to one another, carried on an uninterrupted, now hidden, now open fight, a fight that each time ended, either in a revolutionary reconstitution of society at large, or in the common ruin of the contending classes."[14] These struggles registered in literature, religion, science, arts, music, politics, and every other aspect of hu-man affairs. The base, more closely examined, included the state of technology, as well as machines and factories and the legal rules which governed their ownership. In the full flush of capitalist achievement, appropriate legal rules in-terpreted by sympathetic judges protected capitalists against claims of damages by injured workers and similar suits by customers poisoned by the products of industry.

As the legal tale went, factory owners and factory em-ployees were bound to each other by voluntary contracts. The workers were free to sell their labor to the highest bidders, shift from place to place and employer to em-ployer, in imitation of the search by the owners of non-human resources for the best market. It was a fair sample of Marx's black humor that he declared the workers free in a second sense, free of the implements of production. Because capitalism had deprived them of their land and their tools, all that they had left to sell was their capacity to work—in Marx's terminology their labor power.

Legal change was essential to the success of mature capitalism. Before it could complete its evolution, "the ex-propriation of the agricultural producer, of the peasant, from the soil,"[15] had to be completed. Only then were capitalists confident of a labor supply to use and exploit. As Marx described them, steps in the process included two enclosure movements, expropriation of church lands, and other land transfers which followed the English Glorious Revolution at the end of the seventeenth century. Masquerading as political and religious events, these were in truth milestones en route to the free labor markets of nineteenth-century capitalism.

As success followed success, the victory of the modern factory system became first feasible, then complete. Capitalism was always a society in motion. In the late eighteenth and early nineteenth century, more and more small holders were forced off the land. The few who remained were compelled to eke out meager existences as hired hands. Thus disappeared the distinction, once sharp, between small farmers and the urban proletariat. All were proletarians in the new order. One of the consequences of the repetitive business cycles which punctuated capitalist chronology was progressive simplification of class structures. In each crisis, big capitalists devoured little capitalists and the middle class of small shopkeepers, independent artisans, teachers, and professional workers shrank in size and influence.

As we shall shortly see, the logic of their situation drove capitalists, the Fausts of their time, to seek ever larger output and ever fatter profits. In time, the contradiction between the floods of goods an efficient technology tried to market and the maldistribution of income which limited the number of available customers grew less and less tolerable. Crises and unemployment became more frequent and catastrophic. The misery of the proletariat became less bearable. Objective conditions ripened for revolution and movement from capitalism to socialism, a higher stage of historical evolution. Or to put it slightly differently, when the legal arrangements which had promoted capitalist success turned into "fetters" upon production, then revolutionary action was predictable. Here is Marx's own précis of the events:

Along with the constantly diminishing number of the magnates of capital, who usurp and monopolise all advantages of this process of transformation, grows the mass of misery, oppression, slavery, degradation, exploitation; but with this too grows the revolt of the working class always increasing in number, and disciplined, united, organised by the very mechanism of the process of capitalist production itself. The monopoly of capital becomes a fetter upon the mode of production, which has sprung up and flourished along with it and under it. Centralisation of the means of production and socialisation of labour at last reach a point where they become incompatible with their capitalist integument. This integument is burst asunder. The knell of capitalist private property sounds. The expropriators are expropriated.[16]

This glorious passage isolated the historical irony which ensured the ultimate revolt of Marx's disciplined working class. The capitalist was the unwilling but predestined agent of the discipline. Trained to cooperate in the performance of alienated labor with more and more of his fellow sufferers, the worker, as his straits became more desperate, also became increasingly class conscious. Aware at last of the origins of his daily misery, he was ready to turn the painful lessons of factory discipline against his teachers. The factory is the school of revolution.

Such were the changes to be discovered in the base. The superstructure was responsive to technological and legal shifts within the base. In England, Marx's usual model, political democracy paralleled maturing capitalism because democracy was a convenient device of dominion by capitalists. Precapitalist faiths like Christianity transformed themselves in obedience to economic necessity. In medieval Europe, the Catholic church condemned the taking of interest as usury, a sin whose practitioners ended far down in Dante's *Inferno*. Calvinism gradually came to sanction not only the charging and payment of interest, but the entire apparatus of profit maximization into the bargain. By the time the Pilgrim Fathers discovered Plymouth Rock, riches were taken as the mark of election by God to grace. Great fortunes were to be amassed and conserved by their creators and heirs under the guise of stewardship in the Lord's service.

Economic thought also evolved in response to the needs of capitalism. Adam Smith's simple system of natural liberty in its day signalized capitalism's impending success, just as Marx's own doctrines presaged proletarian victory. The relationship of base and superstructure has been the topic of endless controversy among Marxists. Was the relationship reciprocal? Did changes in superstructure react upon the base? Or did the lines of influence proceed in a single direction from base to superstructure? The Marx of *The Communist Manifesto* argued for nonreciprocity. The elderly Engels, years after his collaborator's death, advanced a more subtle doctrine:

According to the materialist conception of history, the determining element in history is *ultimately* [italics in original] the production and reproduction in real life. More than that neither Marx nor I have ever asserted. If therefore somebody twists this into the statement that the economic element is the *only* [italics in original] determining one, he transforms it into a meaningless, abstract, and absurd phrase. The economic situation is the basis, but the various elements of the superstructure —political forms of the class struggle and its consequences, constitutions established by the victorious class after a successful battle, etc.—forms of law—and then even the reflexes of all these actual struggles in the brains of the combatants: political, legal, philosophical theories, religious ideas and their further development into systems of dogma—also exercise their influence upon the course of the historical struggle and in many cases preponderate in determining their *form* [italics in original]. There is an interaction of all these elements, in which, amid all the endless host of accidents ... the economic movement finally asserts itself as necessary.[17]

The passage poised Engels exquisitely between free will and inevitability. Although the primacy of the economic guaranteed eventual capitalist destruction, timing, type, and even consequences of revolution were left to the human will. It is an excellent revolutionary strategy, after all, to stimulate the doubtful to organize in quest of certain victory.

Marx and Engels insistently distinguished their brand of "scientific" socialism from the utopian visions of Saint-Simon, Fourier, and Owen. Marxism analyzed the machinery of history. The utopians dealt in fabulous tales of better societies and never explained how to proceed from the wretched present to the glorious future. Even Marx and Engels, their major work done, allowed themselves as good children are given candy, the occasional treat of speculation into society after the capitalists were dragged, kicking and screaming, from the stage of history. At that apocalyptic moment,

The struggle for human existence comes to an end. ... Man cuts himself off from the animal world, leaves the conditions of animal existence behind him and enters conditions which are really human. The conditions of existence forming men's environment, which up to now have dominated man, at this point pass under the dominion and control of man, who now for the first time becomes the real conscious master of Nature, in so far as he has become the master of his own social organization.[18]

Marx's longest look at the future, the introduction to his 1871 *Critique of the Gotha Program*, featured a crucial distinction between the socialist society as it emerged from degenerate capitalism and the communist commonwealth toward which it evolved. Because newborn socialism is "in every respect tainted economically, morally, and intellectually with the hereditary diseases of the old society from whose womb it is emerging," the equal right of each citizen to share in the social product is "continually handicapped by bourgeois limitations." Therefore, initially, "rights must be unequal instead of being equal," because "rights can never be higher than the economic structure and the cultural development of society conditioned by it."[19]

After the remnants of bourgeois opposition are eliminated, class struggle at length comes to a full stop. Only then are men and women able to lead fully human lives:

In a higher phase of communist society, after the tyrannical subordination of individuals according to the distribution of labour and thereby also the distinction between manual and intellectual work, have disappeared, after labour has become not merely a means to live but is in itself the first necessity of living, after the powers of production have also increased and all the springs of cooperative wealth are gushing more freely together with the all-round development of the individual, then and only then can the narrow bourgeois horizon of rights be left far behind and society will inscribe on its banner: "From each according to his capacity, to each according to his need."[20]

Under communism, the state withers away. Always before in history, the instrument of class dominion, it loses its function in a classless society. The oppression of the state accompanies the last capitalist out of society.

It is time to treat explicitly the economic concepts entwined with this view of historical evolution. Marxist economics start with a labor theory of value and culminate in doctrines of business-cycle crisis, proletarian immiseration, class polarization, breakdown, and transition to socialism. The classical economists, including Marx, wanted value theory to answer the question why items were traded according to one set of ratios instead of another. Why, Marx asked, did a quarter of wheat exchange for x blacking, y silk, or z gold? Marx's classical predecessors had replied to similar queries that if the silk cost twice as much as the blacking, twice as much human labor must have been devoted to its completion. Marx put this explanation far more philosophically: "... the valid exchange values of a given commodity express something equal ... exchange value ... is only the mode of expression, the phenomenal form, of something contained in it, yet distinguishable from it."[21] Each commodity's essence was "a mere congelation of homogeneous human labor," value itself.

The philosophical exercise was worth the trouble because Marx wished to emphasize value as the core of human relationships in the marketplace and the consequence of capitalist property rights. This proposition emerged from a seeming quibble which was actually of great importance. The value of undifferentiated labor is indeed the source of market price ratios. Labor is itself a commodity, purchased at its value in competitive hiring markets. The value of labor is a wage high enough to support at a subsistence level the worker and his dependents. But what employers purchase when they hire you or me is a quality peculiar to an employee as a commodity, the capacity to create value. The employer, however, pays us less than the entire value we contribute. Instead he hires us for a standard working day only part of which creates the merchandise which, when sold, pays our wages and the remainder of which remains in the hands of capitalists as surplus value. In a twelve-hour day, Marx's typical proletarian slaved six hours for himself, six hours for his master. Profit, rent, and interest, the constituent parts of surplus value, were entirely the consequence of employers' ability to pay less for labor power than the value of the labor generated by that labor power.

Because only labor created value, workers were morally entitled to the whole product of their labor, the traditional claim of socialists who preceded Marx as well. The capitalist was able to extract surplus value from his victims only because his monopoly of tools, machines, and factory premises gave his employees no alternative source of livelihood. From capitalism's very beginnings, the secret of primitive accumulation, the initial hoard of capital invested in the first factories, rested in the methods by which the accumulation took place: the force and fraud which had wrested precious acres from small farmers and tools from independent artisans. Once this "freedom" became universal, rural and urban proletarians alike were exposed naked to the power of their capitalist exploiters.

Naturally, the longer the working day the larger the portion of it extracted as surplus value. According to Marx, in the early years of the Industrial Revolution employers tried to stretch the working day from ten, to twelve, fourteen, or even sixteen hours. However, the process was self-defeating because overworked laborers sickened and died. The Factory Acts which regulated child labor, then female labor, and finally adult male working hours and conditions were a belated defense of their own interests by intelligent capitalists fearful that the very source of profit (surplus value) was being depleted by too rapid a pace of exploitation.

When the work week stabilized, employers concentrated on expanding relative surplus value. Surplus value expanded if only four hours' product of a twelve-hour day were needed to pay a subsistence wage instead of six. The capitalist's share, eight hours in place of six, amounted to a 200 percent rate of surplus value, 8:4, much preferable to its preceding 100 percent rate, 6:6. Labor-saving equipment, improved factory management, a faster pace of operation, and cheaper food all contributed to greater surplus value. The prolonged agitation, organized by capitalists, which culminated in the 1846 repeal of the Corn Laws, was a sensible attempt to diminish the hours workers toiled for their own benefit and enlarge the time they spent in their employers' interests.

Marx's English predecessors and contemporaries took it for granted that the owners of machinery and factory structures deserved financial rewards for buying and using their capital. Nassau Senior held that the abstinence from consumer spending which produced the savings to finance purchases of equipment was just as painful to the savers as their daily exertions were for factory operatives. Marx insisted that machines could never do more than *transfer* the value embodied in them—the number of hours of socially necessary labor time needed to manufacture them.

But if machines failed to add value, why did capitalists

persist in buying them? Marx's solution employed the mechanism of competitive markets. Innovative capitalists who introduced new and better equipment temporarily benefited because relative surplus value increased. Continuing to collect the same prices for finished goods as their less alert rivals, the innovators earned exceptionally high profits. However, this edge soon disappears as the remaining capitalists copy the tactics of their brighter rivals. The flood of merchandise made possible by superior techniques depresses prices. Surplus value declines and the capitalists are worse off than they were before their innovations because they now employ fewer men and women to exploit. The process of mechanization nevertheless continues because it always appears advantageous to some capitalists to steal a march on their brethren.

As the eloquent pages of *Capital* tell the tale, the impact of machinery upon the English working class was almost uniformly tragic. Because many of the early machines required dexterity and capacity to maneuver in small spaces, employers sought out women and children. These unfortunates toiled dreadfully long hours, in wretched surroundings, under stern, often brutal discipline. Male laborers turned themselves into slave dealers, trafficking in the pain of their wives and children. Mortality rates were high among adults and murderous for children. Because men and women mingled in heat and grime, because they had no reasonable expectation of escape, and because only violent entertainments could arouse their dulled senses, they wallowed in moral degradation.

The intellectual desolation of the new mill towns fittingly complemented their spiritual condition. If literate, adults had no time or energy to read and their children no opportunity to become literate. When eventually compelled by the Factory Acts to attend some institution labeled a school, the children, exhausted, slept instead of learned. Quoting the reports of the Factory Act commissioners, Marx cited pit boys who could not identify Jesus Christ and other youths who could not name the Queen of England.

Machinery's single virtue was its aid to class consciousness and proletarian organization, for the mechanized factory operated effectively only when managers coordinated and supervised highly disciplined groups of workers. One day they would divert their training to equally disciplined revolutionary action. For that time of deliverance, strikes were a preparation and their bloody repression a salutary lesson in the facts of capitalist power and injustice.

Since the 1870s, conventional economists have substituted for the labor theory of value in either Ricardian or Marxist versions, the marginal-productivity explanation of income shares. The contributions of capital and land to economic activity justify profit, interest, and rent, just as the efforts of employees deserve the rewards of wages and salaries. The theory contains no explanation of the origins of capital and makes no invidious distinctions between income from property and income from labor.

Among living Marxist economists, a minority, of whom the well-known English economist Joan Robinson is the most prominent, argue that the validity of the labor theory of value is not essential to Marxist interpretations of class struggle, exploitation, and the internal contradictions of capitalism. Professor Robinson has insisted that "no point of substance in Marx's argument depends upon the labour theory of value. Voltaire remarked that it is possible to kill a flock of sheep by witchcraft if you give them plenty of arsenic at the same time. The sheep, in this figure, may well stand for the complacent apologists of capitalism; Marx's penetrating insight and bitter hatred of oppression supply the arsenic, while the labour theory of value provides the incantations."[22]

Right or wrong, essential or marginal to the corpus of Marxist doctrine, the labor theory of value continues to convey a potent charge of moral indignation and a basically simple explanation of how the capitalists are exploiting the rest of us. Happily, not forever. Marx foresaw growing concentration and centralization of capital, declining rates of profit, rising average unemployment, more and more proletarian misery, stronger class consciousness among workers, and eventual proletarian revolt.

Marx defined concentration as the trend toward larger factories in each industry. With size, efficiency increased because processes could be more finely subdivided and more intricate machinery deployed. Smaller capitalists either could not afford such equipment or lacked the outlets for its products. Centralization related to the number of enterprises in each branch of industry. The market for finished consumer goods was limited by the small purchasing power of an underpaid proletariat. Hence if average factory size rose, the number of enterprises in each industry necessarily shrank. As smaller capitalists filed their petitions of bankruptcy, their larger rivals swelled to even grosser dimensions.

Crises hastened these trends. For several reasons, business cycles of rising violence were unavoidable. Disproportions between capital goods and consumer goods production eventuated in gluts in one sector or another. In its best moments, capitalism is a jumpy affair. Fits of investor gloom and euphoria are accompanied by depression and boom in capital investment. But the mortal weakness of capitalism as ever was the disparity between its productive efficiency and the limited capacity to purchase the Niagaras of goods which the factories poured out. In Marx's words, "The enormous power, inherent in the factory system, of expanding by jumps, and the dependence of that system on the markets of the world, necessarily begets feverish production, followed by overfilling of the markets, whereupon contraction of the markets brings on crippling of production."[23]

For capitalists the infallible thermometer of the system's fevers was the behavior of the rate of profit. In the long run, it could only fall, for as industry grew larger, machinery (constant capital) expanded more rapidly than labor (variable capital). Inasmuch as surplus value sprang solely from the exploitation of labor power, rates of profit necessarily declined unless capitalists were able to perpetually enlarge rates of exploitation. Marx assumed that they could not.

However, he did identify forces which in the short run might delay decline in profit rates. Temporarily the rate of exploitation could be forced upward. For short periods wages might be depressed below subsistence. Cheaper machinery was another device. Foreign trade was capable of cheapening raw materials and thus factory costs, as well as the laborer's food. These were delaying actions at best. Higher rates of exploitation diminished working-class incomes and narrowed the markets of their exploiters. Substitution of machines for human hands reduced the sources of surplus value. Revolution was the only exit from the inherent and increasing contradictions of capitalism.

Profit was the crucial measure because capitalists measured success and failure according to its fluctuations. When profits fell, capitalists became so alarmed that they tried almost anything to restore them. But, as we have already seen, these efforts were self-defeating. Mechanization, and more vicious competition, destroyed the small sharks and fattened the big ones. But the world was finite and the supply of new customers in new markets soon exhausted. Practically every defensive tactic of capitalism inflamed its condition by maldistributing income and wealth ever more outrageously. By first destroying its own customers, capitalism guaranteed its own destruction.

Crises were accompanied by simpler and sharper class struggles. Conflict polarized between capitalists and workers. Class position was defined by ownership. Capitalists owned the instruments of production, proletarians nothing beyond their own labor power. The internal logic of capitalism was allied to a two-class system, much as the logic of socialism led to a single class. These were facts of life that capitalists desperately sought to conceal, often with temporary success. Workers in many instances suffered from the false class sentiments which led them to identify with capitalists —tellers with their banks, life insurance salesmen on commission with Equitable and Prudential, and assembly line workers with General Motors. With rather more plausibility, small proprietors, doctors, dentists, and lawyers, and other white-collar types placed themselves in the company of capitalists.

One of the consequences of business-cycle crisis was clarification of genuine class identity and interest. Small businessmen who became bankrupt sank into the proletarian mass. Big farmers, the rural branch of capitalism, took over the property of small farmers. Once dispossessed, the former owners were forced either into the rural proletariat as farm laborers or compelled to swell Marx's reserve army of the unemployed in the cities. Even respectable skilled workers encountered cyclical unemployment. When they unionized, employer reprisals were swift and bloody. Each crisis enlarged the working class and sharpened the class struggle.

When and where inevitable revolution arrived could not be forecast with precision. Marx's own guesses wavered among England, Germany, and even Russia. The historic mission of capitalism was to develop technology as far as its system of property ownership allowed and then yield to a higher mode of organization, socialism. "It is," commented Marx, "one of the civilizing sides of capital that it enforces this surplus labor in a manner and under conditions which promote the development of the productive forces of social conditions, and the creation of the elements for a new and higher formation better than did the preceding forms of slavery, and serfdom . . . it creates the material requirements and the germ of conditions which make it possible to combine this surplus labor in a higher form of society, with a greater reduction of the time devoted to material labor."[24]

Obviously in the industrial West the revolution has been delayed. In Europe and the United States the misery of the masses has increased neither absolutely nor relatively. The middle classes are much with us. Workers are not nearly as hostile to owners as Marxist forecasts of impending polarization specify. From the radical point of view, the pervasiveness particularly in the United States of false class consciousness is an international scandal. It must sadden any true believer to contemplate hard-hats parading through Wall Street waving banners whose legends order that "God Bless the Establishment."

Nevertheless, communist and socialist parties are strong in Western Europe and numerous revolutions in developing nations appear Marxist in ideological inspiration. Whatever the accuracy of its prophecies, Marxism continues to attract admirers because it offers them coherent doctrine, a gallery of heroes and villains, a code of morality, and, best of all, a hope for the future. Marxism, the greatest of the intellectual fighting faiths, seems more and more relevant to the struggles over the world's resources which have already broken out and the internal conflicts between capital and labor in rich societies which are certain to be exacerbated by declining growth rates.

Marxism may not be the best explanation of these large events. But its critics would be in a stronger position if they could offer any explanation of the disorders of capitalist economies even approximately as plausible.

All told—if it were possible—it will be evident that the aggregate of human talent currently consumed in the fabrication of vendible imponderables in the nth dimension, will foot up to a truly massive total, even after making a reasonable allowance, of, say, some thirty-three and one-third percent, for average mental deficiency in the personnel which devotes itself to this manner of livelihood.

—THORSTEIN VEBLEN

A Western European phenomenon, Marxism is a latecomer to the United States. Only recently has it attracted sizable numbers of recruits among economists and other social scientists. The closest native approximation to the Marxist strain of radical criticism of capitalism is the institutionalism of Thorstein Veblen. As an explanation of

American business, industry, and society, Veblen's speculations were altered and promoted in the work of John Commons at the University of Wisconsin. At a remove, Ralph Nader, John Kenneth Galbraith, John Blair, Allan Gruchy,* and Warren Samuel act and write in the general tradition of institutionalist thought.

As the assortment of names implies, institutional economics has been more a thing of attitude than of dogma. Institutionalists like Marxists differ among themselves, but unlike Marxists, they have no authoritative source powerful enough to resolve disputes, for institutionalist doctrine always has been subtle enough to elude the writers of primers. Veblen's first major work, his 1899 *Theory of the Leisure Class*, seemed to be a nasty attack upon the manners and morals of the rich. In the Gilded Age, the hostility of most reviewers was a foregone conclusion. Veblen's style was involved, the economic points concealed, the tone acerbic, and the conclusions ambiguous.

By good fortune the tract became a cultural sensation when William Dean Howells, the Edmund Wilson of his day, reviewed it glowingly as a masterpiece of social satire. Certainly it resembled none of the traditional economic treatises. Although Veblen's second major volume, *The Theory of Business Enterprise*, bore more of the superficial characteristics of economics, it too was strange fare, jammed with anthropological, evolutionary, historical, and sociological references, studded by footnotes which if seri-

---

* The Association for Evolutionary Economics (AFEE) is a subgroup of economists attached to institutional economics. It sponsors the *Journal of Economic Issues* and annually presents to a suitable candidate the Veblen-Commons award. The 1975 winner was Gunnar Myrdal.

ous were subversive and if frivolous undignified, and addressed to no identifiable audience. Was Veblen to be believed when he solemnly averred that "the nation remains a predatory organism, in practical effect an association of persons moved by a community interest in getting something for nothing by force and fraud?" Did he make up his account of the French king who allowed himself to burn to death in front of an open fireplace because the servant charged with shifting the royal person was absent and the king's sense of status did not allow him to move himself? Was he teasing his colleagues with stuffy scholarship like this: "Such seems to be the evidence, for instance, for Cybele, Astarte (Aphrodite, Ishtar), Mylitta, Isis, Demeter (Ceres), Artemis, and for such doubtfully late characters as Hera (Juno),—see Harrison, *Prolegomena to the Study of Greek Religion*, Frazer, *Adonis, Attis, Osiris* and *The Golden Bough*. Quan-on may be a doubtful case, as possibly also Amaterazu." No economist alive, aside from Veblen if he were an economist and really cared, gave a damn about Quan-on, or preferred Harrison and Frazer on Greek mythology and modern superstition to the latest issue of the *American Economic Review*.

His learned foolery apart, Veblen was a man possessed by a single idea, a key distinction around which all of his books and essays were organized. This master notion was the persistent contrast in capitalism between business enterprise and the machine process. By the latter he meant the technology of factory production and the coordination of men and technology by engineering logic. Still more vital to a grasp of the machine process was comprehension of the habits of thought which working with machines encouraged and reinforced. Veblen admired the machine process because its reasoned procedures, standard measurements, and matter-of-fact animus offered outlet for the instinct of workmanship with which each of us is blessed at birth. Veblen identified the machine process at work "wherever manual dexterity, the rule of thumb, and fortuitous conjunctures of the seasons have been supplanted by a reasoned procedure on the basis of a systematic knowledge of the forces employed," for "there the mechanical industry is to be found, even in the absence of intricate mechanical contrivances."[25] The objectives of the machine process were friendly to human survival, for its serviceable products gratified biological needs to eat, keep warm, work at constructive tasks, and satisfy the instinct of idle curiosity.

Brought up on a farm, though none too eager to do his share of the chores, Veblen all his life generalized from the usual collection of activities successful farmers routinely engaged in. Capitalist prosperity was the gift of the sheer efficiency of the machine process guided by the benign criteria of workmanship and idle curiosity. Unobstructed, these instincts guaranteed the abundant life to everybody.

Unfortunately capitalism, or rather business enterprise, constructed higher and higher barriers to the fulfillment of these life-enhancing and species-conserving instincts. As an institution, business enterprise directed itself at objectives directly contrary to those of the engineers, technicians, and ordinary operatives who served the machine process. Only one goal interested businessmen, pecuniary gain. Serviceability was secondary, although, other things equal, businessmen preferred the serviceable to the useless. Other things were seldom equal.

Businessmen were not bloodthirsty fiends. However, because of their obsession with vendibility as the prerequisite of profit, they were necessarily utterly indifferent to the safety, durability, or aesthetic appearance of their commodities. Can it be sold at a profit? That was the proper question. Its answer frequently required business enterprisers to prefer the meretricious and flashy to the sober and durable. Merely fashionable clothes soon displeased their wearers and stimulated delightfully profitable replacement. For such profit-and-loss reasons, hucksters altered women's fashions annually. Each season's *dernier cri* looked better than last year's, if only because the new horror afforded the momentary pleasures of novelty. Not for a moment did Veblen share the assumption of standard economics that vendibility and serviceability coincided.

Businessmen were the occasion of other damage. Business leaders were not always best pleased when the economy ran smoothly, when their profits might increase by a little judicious disruption and manipulation of the stock market and the industries whose stocks and bonds bought and sold at the right time were financially highly lucrative. To prove his point, Veblen sketched the events which preceded the creation of United States Steel. In Veblen's telling, the completed merger was a triumph of commercial maneuver which accomplished no industrial end, caused much unrest in financial markets, and profited only its promoters. Among the latter were J. P. Morgan & Company, which collected some $65 million as reward for inspired efforts in marrying, on paper, a large number of previously independent steel firms. At the end of the operation, no extra ton of steel was poured but a number of speculators and promoters were magically much richer. Here and in less spectacular instances relentless pursuit of financial gain caused unemployment, higher prices, diminished efficiency, delayed innovation, and encouraged what Veblen termed "conscientious sabotage" of the machine process.

The business cycle itself was the natural consequence of business enterprise. Depressions, Veblen told his readers, were a "malady of the affections," a financial rather than an industrial illness. "The discrepancy," according to Veblen, "which encourages businessmen is a discrepancy between that normal capitalization which they have set their hearts upon through habituation in the immediate past and that actual capitalizable value of their property which its current earning capacity will warrant."[26] Commerce was done on credit. Businessmen borrowed on the basis of their expected earnings and their actual inventory of merchandise. When businessmen borrowed in unison in order to add to their stocks of goods, they bid prices up and the value of the collateral they had pledged to their banks sympathetically rose as well. For a time the process might proceed merrily but at some point as loans began to set new records, businessmen and bankers began to wonder whether prices and profits could continue high enough to support the huge structure of credit. On occasion, astute operators, scenting profits in a financial crash, spread the rumor that the event was impending. Always a fragile emotion, business confidence faltered, banks called in loans, manufacturers demanded payment by wholesalers and wholesalers by retailers, weak enterprises faltered and failed, and depression spread and persisted until readjustments of debt to prospective sales were completed. None of these events was the natural consequence of the workmanlike activities of the sensible folk who ran the machines and managed the factories. All were damaging effects of the normal routines of people who live in a universe of currency and contracts.

The similarities to Marxist theory were striking. Crises were recurrent. Big operators swallowed little ones. Technology was efficient. Capitalist institutions sabotaged technology in both Marx and Veblen.

On matters of causation, the two diverged. Crises in Marx occurred partly because efficient factories flooded markets with more goods than there were customers. Veblen argued that the huge volume of resources wasted by business enterprise on fashion, advertising, and deliberate interruptions of normal production tended actually to diminish output, at least of biologically serviceable items. Contrasting diagnoses evoked contrasting prophecies. Marx's revolution came when the conflict between the material interests of capitalists and proletarians became sufficiently acute. As soon as workers learned their true class interest, they rationally sought to advance down the road that ended in revolution.

In Veblen groups fought over different issues. The future shape of society evolved from the struggles among three hostile cultural tendencies: business enterprise, the machine process, and yet a third nominee. The last cultural actor was affiliated with warlike or predatory impulses—archaic echoes of the Middle Ages. Men and women dominated by any one of these habits of thought had little in common with the votaries of either of the others. Social conflict was, thus, less an argument about property than a clash of ideologies. Business enterprise insisted on the validity of natural-rights concepts. A proper businessman fervently believed that God and nature validated his title to property and sanctified his every contract. Although the more learned invoked the authority of John Locke, business apologists rewrote Locke to turn each businessman into the "putative producer of whatever wealth he acquires," however little of his own labor was mixed with the products he sold.

Businessmen and their allies fretted over legal rights, judicial precedent, and the rules of inheritance, each equally irrelevant to industrial efficiency, but directly supportive of pecuniary achievement. The indispensable ally of business enterprise was the lawyer, a good soul "exclusively occupied with the details of predatory fraud." As much as possible, true businessmen kept out of factories and avoided contaminating information about actual industrial processes.

How different were the attitudes of engineers, technicians, and craftsmen we have had occasion already to describe! Efficient, self-respecting, proud of their work, products, and their own role, they were aggravated by the paper-cherishing, legalistic, pecuniary preoccupations of their masters whenever these preoccupations interfered with their own benevolent activities. The sacredness of property provoked no affect in engineers. Pecuniary aims in general struck them as irrelevant or worse. They cared as little for the hobbies and pastimes of business enterprisers —religion, sport, and politics.

If, said Veblen, the argument were between these two groups only, the outcome was in no doubt, the partisans of the machine process were clear winners. Engineers and workmen could readily get along without businessmen. They would never countenance sabotage of sound engineering design in the interests of flashy salability. Businessmen, devoid of the capacity actually to run a factory, needed the people who had such abilities. In one of his late books, *The Engineers and the Price System*, issued in 1921 by Veblen's loyal New York publisher, Viking Press, he almost flatly predicted that the guardians of the machine, provoked beyond endurance, would certainly take the industrial system into their own hands and operate it henceforth solely according to the canons of mechanical efficiency and biological serviceability.

Veblen died in early 1929, just before the Great Crash which he surely would have enjoyed. During the depression which followed the collapse of the stock market, Howard Scott's Technocracy, a crackpot movement, adopted as its manual *The Engineers and the Price System.* For a time, the movement's world headquarters were located in the utterly respectable Columbia University School of Engineering. Veblen, no optimist, would not have been astonished in death to be honored by the scatterbrained as in life he was ignored by the supposedly intelligent.

The triumph of the engineers was less than foreordained because of the actions of the third runner in the race for power, the remnants of still "older conventions," the living anachronisms personified by "soldiers, politicians, the clergy, and men of fashion." Their habits of thought were hardened in amber long before the natural-rights philosophy of business enterprise emerged in the seventeenth and eighteenth century. The expanding operations of business enterprise called increasingly on the military. Businessmen of assorted nationalities, backed by governments which almost invariably represented their interests, fought over available markets. Their objective was, according to their invariable custom, simple pecuniary gain. Soldiers loved war and destruction for their own sweet sakes. Begun in greed, wars gave the generals the opportunity to return capitalist societies "to a more archaic situation that preceded the scheme of natural rights ... absolute government, dynastic politics, devolution of rights and honors, ecclesiastical authority, and popular submission and squalor."[27]

Nevertheless, business enterprise was slated for bankruptcy whoever became the receiver, generals or engineers. When the hour of grim truth struck, businessmen and their allies were fated either to revert to archaic absolutism under military dominion or submit to the enraged partisans of the machine process. Writing in 1915, Veblen cited the Kaiser's Germany as a contemporary example of reversion to archaic modes of thought. Quite presciently since Japan was at the time an American ally, he wondered whether that country might lapse into the same category.

As Veblen defined them, institutions were "prevalent habits of thought with respect to particular relations of the individual and of the community."[28] In optimistic moods, Veblen true to the evolutionary creed hailed the certain triumph of the engineers. As Darwin taught, variations favorable to the survival of a species tended to be passed on generation after generation. If human evolutionary goals were really biological improvement, the machine process supported them infinitely better than wars and business manipulations. Perhaps this agnostic passage echoed Veblen's settled opinions most closely:

Natural rights being a by-product of peaceful industry, they cannot be reinstated by a recourse to warlike habits and a coercive government, since warlike habits and coercion are alien to the natural rights spirit. Nor can they be reinstated by a recourse to settled peace and freedom, since an era of settled peace and freedom would push on to the dominance of the machine process and the large business which would break down the system of natural liberty.[29]

Veblen's lingering influence is difficult to estimate. Substantial portions of the Veblenian vision are outmoded. Instinct psychology has lost its vogue. Veblen's anthropological musings about Scandinavian heroes and biologically gifted dolichocephalic blonds were perhaps innocent enough when he wrote but discomforting to read in the post-Holocaust era. Evolutionary doctrine is more complex in 1976 than in 1904. Species perish as well as survive.

Moreover, as a revolutionary elite, engineers are as plausible as dentists or accountants. They probably vote Republican, the purest of the natural-rights parties, even more heavily than lawyers and account executives in advertising agencies. In the industrial West, according to standard measurements, incomes have steadily risen in spite of business sabotage of industrial operations. A Veblenian might with justice retort that the national income categories themselves conform to the requirements of business enterprise. If engineers reformulated them, GNP might be much smaller and decreasing instead of increasing.

Neo-Keynesians and neoclassicists dominate the nation's graduate departments of economics. Young economists, clutched by the intricacies of econometrics and subtle theories of price, read no Veblen. The lonely Norwegian scholar, the drifter among American universities, the persistent dissenter from the American celebration, and the suspected World War I subversive founded no party and acted as patron saint to few departments of economics. In each presidential season, the major parties nominate excellent friends of business enterprise.

This is not quite the whole story. High-school and university students still are assigned Veblen. Veblen's strange, convoluted, mock-ponderous manner takes more than the five minutes between television commercials to appreciate, but like addictions to shellfish, martinis, and Monty Python's Flying Circus, affinity increases with familiarity. Once a person is hooked, he or she derives continuing delight from Veblen's wicked wit, felicity of phrase, and unexpected turns of thought. He treated the military, one of his favorite targets, to this salvo:

> With the complement of archaic virtues that invests these adepts, there is also associated a fair complement of those more elemental vices that are growing obsolete in the peaceable civilized communities. Such debaucheries, extravagances of cruelty, and general superfluity of naughtiness as are nameless or impossible in civil life are blameless matters of course in the service. In the nature of the case they are inseparable from the service. The service commonly leaves the veterans physical, intellectual, and moral invalids.... But these less handsome concomitants of the service should scarcely be made a point of reproach to those brave men whose devotion to the flag and the business interests has led them by the paths of disease and depravity. Nor are the accumulated vices to be lightly condemned, since their weight also falls on the conservative side; being archaic and authenticated, their cultural bearing is, on the whole, salutary.[30]

The linguistic twirls apart, Veblen meant what he said. If military veterans perished either at each other's hands or in hospitals where their "superfluity of naughtiness" landed them, peaceful citizens would sleep more quietly in their beds and the cause of evolution would be better served.

Enduring wit demands enduring targets. Systematic critics of Pentagon budgets like Seymour Melman and J. K. Galbraith seem to echo Veblen's mordant judgment of military aspirations. They fear waste of resources, but even more the influence of the military mind. The diverse legions of environmentalists and consumerists carry on the Veblenian distinction between the serviceable and the meretricious. Ralph Nader's and Emma Rothschild's assaults upon the auto industry focus on both unsafe cars and meretricious designs. One hopes that, wherever he now is, Veblen chuckled in appreciation at these words of Galbraith's:

The family which takes its mauve and cerise, air-conditioned, power-steered, and power-braked automobile out for a tour passes through cities that are badly paved, made hideous by litter, blighted buildings, billboards, and posts for wires that should long since have been put underground. They pass on into a countryside that has been rendered largely invisible by commercial art. The goods which the latter advertise have an absolute priority in our value system. Such aesthetic considerations as a view of the countryside accordingly come second. On such matters we are consistent. They picnic on exquisitely packaged food from a portable icebox by a polluted stream and go on to spend the night at a park which is a menace to health and morals. Just before dozing off on an air mattress, beneath a nylon tent, amid the stench of decaying refuse, they may reflect vaguely on the curious unevenness of their blessings. Is this, indeed, the American genius?[31]

With Veblen of all people, one ought to refrain from advertising his product beyond its mechanical merits. Still, credit is due to a thinker who identified three persistent institutional themes of American capitalism, embodied in the arts of engineering and technology, salesmanship and advertising, and war and military glory. Misguided adventures like the *Mayagüez* incident attest to the capacity of any president, even at the end of a disastrous military enterprise, to whip up the dormant martial emotions of the public. To appreciate Veblen and to adapt his ideas it is unnecessary, indeed barely possible, to endorse every assumption and every speculation. Like Marx, Veblen, endowed with a powerful moral vision, saw society as a whole and grappled with its future.

———————

As Keynes has been domesticated by textbooks and politicians, he is scarcely identifiable as the closet radical and rebellious member of the English intellectual establishment whom his friends and followers admired in his lifetime. Child of Cambridge University, favorite pupil of Alfred Marshall and Marshall's successor A. C. Pigou, peer of the realm at the end of his career, Keynes nevertheless struck the public eye first as an ingrate who had turned maliciously against his political superiors. For when he resigned in disgust from the British delegation to the 1919 Versailles Peace Conference, he was an important adviser to Prime Minister Lloyd George, and one of a Big Four whose other members were no less than Woodrow Wilson, Georges Clemenceau, and Vittorio Emanuele Orlando. Deeply distressed though he was by the cynicism and treachery of the others, Keynes according to polite convention should have resigned and kept his mouth shut. Lloyd George would surely have written him a pleasant letter of regret.

Silence seldom struck Keynes as the best course of action, then or later. At the end of 1919, he published one of the great polemics of the century, *The Economic Consequences of the Peace*. By respectable criteria, this detestable volume did everything wrong. Keynes attracted his readers' immediate attention with four mordant sketches of the central actors at Versailles. Lloyd George had encouraged Britons to believe that the devasted German economy could pay vast sums in reparations to the winners, at the same time as the winners refused to buy German exports—the only conceivable source of the reparations. No doubt to the victors belonged the spoils. But, cried Keynes, just imagine that the losers' cupboard is bare. What price spoils then? The guts of the book were its statistical and analytical demonstration that German resources and commercial opportunities were much too sparse to justify any but very moderate reparations.

Keynesian magnanimity, if it had become Allied policy, might have removed the injustices of Versailles as a major theme of German politics during the Weimar period. If the German economy had been allowed to recover more quickly after 1918, the country presumably might have avoided the hyperinflation which wiped out middle-class savings and made that class ripe for recruitment by the Nazis. It is also possible that a consistently Draconian policy of repression might have kept Germany so weak that even Hitler would have hesitated to start a new world war. The vacillations of actual Allied policy between indulgence and harshness preserved German grievances and prevented full recovery of prewar prosperity.

History cannot be rerun. The aspect of *Economic Consequences* most relevant to the 1970s was Keynes' concern for the stability of capitalism. Keynes spent much of his time searching out innovative economic policies to salvage his own beloved England. "Here," he sighed in 1931, "are collected the croakings of twelve years—the croakings of a Cassandra who could never influence the course of events in time."[32] What terrified Keynes especially was the fragility of democratic institutions, the delicacy of public psychology, and the weakness of the economic arrangements which institutions and psychology had made possible. Looking back in 1919 upon the comparative success of Western society between 1870 and 1914, Keynes discerned the operation of a good deal of luck:

Europe was so organised socially and economically as to secure the maximum accumulation of capital. While there was some continuous improvement in the daily conditions of life of the masses of population, society was so framed as to throw a great part of the increased income into the control of the class least likely to consume it. The new rich of the nineteenth century were not brought up to large expenditures, and preferred the power which investment gave them to the pleasures of immediate consumption. In fact, it was precisely the *inequality* of the distribution of wealth which made possible those vast accumulations of fixed wealth and of capital improvements which distinguished that age from all others. Herein lay, in fact, the main justification of the capitalist system. If the rich had spent their new wealth on their own enjoyments, the world would long ago have found such a regime intolerable. But like bees they saved and accumulated, not less to the advantage of the whole community because they themselves held narrower ends in view.

Unfortunately these moderately benign arrangements were inherently unstable because,

. . . this remarkable system depended for its growth on a double bluff or deception. On the one hand the labouring classes accepted from ignorance or powerlessness, or were compelled, persuaded or cajoled by custom, convention, authority, and the well-established order of society into accepting a situation in which they could call their own very little of the cake that they and nature and the capitalists were co-operating to produce. And on the other hand the capitalist classes were theoretically free to consume it, on the tacit underlying condition that they consumed very little of it in practice.[33]

Keynes thought it unlikely that in the postwar atmosphere either the thrift of the affluent or the docility of the working class could be restored to prewar standards. For one thing, "the war had disclosed the possibility of consumption to all, and the vanity of abstinence to many."[34] For another, capitalists were so unconfident of the future that they took to spending their incomes on immediate pleasures rather than saving them for investment in an uncertain future. Far less deferential to their betters who were setting this poor example, workers and unions demanded with mounting determination larger slices of the cake they had helped to produce.

During the 1920s, Keynes' gloom deepened as the English economy sank into a sea of troubles. Even before 1914, English merchants and producers had been losing ground steadily in world markets to more vigorous German and American competitors. Victory failed to interrupt this long trend, and errors of policy compounded the adverse effects of slow growth in English productivity. In a misguided attempt to recall the imperial glories of the past, a Conservative government and a conservative chancellor of the exchequer, none other than Winston Churchill who understood glory better than exchange rates, revalued the pound in 1925 at its old parity with the American dollar. However, in 1925 the pound was worth much less and the dollar far more. English exports after 1925 became artificially more expensive and English imports of American merchandise unrealistically cheap.

The consequent threat to the English balance of payments could be overcome by devaluation of the British pound—a political impossibility; an industrial investment boom—an economic implausibility; or a reduction in costs especially of wages. The English government, adopting the third remedy, soon discovered that it was equally implausible. Attempted wage reductions sparked a general strike which has embittered labor-management relations ever since.

For nearly the decade which preceded the 1929 crash of the world economy, English unemployment was at depression levels in the Welsh coal valleys, the Scottish shipyards, and the manufacturing towns of the midlands. In the 1920s, the dole became as much a way of life for the long-term unemployed as welfare for many inner-city American families in the 1960s and 1970s.

What could be done? A man of endless ingenuity, Keynes turned first to currency reforms. If England went off the gold standard, or at least valued the pound more sensibly, English exporters could do better in world markets and English merchants would be less menaced by competition from American, Japanese, and German imports. Falling imports and rising exports are the usual tonic for any country's balance of payments. England, a country exceptionally dependent upon world trade, needed the tonic in generous doses. No English government was willing to accept Keynes' "croakings."

Keynes was by nurture and conviction a free trader. In desperation, he came to advocate, as a temporary measure, tariffs to protect English business. Against the grain of conventional opinion, he proposed to tackle unemployment directly. Making up his quarrel with Lloyd George, now an opposition leader, he composed a pamphlet *Can Lloyd George Do It?* which advocated public works, financed by government deficits, to absorb the unemployed in useful projects. He encountered another stone wall. The experts in the British Treasury solemnly averred that if the government borrowed more, less would be available for business investment. At most then, less important public jobs would replace economically more valuable jobs in the private sector.

Fallacies often have long lives. In 1974 and 1975 Treasury Secretary William Simon, the Ford administration's most vigorous exponent of economic error, repeatedly warned Congress that more stimulus to the economy would "crowd out" private borrowers, renew inflation, and lead to even worse recession. Minds unbefuddled by reading too many of Mr. Simon's statements might have concluded that when unemployment was running at 9 percent levels, eight or nine million people were looking for jobs, factories were operating at 70 percent of capacity, and inventories were stacked in warehouses, there were plenty of resources available to be put to work by money borrowed by both sectors of the economy—private and public.

Keynes' warnings went unheeded partly because employed blue-collar workers and most of the middle class were doing reasonably well. There was a second reason why the experts could safely brush Keynes aside. Keynes' job creation proposals were, on practical grounds, obviously sensible. He simply brought together idle men and women and useful tasks to engage their energies and restore their self-respect. Keynes' pamphlet, however, supplied no theoretical rationale for his economic therapy. Among economists this is a grave deficiency. By and large, the profession prefers good theory to bad, but even bad doctrine to none at all.

Between them the disasters of the 1930s and the analytically elegant *The General Theory of Employment, Interest and Money* removed both impediments to acceptance by the public, politicians, and professional colleagues of the Keynesian faith. Rates of unemployment as high in the United States as 25 percent caused widespread distress among the middle class. Doctors, lawyers, and businessmen were all caught in the economic storm. In the face of such calamities, no sensible citizen was likely to retain his confidence in politics as usual and policies based on conventional economics.

The General Theory, as abstruse and difficult to comprehend as the most carping theorist could require, was Keynes' answer to two questions: What causes mass unemployment? How can the malady be treated and the patients cured? The crucial element in Keynes' responses was his substitution of human will for automatic market processes. For much too long a time, economists, bankers, and Treasury knights had been telling all who listened that, if only we were all as patient as they were, the normal mechanisms of a capitalist economy could be counted upon to restore full production. Clumsy interventions by the politicians simply sabotaged these mechanisms by postponing salutary bankruptcies by inefficient enterprises, and necessary reductions in wages.

Keynes, a manager of everything that caught his interest, from ballet companies and liberal journals of opinion to banks, life insurance companies, Cambridge colleges, and complex international negotiations, simply refused to believe that the human intellect was helpless to handle unemployment, inflation, or any other economic trouble. With unusual rapidity his defense of human competence began to influence public policy, economic research, and statistical practice even before the onset of World War II. By that time England and the United States had installed systems of national income accounting faithful to Keynesian definitions. The New Deal response to the sharp 1937–38 contraction was an explicitly Keynesian resort to public works and new deficits.

Politicians, not the fastest of learners, had come to understand that unemployment, no act of God, was the almost banal consequence of inadequate spending by three kinds of customers—ordinary consumers, investors, and public agencies. To increase employment, somebody needed to spend more: simple as that. If the consumers could not be coaxed to buy more and save less, the government itself must take action. Lower interest rates encouraged hesitant investors, but if the best efforts of the Bank of England or the Federal Reserve were not enough, Congress or Parliament need only appropriate the money to construct additional hospitals, schools, subways, and houses, or, less sensibly, more tanks, bombers, missiles, and naval vessels.

Keynes recommended redistribution of income in the direction of equality partly on the ethical ground that extremes of wealth and poverty were disgraceful, but also because the poor spent more of their income than the rich. An excellent way to stimulate aggregate demand, accordingly, was to tax the rich to employ the poor. Full employment was the necessary means to the larger objectives of existence, the highest possible quality of civilized enjoyment, diffused among the entire population. Keynes, a creature of Bloomsbury as well as Cambridge, worried as much about life's quality as John Stuart Mill before him and contemporary partisans of the environment after him. Most American and British Keynesians have been almost unqualified partisans of rapid growth in GNP. Not so their master.

Our wishes sometimes are granted in unpleasant ways. It was World War II, a gigantic experiment in the macro-economics of aggregate demand, that finally convinced the universe of the validity of Keynes' emphasis upon the symbiosis between employment and total spending. Just before the war began, unemployment in the United States was a distressing 14 percent. Mobilization of people and resources to win wars in the Atlantic and the Pacific reduced unemployment practically to zero, provisioned and munitioned thirteen million men and women in uniform, and miraculously raised domestic living standards at the same time. Massive military outlays generated an enormous federal deficit—and full employment.

In Keynesian terms what counted was the size not the shape of spending, a lesson too well learned by some followers of Keynes. Communities enlightened enough to finance universal health care, free public transportation, and free tuition in universities, as well as museums, libraries, orchestras, art galleries, and opera companies, could enjoy the simultaneous delights of full employment and civilized pleasure.

Even though successful politicians in high office quietly applied Keynes and, after 1948, successive editions of Paul Samuelson's *Economics* (and numerous imitations) carried the Keynesian word to legions of students, something more was required to complete public triumph. For in their public pronouncements, Republican and Democratic politicians remained curiously reluctant to surrender outworn celebrations of balanced budgets and misleading analogies between the conduct of family finances and the management of national economies.

Only in the 1960s, after appropriate domestication to the

desires and interests of powerful corporations and wealthy individuals, was Keynesian vision translated into conventional wisdom. In December 1962, persuaded by Walter Heller his principal economic adviser, John F. Kennedy asked Congress to reduce taxes on personal and corporate income even though the government was already running a deficit and the economy was languidly recovering of its own accord. The president explicitly connected an even larger deficit with acceleration of economic growth and a faster march toward his administration's 4 percent unemployment "interim" target. *Business Week* saluted eventual congressional passage of the tax cut in February 1964 as the triumph of an idea. Two presidents and Congress thus ratified the Keynesian premises upon which earlier administrations had privately operated.

With reason these days economists usually identify their occupation apologetically rather than boastfully. A decade ago, Keynesians were proud souls. The tax cut they had promoted was operating just as predicted. Between 1961 and 1969 the economy expanded without interruption from recession, one of the longest booms of business-cycle record. Almost best of all, until mid-1965 when irrational Vietnam escalation distorted all other federal actions, prices behaved beautifully, creeping upward at a discreet 1 or 2 percent each year. For a golden moment, growth became the magic author of many good things. The middle class and the wealthy rejoiced in lower taxes, larger profits, and higher dividends. For the poor, black, young, and urban, Great Society spectaculars unfolded a bewildering array of novelties—Lyndon Johnson's "unconditional" war against poverty, medicare, medicaid, Title I funds for impoverished school districts, Head Start, model cities, community action, neighborhood legal services, and more, much more. As the economy baked bigger pies, everybody ate better, even though in obedience to precedent the rich gobbled the bigger pieces and the poor feasted on the crumbs.

The moral appears to be that in conservative societies dominated by corporate interest Keynesian measures operate successfully during large and popular wars or, as in the early 1960s, during spells of economic growth rapid enough to offer a little something to the officially poor who populate the bottom fifth of the income distribution. What happens when growth potentials diminish is illustrated by Nixon-Ford responses to the challenge of inflation and unemployment. Their administrations arranged the mild 1969–70 recession and prolonged and deepened the 1974–75 mini-depression. The second episode in particular imposed major burdens of unemployment on the most vulnerable groups—women, blacks, teenagers, and urban poor. In all probability, income has been redistributed from poor to rich. Keynesian economics have been redirected from full employment to the pursuit of price stability.

As Keynes himself assumed, no economic technique or doctrine ever substitutes for the play of selfish interest and ideology which power the machine of democratic politics. It is therefore highly unlikely that by themselves Keynesian fiscal and monetary tools will ever again suffice to repeat the triumphs of 1961–65. Growth for the rest of this century and beyond is likely to be slow. Resource shortages, population pressures, declining American influence in the world, and altered relations between rich and developing societies argue against resumption of the 4 percent annual growth rates of American history which softened past struggles over the distribution of the national product.

When growth slows or stops, the gains of one group are the inevitable losses of another. If the poor get more, the rich get less. Gains by blue- and white-collar workers must be matched by losses of income by doctors, lawyers, and other professional workers. Without democratic national planning and conscious selection of income priorities through the political process, slow growth eventuates either in perpetual inflation, persistent unemployment, a combination of the two, or an alternation of inflation and unemployment.

In the 1970s and after, Keynesian economics in their current, dominant conservative guise are an inadequate response to the transformation of national and world economies that has bewilderingly occurred. Economists need to read or reread portions of *The General Theory* usually ignored. Keynes was not only an advocate of income redistribution, he also foresaw probable need for a "somewhat comprehensive socialisation of investment." Addressing himself above all to the scandal of mass unemployment, he failed to foresee the trend toward even greater concentration of economic power in huge corporations. At a time of enormously deficient aggregate demand, Keynes devoted little attention either to inflation or the capacity of large units in concentrated industries to raise prices in good and bad times without discrimination.

Within the framework of socially chosen goals, Keynesian economics will again flourish. In the United States at the moment, conservative presidents and their corporate allies have learned, alas for the unrich and the nonpowerful, how to generate unemployment high enough to preserve and even improve their share of American wealth.

In their way great social thinkers are a permanent second government. Marx is better remembered than Millard Fillmore, his contemporary. Veblen sends clearer messages than Chester Arthur. Keynes will be remembered when Stanley Baldwin and Ramsay MacDonald are forgotten. Keynes concluded *The General Theory* with this affirmation of the power, even the primacy of ideas:

> . . . the ideas of economists and practical philosophers, both when they are right and when they are wrong, are more powerful than is commonly understood. Indeed the world is ruled by little else. Practical men, who believe themselves exempt from any intellectual influences, are usually the slave of some defunct economist. Madmen in authority, who hear voices in the air, are distilling their frenzy from some academic scribbler of a few years back. I am sure that the power of vested interests is vastly exaggerated compared with the gradual encroachment of ideas. Not indeed immediately, but after a certain interval; for in the field of economic and political philosophy there are not many who are influenced by new theories after they are twenty-five or thirty years of age, so that the ideas which civil servants and politicians and even agitators apply to current events are not likely to be the newest. But, soon or late, it is ideas, not vested interests, which are dangerous for good or evil.[35]

Six million Jews died because Adolf Hitler spent an unhappy youth reading anti-Semitic pamphlets and newspapers. The normal aggressions of large states are in Russia reinforced by the vulgar Marxism of its leaders. For good or evil, ideas rule society—whether they are implanted by God and nature, whether they reflect conflicts in the economic base or are responsive to evolutionary imperatives, or, as Keynes preferred to believe, are the fruits of unimpeded, free intellectual speculation.

Contemporary critics of economic thought and action continue to draw inspiration from Marx and Veblen. The economic profession's shrinking and disheartened legions of celebrants mix a brew of Keynes and Adam Smith that displeases even the brewers. In the absence of superior alternatives, they content themselves with fiscal manipulation and an almost touching confidence in the operation of free markets. It attests to the power of past thought and the feebleness of contemporary social analysis that the venerable quartet, Smith, Marx, Veblen, and Keynes, speak in louder voices than the bearers of fresher tidings and the creators of newer visions.

7

the revival
of economics?

Discoursing some sixty years ago on the text, "Choose equality
and flee greed," Matthew Arnold observed that in England
inequality is almost a religion. He remarked on the incom-
patibility of that attitude with the spirit of humanity, and sense
of the dignity of man as man, which are the marks of a truly
civilised society. "On the one side, in fact, inequality harms by
pampering; on the other by vulgarizing and depressing. A system founded on it is against nature, and, in the long run, breaks
down."

—R. H. TAWNEY

I think of equality, not as an end-state, but as the direction or
trend of a social process that, as it leads to social change, creates
costs as well as benefits.

—HERBERT GANS

265

Economics eagerly awaits its next great visionary. One can legitimately wonder whether he or she will emerge from any of our leading graduate schools. Such intellects do not appear on order. The 1920s, it is now plain, were pre-Keynesian. What, if anything, are the 1970s preparing to receive in the shape of economic revelation?

At the end of this lament for the beloved subject, I can do no better than sketch a prospectus for potential saviors. In its best moments economics has commanded respect and influenced events because its ablest practitioners placed themselves and their societies in the stream of history. Within history, they sensitively grappled with the origins and prospects of contemporary institutions. They brought to their inquiries their own special perceptions of how a better society might organize its work, recreations, and politics. Shorn of morality and history, economics is reduced to techniques, no doubt useful and lucrative for economists and their clients, but as guides to social policy no better than the ruminations of accountants, lawyers, and philosophers of advertising, marketing, and public relations.

In its analysis of consumer behavior, standard economics has exaggerated the autonomy of average Americans and drastically understated the manipulative arts of advertisers and sellers. The analytical lapse, no accident, is the effect of one of the profession's gravest failures of institutional understanding, the long-standing reluctance of economists to struggle with giant corporations—the dominant commercial institutions of the century. Standard economics compounds its sin by almost ignoring trade unions and treating with unpardonable naïveté the consequences for analysis and policy of the close ties between political institutions and private interest groups.

The spell of the competitive market cast by Adam Smith two centuries ago still operates upon respectable members of his trade, even though it daily becomes more difficult to locate actual markets which even approximate the requirements of pure competition. Where are the hordes of buyers, multitudes of sellers, and utterly standardized products by which the textbooks define a properly competitive market? For the most part, these paragons are to be found only in the textbooks themselves.

In their newest and least understood mode of organization, corporations have begun to restrain competition on an international scale. In pursuit of their own interest, global corporations find it convenient sometimes to stimulate inflation, at other times unemployment, in one country or another. The fabled mobility of their capital interferes with parochial attempts by mere national governments to manage their own economies. Without effective regulation, slipping through the legal crevices of assorted legal codes, the multinationals in mysterious ways influence the distribution of income and wealth within and between nations. Power, seldom a favorite topic of economists, is at the head of any agenda of neglected issues in the typical graduate curriculum.

It follows that the revival of economics necessitates rescue from the curiously abstract, empirically empty finger exercises of received price and income theory. Young economists emerge uneducated, Ph.Ds in hand, for want of knowledge of the history of their own subject. No one has told them that one major task before them is how to control the dominant corporations whose origins and development no one has seen fit to tell them about. A more realistic economics will not surrender its interests in choice and allocation, although it will speak better sense about how the allocations and choices are made after it comes to terms with the politics of allocation and the limitations of individual choice.

The distribution of income and wealth is a topic on which much remains to be learned. One of the fascinations of the congressional hearings on Nelson Rockefeller's nomination as vice president in 1974 was some tantalizing hints of the complexity of an enormously wealthy family's interests and the sheer reach of its influence upon banking, industry, philanthropy, and the arts. At the moment, the secrets of power are locked in a great many private archives of other family dynasties. Distribution, for reasons previously stated, is clearly fated to be the crucial political and economic issue of this and the next generation. Economists have done too little research into its statistical mysteries. They have unnecessarily handicapped themselves by a foolish reluctance to compare the rich and the poor and to make the choices of research topic and actual policy which depend on such comparisons.

It would be well for the profession and possibly for the public were economists to descend from the mountain peaks of high theory and once more grub in historical and statistical data. These are the potential sources of generalizations better related to the evolution of their understanding of their own and other societies. Indeed until they do this they are and will continue to be the astonished victims of unexpected happenings which fail to accord with their conventional analysis, for the sufficient reason that less and less of what occurs out there is caught in the net of outworn analytical assumption and inappropriate institutional specification.

I hasten to interpolate that even in its present state of intellectual disarray economics has its humble uses. Economists work comfortably in large corporations which pay them salaries large enough to imply a high valuation of their services. Quite possibly their expert counsel on such topics as the industry's sales prospects, the consequences of public regulation, the prospect of profit in foreign markets, and other matters of direct pecuniary concern is sufficiently more frequently right than wrong to argue in their favor. Public agencies are populated with men and women whose title is economist. And students continue to enroll in university departments of business and economics in the confidence that they are more likely when paroled to get a job some place than fellow students foolish enough to prefer philosophy, ancient history, fine arts, or classical Greek.

As no one can gainsay, the forecasts of business analysts of all schools have in recent times been strikingly wrong. I have not neglected to mention glaring examples earlier in this chronicle. Nevertheless, business and government keep reading and even buying prophecies of the future. In our apprehensive era, economics serves the priestly function of reassuring the despondent by piercing the veil of mystery which separates today from tomorrow. And like the Delphic oracle of old, economists often speak in riddles obscure enough to prove that they were right or at least not wrong however events turn out.

To be an economist is perfectly respectable. No parent need feel shame when a son or daughter confides economics as his or her vocational aspiration. Medicine and law are considered preferable specialties but university teaching has somehow retained the respect of those who are neither teachers nor students in universities. Most economists of course are, have been, or will be members of university departments. Upwardly mobile middle-class folk who have achieved reasonably satisfactory personal goals tend to accept the social and political institutions of a society which has had the grace to allow them to earn a decent income and attain a degree of status. This inclination and the reinforcing disciplines of the graduate school turn thoroughly socialized young practitioners into institutional conservatives, wary of structural change, dependent upon official sources for data, and skeptical of inquiry into emerging institutions and impure issues which combine politics and economics.

To the laity the topics economists enjoy talking about and discussing at their conventions usually seem not very important if not downright trivial. Appearances do not deceive. The journals are filled with matters of interest only to economists.

As the prophet has said, where there is no vision the people perish. Economists who think small thoughts condemn themselves to be intellectual hirelings, instruments of other people's purposes. The places to look for renewed moral vision are both old and new. Relatively novel is the global demand for justice among nations. Fairly or otherwise, poor countries without resources, and suddenly rich oil lands, cry for reparations from richer, already industrialized lands. Their list of demands is long. The Third World endowed with oil and minerals and the Fourth World rich only in population want to buy the technology of the West on favorable terms. They want to sell their own oil, minerals, and other raw materials at guaranteed (high) prices. In the wake of OPEC, producers of tin, bauxite, copper, coffee, sugar, and other foodstuffs or raw materials have with varying results sought to organize their own cartels. The advanced nations have before them delicate problems of ethics and power. How justified are the demands of these countries? Does the West possess the resources to meet even justified demands? What assurance is available that favors granted governments will benefit ordinary citizens? Can vast resource transfers such as those engendered by OPEC be accomplished without disrupting the economies of givers and takers alike.

The conceptual difficulties are enormously difficult. They require not only detailed knowledge of the societies affected but also clear ethical principles of guidance. As even Henry Kissinger has recognized, a nation's conception of morality influences its perception of national interest. National interest is the guide to hardened practitioners of realpolitik like our own Secretary of State. It is none too soon for economists to collect the information about the institutional forms that shape modern society, the major corporations, the large unions, and the elite institutions which train and indoctrinate our leaders; but it is far from easy. Harder still is the formulation of the distributive principles which must guide both the search for information and the ultimate policies of this country and its allies in the West.

Clearly, the place to look for help is in American tradition and history. As Alexis de Tocqueville traveled around the United States in the 1830s, liking little of what he observed and heard, he was especially impressed by the passion of the natives for equality. He put his impression in these memorable words:

The more I advanced in the study of American society, the more I observed that ... equality of condition is the fundamental fact from which all others seemed to be derived, and the central point at which all my observations terminated. ... The gradual development of the principle of equality is, therefore, a providential fact. It has all the chief characteristics of such a fact: it is universal, it is lasting, it constantly eludes all human interference, and all events as well as all men contribute to its progress.... [It is] an irresistible revolution which has advanced for centuries in spite of every obstacle.[1]

Equality, occasionally a synonym for justice, is a word which courses through the most solemn of constitutional safeguards and statutory declarations of the rights of Americans. The Fourteenth Amendment to the U.S. Constitution, ratified in 1868, prohibits any state from so acting as to "deny to any person within its jurisdiction the equal protection of the law." In a civil-rights act of the same vintage Congress promised that "all citizens of the United States shall have the same rights, in every State and Territory, as are enjoyed by white citizens thereof to inherit, purchase, lease, sell, hold, and convey real and personal property."

In its renewed thrust toward racial equality, Congress a century later enacted in 1964 a landmark Civil Rights Act. Title VII, applicable to employment, extended its commitment to fair treatment even beyond the black community which had been the object of congressional attention in the 1860s:

"It shall be an unlawful employment practice," read Title VII, "for an employer to fail or refuse to hire or to discharge any individual, or otherwise to discriminate against any individual, with respect to his compensation, terms, conditions, or privileges of employment, because of such individual's race, color, religion, sex, or national origin."[2]

It is accurate to say that the hunt for equality, of some kind, in some degree, according to favored criteria, is the multipartisan passion of liberals, radicals, and conservatives.

In the process of casting a cold glance on testing and educational qualifications for jobs of a superficially racially neutral kind, Chief Justice Warren Burger, Nixon's own highly praised student of constitutional strict construction, uttered these libertarian remarks:

> Congress has now provided that tests or criteria for employment or promotion may not provide equality of opportunity only in the sense of the fabled offer of milk to the stork and the fox.... The Act proscribes not only overt discrimination but also practices that are fair in form, but discriminatory in operation.*

As the Department of Health, Education and Welfare and other federal agencies interpret congressional intent, universities, corporations, and, in some instances, certain craft union locals have been obliged to pledge themselves to affirmative-action remedies for the injustices inflicted in the past against blacks, women, American Indians, and Spanish-speaking citizens.

It is time to pause and sort out the two meanings attached to the word *equality*. Mr. Burger focused his concern upon the denial of equality of opportunity. He held that this aspiration was frequently thwarted by tests and educational requirements which were little connected with successful

---

* Mr. Burger reminded the sketchily educated who might have forgotten their Aesop that the fox in the fable invited the stork to dinner and played upon his guest the dirty trick of serving milk in two shallow bowls. The fox lapped up his meal with evident pleasure. The hungry stork, futilely dipping his bill into the bowl, got barely a taste. Biding his time, the stork courteously extended a dinner invitation of his own to the fox. This time the milk arrived in two narrow jugs. Roles were reversed: the stork inserted his beak and drank, the fox was reduced to lapping the neck of his jug. Moral: things are not necessarily what they seem.

performance on the job and usually discriminated against black applicants who in disproportionate numbers score poorly on these inappropriate tests, the point of the chief justice's retelling of Aesop.

Equality of opportunity has also been the standard applied by the courts to school funding controversies. If one school district, populated by the wealthy, spends three times as much per public school pupil as a neighboring district, have the children in the second school been denied fair chances in life? Does it offend constitutionally that the Greak Neck schools are more lavishly financed than the Levittown facilities? In its influential *Serrano* v. *Priest* decision, the Supreme Court of California answered these questions affirmatively. In its even more important five-four *Rodriguez* v. *San Antonio Independent School District* decision, the Supreme Court of the United States came to opposite conclusions. Mr. Justice Powell, writing for the majority, refused to declare education a "fundamental" right shielded by the equal-protection clause of the Fourteenth Amendment. So long as even the poorer school districts, with the help of state aid, offered adequate education, no child was really injured by the better luck of agemates in better-supported schools.

In spite of *Rodriguez*, California, New Jersey, and a number of other states, obedient to state court interpretations of state constitutional requirements, have begun to rearrange and equalize educational expenditures per pupil. Under a new governor who is exceptionally open to innovation, California has increased funding for early childhood education. It is in the first years of life that middle-class boys and girls acquire the advantages of motivation, vocabulary, cultural experience, and self-esteem which endow them with a permanent edge over the children of poor and working-class parents. The inherent logic of equality of opportunity runs in the direction of public compensation, as far as is possible, for the shortcomings of home environments.

The jurists, social scientists, and plain citizens who favor equality of opportunity as an appropriate American aspiration rarely pursue the radical implications of their goal. When income and wealth are extremely unevenly distributed, how much equality of opportunity is genuinely available? Would Nelson Rockefeller be vice president if his grandfather had been an oil-field roustabout instead of an oil billionaire?* In the absence of his father's financial backing, would John F. Kennedy have made it to the White House? As in politics, so in business and banking. No special gift of cynicism is needed to suspect a degree of family advantage in Henry Ford II's tenure as chairman of the board of the Ford Motor Company or David Rockefeller's comparable position at the head of the Chase Manhattan Bank, one of the Rockefeller family's many holdings. To put the matter as softly as possible, tension must exist between virtually unlimited rights of inheritance and genuine equality of life chances for individuals of similar personal and intellectual qualities.

As a social goal, then, equality of opportunity is susceptible to radical interpretation. It appears to require at the

---

* Nelson Rockefeller, according to the Citizens Research Foundation, spent more of his own and his relatives' money seeking political office than anyone else in American history. Between 1952 and 1970, this sum totaled no less than $27 million. As one wit put it, "This kind of thing tends to make the people's grant of unique opportunities for public service more likely." See Edwin Newman, *Strictly Speaking* (New York: Bobbs-Merrill Co., 1974), p. 86.

least substantial rearrangements of public education, employment policy, the Internal Revenue Code, and the laws of inheritance. However, equality in its second sense, as requiring the equality of condition which so impressed de Tocqueville, is even more subversive of traditional institutional practices. In the last fifteen years, this more potent version of equality has become popular among members of groups as diverse as women's liberationists, blacks, the elderly, the Hispanic, and the homosexual. Spokeswomen and spokesmen typically begin with demands for nondiscriminatory evaluation as potential employees, next insist upon fair promotion, and frequently conclude by defining as the appropriate criterion of justice placement of their members in good and bad jobs according to the majority pattern.

Especially in periods of economic adversity, individualistic interpretation of equality as fair chances clashes with the equally powerful measurement of equality as it is registered in the progress of the group. Consider, for example, Marco de Funis, the most famous law student of his generation. After many legal vicissitudes, Mr. de Funis graduated in 1974 from the University of Washington School of Law. A Sephardic Jew who a generation ago might well have been rejected because of his religion, Mr. de Funis applied to the University of Washington School of Law in 1970. His undergraduate record at the same university had been an excellent 3.71 on a scale of 4.00. Nevertheless, the law school rejected him, though he was advised to try again a year later. While he waited, he earned twenty-one points of "A" credit in graduate school and managed simultaneously to hold a full-time job in the Seattle Park Department. Although his scores on three Law School Admissions

Tests (LSAT) averaged only 582, his 668 in the third test put him in the top 7 percent nationally. Again de Funis was rejected.* During the same admissions season, the law school admitted a total of forty-four minority candidates, thirty-six of whom had lower predicted first-year averages than de Funis.†

Marco de Funis had recourse to a traditional American remedy: he sued the law school. As one of the judges who heard his suit pointed out, among the successful minority applicants, "were some whose college grades and aptitude scores were so low, that, had they not been minority students, their applications would have been summarily denied." Nevertheless, in a decision upholding the law school's policy, the state supreme court of Washington asserted that racial classifications were not necessarily unconstitutional, unless they invidiously stigmatize a *minority*. The court implied that members of a majority were not subject to stigma. The court proceeded to hold that the law school's good faith effort to ensure a "reasonable representation" of

---

* The de Funis case figures in an excellent debate between two civil libertarians on the merits of preferential admission in higher education. In supporting separate standards for minority applicants, one lawyer argues that the lingering effects of past discrimination require powerful remedies, among them preferential treatment of minority applicants by professional schools. His opponent, another lawyer, asserts with equal passion that dual admissions criteria are inherently racist and certain to stigmatize those who apparently benefit with a badge of permanent inferiority. See the *Civil Liberties Review*, Spring 1975, pp. 95–116.

† The preferred minorities were Phillipine-Americans, Chicanos, blacks, and American Indians. As critics were quick to point out, why weren't additional minorities also preferred? Poles, Slavs, and Italians have also encountered professional school discrimination. They too are underrepresented in the legal profession.

As the law school computed predicted first-year averages, LSAT scores and junior-senior undergraduate averages were accorded equal weights.

minority students was admittedly "color conscious," but acceptable in a good cause, for it sought "to prevent the perpetuation of discrimination and to undo the effects of past segregation."

By direction of Justice Douglas, de Funis was admitted to law school and by the time his cause was argued before the entire Supreme Court he was only a month or two away from graduating. Although de Funis' personal situation gave the majority of the Court a chance to dodge the case on the ground that there was no longer an issue to be decided, Douglas dissented ringingly. He attacked admissions preferences based on race or ethnic origin. However, he accepted as constitutional classifications according to wealth and poverty, and comparative life experiences. He strongly indicated that a university might legitimately prefer applicants who were similarly handicapped by family poverty or low-quality previous education. The white child of a West Virginia coal miner and the black son or daughter of an Alabama farmworker who scrambled through inferior state colleges might *both* merit preference over a bright but lazy Ivy League graduate. Character and personality may be as relevant to future professional success as measures of previous educational achievement.

One doubts that economists' trade-offs can do much to clarify, much less resolve, these clashes of principle. Can a society trade off a quantity of equality of opportunity for a measure of group advancement? One reason why affirmative-action schemes often strike their opponents as ambiguous or hypocritical derives from the attempts of the designers to satisfy simultaneously both conceptions of justice. Such appears to be the case at Berkeley, where after four years of negotiation with HEW, the university unveiled an institution-wide affirmative-action hiring and promotion policy. Its authors conscientiously analyzed by race and sex each of the campus' seventy-five academic departments. It compared its findings with the characteristics of the people who held doctoral degrees in the entire country and then, for each department, proposed a hiring goal and timetable. Over the next thirty years, Berkeley promised to replace 178 of its white males with the same number of women, blacks, Asians, and Chicanos. In early 1975 the total academic staff was 1,489.

Naturally the extent of remedial action differed from department to department. The English department, only 9 percent of whose faculty are women, can draw from a national pool of qualified candidates which includes a 30 percent female contingent. In six years, this department must enlarge the number of women at the lowest faculty rank to the full 30 percent. In the long march to equality, twenty-nine years later women will also be 30 percent of the full professors. For women, things were far worse in some other Berkeley departments. An evident citadel of male chauvinism, the chemistry department employs forty-eight males and not a single female. It is instructed to hire three women assistant professors within nine years and promote them (or their replacements) to full professor in thirty years.

HEW wields a big stick. Should the university fail to reach its objectives, then "administrators must explain their hiring practices and risk losing $9 million in federal contracts if found negligent."[3] Few instances of intended benevolence can have aroused more varied responses. Peter Holmes, director of the Federal Office of Civil Rights, praised the Berkeley plan as "the best thing we've come up with." He promised (threatened?) to take Berkeley as his model. Others contained their enthusiasm more readily. Ms. Isabel Welsh Pritchard, leader of a campus women's group, thought the number of new jobs in prospect was ridiculously small. Paul Seabury, a political scientist, termed the agreement "ludicrous" and "absurd" because after so many years of labor, it reached such minor conclusions. "It is a gigantic enterprise," he acidly remarked, 'in which no one wins except the bureaucrats.''

I cite de Funis, Berkeley, and the many instances in 1974 and 1975 when in factories and offices the rules of seniority came into conflict with affirmative-action hiring and promotion promises,* because they are aspects of moral choice which affect all sorts of resource allocations now and in the future. American society is at almost the beginning of its attempt to do justice to individuals and groups in the context of diminishing rates of growth.

Economists can sustain their portion of this inquiry by turning for ethical sustenance to their own, partially discarded tradition. Jeremy Bentham, I wrote in an earlier chapter, shared Adam Smith's belief that, as vessels of pain and pleasure, human beings were more or less alike, at least until environment made them different. Bentham added the crucial assumption that money, like any of the things money buys, yielded diminishing pleasure as a man or woman collected more dollars. It followed, other things equal, that redistribution from rich to poor increased the community's aggregate pleasure. Take $10,000 from the millionaire of

---

* With one exception, courts have decided in favor of union seniority clauses and against the blacks and women who were laid off first because they were hired last.

your choice and give it to a member of the United Farm Workers. Imagine a large number of such transfers. Common sense leads to the conclusion that the pleasures of the beneficiaries would exceed the sufferings of the millionaires. As a twentieth-century Benthamite generalized these individual instances,

> . . . it is evident that any transference of income from a relatively rich man to a relatively poor man of similar temperament, since it enables more intense wants to be satisfied at the expense of less intense wants, must increase the aggregate sum of satisfactions. The old "law of diminishing utility" thus leads securely to the proposition: Any cause which increases the absolute share of real income in the hands of the poor, provided that it does not lead to a contraction in the size of the national dividend from any point of view, will in general, increase economic welfare.[4]

The proviso referred to the possibility that too much redistribution might diminish individual incentives to save, invest, and innovate.

These are the psychological justifications for progressive income taxes, and heavy levies on large fortunes. Benthamite psychology also supports negative income tax and other income maintenance devices. In the nineteenth century John Stuart Mill's opposition to progressive income taxes but advocacy of sharp taxes on bequests was the consequence of Mill's belief that the first tax discouraged incentives and the second did not. The dead can contribute nothing to GNP, and their heirs might actually work harder and produce more if the taxman removed the alternative of idle luxury.

There is no abstract answer to the key question of how much can be redistributed from rich to poor without rebellion on the part of the wealthy and withdrawal of their resources and energies from productive activity. Sweden, which according to some measures is the world's richest country, extracts from its citizens mostly by progressive taxation 43 percent of the Swedish national product—11 percent more than Americans pay. Economists and others need to explore further the psychology of competition. It may be that what counts is not the margin by which you or I or any person best our rivals but the sweet fact that we have bested them at all. In the baseball standings 2–1 victories are just as good as lopsided 15–0 scores. Corporate executives, it is safe to say, enjoy their salaries as well as their power and position in the land. Would a company president retire in disgust if his after-tax income were only a trifle higher than the take-home pay of the mere vice presidents? It may be that because of the way we are socialized we need to run races. However, the evidence is scant that the distance between winners and losers need be as tremendous as it now is in the United States. The issues are empirical. Economists have presided over income maintenance experiments in New Jersey and elsewhere. It would be harder but potentially more important to design a series of experiments aimed at relating various levels of positive taxation to individual incentives.

Bentham carries economics into interesting practical policy discussions. John Rawls, a Harvard philosopher, presents the profession with an alternative, even stronger argument for equality as the central principle of income distribution. Rawls advocates as preferable to utilitarianism[5] a version of social contract theory whose consequences are even more drastically redistributive. Rawls asks his readers to perform a mental experiment. Each of us is to imagine that we know nothing about the wealth or poverty of our parents, and nothing about the market's valuation of our own ability. Enveloped by this veil of ignorance, we must now answer the question, "What is a fair principle of income distribution?" Rawls argues that under his conditions men and women would opt for equality of reward, out of apprehension that any other arrangement would place them among the losers. In the real world, real people start of course with information about all of Rawls' excluded topics.* Moreover, the more affluent will hang on to their perquisites except in those rare instances where their sense of justice is strong.

In Rawls this general preference for equality is subject to modification on one ground only. The "difference principle" justifies continued or even increased inequality upon the demonstration that the inequality acts to improve the situation of the least advantaged members of the society. In Rawls' phrasing,

Assuming the framework of institutions required by equal liberty and fair equality of opportunity, the higher expectations of those better situated are just if and only if they work as part of a scheme which improves the expectations of the least advantaged members of society. The intuitive idea is that the social order is not to establish and secure the more attractive prospects of those better off unless doing so is to the advantage of those less fortunate.[6]

---

* Arthur Okun has pointed out that a man or woman with a taste for risk might prefer a less equal distribution in the hope of becoming one of the winners. People who bet on races know that most of the time they lose. They continue to bet in the hope of the occasional big win. See his *Equity vs. Efficiency, the Big Tradeoff* (Washington, D.C.: Brookings Institution, 1975).

The tests are again empirical. It is even conceivable, though improbable, that reductions in corporate taxes which are of direct and immediate benefit to corporate stockholders only, rarely to be found below the poverty line, are capable of generating substantial employment for the poor. At their very best, trickle-down devices extract substantial service charges paid to the unneedy.

The philosophical distinctions between Bentham and Rawls are substantial. Nevertheless, adherence to either standard of public conduct probably implies similar social and economic action. Social contractarians and utilitarians alike are biased in favor of egalitarian redistributions of income and wealth. Each qualifies a flat egalitarian recommendation by a significant proviso. In Pigou, redistribution is desirable unless it diminishes national product. Rawls' difference principle, a somewhat stronger guide, disfavors redistribution from the more to the less wealthy where those who gain are not at the very bottom of the income distribution. But Rawls, too, would presumably oppose redistributions to his least advantaged group which left that group worse off absolutely than they were before the change in their relative position.

In the short run certainly, the ideas of economists are less likely to determine in our bad century the distribution of either American GNP or the world's resources than are assorted democratic politicians, authoritarian rulers, corporate tycoons, and military juntas. Contemporary American society faces an agonized and lengthy national exploration of the principles of distributive justice in a time of diminishing growth.

It is earnestly to be hoped that economists will play a role of consequence in that exploration because thus far certainly economic recommendations and economic decisions are being made with only scant awareness of their ethical consequences. Recall, for example, the argument incessantly made by Treasury Secretary William Simon to the effect that the nation now suffers from a serious capital shortage which can best be alleviated by tax cuts on corporate profits and income from dividends. Mr. Simon proposes to replace the lost revenue out of higher taxes on other members of the taxpaying public. By historical standards, American investment has been higher in recent years than average rates of capital formation in this century. In 1974 and 1975, capital investment faltered for the sufficient reason that American factories were operating at 70 percent or less of their capacity and inventories were piling up in stores, showrooms, and warehouses. However, even if Mr. Simon's factual case were more plausible, its ethical implications are strikingly unequal, for he proposes that families of average and low income actually transfer a portion of their modest rewards to the already affluent. If there were no other way, on Mr. Simon's premises, of encouraging desirable levels of investment, then the public might reluctantly pay the price he stipulates, and reward or bribe the unneedy into actions on behalf of the remainder of the community. An alternative more acceptable to egalitarians *does* exist. It is expansion of the economy at rates high enough to hire the unemployed, restore factories to capacity rates of operation, and cheer businessmen up to the point where they buy new machines and construct new facilities.

The Ford administration's unconcealed preference during the remainder of this decade for lower business taxes, higher levies on average families, and 7–8 percent unemployment is premised upon undebated distributional assumptions, on the supposed desirability of increasing still further existing inequalities of income and wealth. It regards as inadequate the favors granted in the last decade and a half to the corporations and investors. By one informed estimate, these are worth $31.4 billion each year,[7] a sum larger by nearly a half than the program of rebates and reductions enacted by Congress in early 1975. Commenting incidentally on the capital-shortage justifications offered, Walter B. Wriston, no radical, chairman of Citicorp, observed that "even in a booming stock market, very few people I run into want to buy a security of a company that doesn't earn money."[8]

Lower taxes on corporate income reward corporate managers and corporate stockholders directly and quickly. For the community the benefits, if there are any, are indirect and delayed. If investment does rise, if corporations build factories and install equipment in the United States in preference to other locations, and if these investments really would not have been made in the absence of new tax incentives, then, possibly, some new jobs will become available. Of course the wages paid to new workers as well as the already employed will be held down by the continuation of planned unemployment. In Hoover days, this sort of policy was derided as trickle-down economics. Twenty years ago Dwight Eisenhower's neo-Hoover advisers revived this ungolden oldie among economic records. With scarcely the change of a note, the tune is being replayed yet again. It appears to be a mistake to elect Republican presidents.

To their credit, liberal Keynesians now and earlier have identified and attacked the injustice of managing the economy to suit the tastes of the rich and powerful. But even liberal economists had their lapses during the Kennedy years when growth superseded distribution as the target of national policy. There are signs of awareness in Congress and the actions of some economists that conscious selection of coherent employment and energy programs involves important distributional consequences.

Thus the Hawkins-Humphrey Equal Opportunity and Full Employment Bill (H.R. 50) harks back to the original goals of the 1945 Full Employment Bill which, as a result of the political events described in chapter 2, survived in attenuated form as the Employment Act of 1946. H.R. 50 is a job guaranty measure. A national promise of full employment is necessarily egalitarian. Unpleasant or dangerous jobs will find takers only at wages high enough to compensate for the distasteful features of the work required. Higher rewards at the bottom of the occupational ladder soon translate themselves into demands for improvement in the rewards of those who occupy the rungs slightly farther from the bottom. As the wage structure shifts upward, prices will surely rise at accelerating rates unless controls are imposed on prices and profits and taxes are levied on the affluent. Full employment without inflation *requires* a substantial shift of net income from the affluent and prosperous to the remainder of the community.

There is a further implication of full employment as deliberate national policy, a glaring necessity for democratic national planning. Again a number of progressive legislators at least started a national debate. The Javits-Humphrey Balanced Growth and Economic Planning Act (S. 1795) is also sponsored by several past or present Democratic presidential hopefuls, among them Senators Jackson, McGovern, and Bayh. Several economists were active in the citizen's group called the Initiative Committee for National Economic Planning* whose discussion eventuated in S. 1795's call for an Office of National Economic Planning to collect and collate planning information and formulate plans of varying duration for congressional debate.

France, Canada, and Japan are among the industrial societies which since 1945 have experimented with generally successful results in various designs of indicative planning, the sort of guidance to the economy which relies on information and incentives rather than coercion. Indicative planning tends to offer the carrots of favorable access to credit and capital, selective tax preference, direct public loans, and the like to private corporations which operate in conformity to congressionally chosen production priorities.

It is possible (nothing in politics can be certain) that a planning mechanism in operation during 1974 and 1975 would have led to an enlightening public debate over the best way to restore prosperity. The Ford administration's priorities would have registered themselves in the plan it submitted to Congress. Alternative sets of priorities in and out of Congress might be more sharply and forcibly advanced because of the very existence of the president's proposal. All parties would be compelled to identify their social goals.

Planning requires the services of economists. The aid is reciprocal. As the national argument over the proper degree of public direction of the private economy continues,

---

* Members included Leonard Woodcock of the UAW and Wassily Leontieff, Nobel Laureate in economics, co-chairmen; Anne Carter, a Brandeis University economist; John Kenneth Galbraith; Robert Heilbroner; Robert Nathan; Robert Roosa; and the author of this advertisement: one labor leader and seven economists.

economists' infatuation with competitive markets should diminish and their renewed attention to unneutral values increase. Even at the current, primitive stage of planning discussion, planning has evoked reactions which reveal the hopes and fears of several varieties of ideologists. Some radicals insist that national economic planning is just another device of corporate capitalism to tighten its control of American society and enrich itself still more at communal expense. With accuracy, they point to the precedent in the history of public regulation. Almost invariably the regulated industries have captured and often later employed the regulators.

Free-market economists and corporate executives who somehow fancy that they are engaged in real competition question the propriety of *any* political specification of priorities. As Chicago economists would have it, priorities sort themselves out automatically when consumers and entrepreneurs freely make their own choices and decisions. Milton Friedman has charged that "the central planners want planning by them for us. They want the government—by which they mean themselves—to decide 'social priorities' . . . take from some of us to give to others."[9] General Motors' chairman, Thomas A. Murphy, who runs the world's second largest planned enterprise (Exxon is first), warns his countrymen that "sooner or later, the Government plan, if it is going to serve any purpose at all, is going to mandate a different mix of goods and services than the free market would spontaneously provide. In other words, inevitably someone —maybe all of us—would lose some freedom."[10]

If conservatives and radicals both fear that their enemies will control the planning decisions, it is tempting to conclude that both groups are wrong and that the community at large will have rather more influence on political choices than they do on the decisions taken by General Motors and its few peers. Democratic planning holds the promise of increased public participation in the making of allocative choices and clarification of the values which ought to shape these choices.

———————

All is not yet lost for economists. Much in their own tradition is still recoverable: Veblen's fruitful distinction between technology and business, Marx's powerful analysis of capitalist development, Keynes' alliance of full employment and diffusion of civilized pleasure, even Adam Smith's hope of public benefit from genuinely competitive markets. Like the rest of humanity, economists take what suits their mood from their predecessors. Keynesians in the 1960s and perhaps again more recently emphasized mere growth above the objectives Keynes himself cherished. In the United States, free-market economists have eagerly embraced Smith's distrust of government. But they have been less eager to break up large corporations which control the markets to which they ought to be responding.

The chastening consciousness of their present intellectual disarray should help economists to return to the patient investigations into corporate and union behavior which they have been neglecting. The operations of OPEC should dispel the parochial inclination of American economists to concentrate on the behavior of their own economy almost to the exclusion of international events. As awareness of the limitations of market analysis spreads, economists will begin seriously to evaluate alternative structures, planning, local cooperatives, entitlements to jobs and medical treatment, and democratization of corporate management.

If economics is once more to be an aid to understanding, its exponents will need to come to grips with a world less friendly to growth and decidedly less sympathetic to rich industrial nations than the world in which middle-aged economists grew up. A sense of history, a concern for the ways in which corporations and other economic institutions actually function, and a more cosmopolitan perspective upon the world, all are obviously desirable improvements in the education and behavior of economists. So also is the rebirth of moral vision which naturally accompanies and stimulates the more creative efforts of social science to understand and transform the behavior of men and women in organized societies.

notes to chapter 1

1. Richard M. Nixon, *The Economic Report of the President*, January 1973, p. 82.
2. See *New Republic*, December 28, 1974, p. 14.
3. *Business Week*, December 21, 1974, p. 51.
4. *New York Times*, April 21, 1975, pp. 1 and 46.
5. *Wall Street Journal*, May 15, 1975, pp. 1, 23.
6. *Business Week*, December 21, 1974, p. 51.
7. *New York Times*, December 28, 1974, p. 6.
8. *Fortune*, January 1975, p. 9.
9. John F. Kennedy, *The Economic Report of the President*, January 1962, p. 120.
10. The story is vividly told in chapter 4 of Hobart Rowen's *The Free Enterprisers* (New York: G. P. Putnam's Sons, 1964). Shorter accounts are to be found in Arthur Schlesinger, Jr.'s *A Thousand Days* (New York: Houghton Mifflin Company, 1965), pp. 635–640 and my own *The Age of Keynes* (New York: Random House, 1966), pp. 255–263.

11. Hobart Rowen, *The Free Enterprisers* (New York: G. P. Putnam's Sons, 1964), pp. 101–02.

12. Ibid., p. 62.

13. Ibid.

14. Leonard Silk, *Nixonomics* (New York: Praeger Publishers, 1972), p. 205.

15. Ibid.

16. "Statement of the Honorable William E. Simon before the House Ways and Means Committee," January 22, 1975, p. 5.

17. Rudolf Klein, "The Trouble with a Zero-Growth World," *New York Times Magazine*, June 2, 1974, p. 14.

18. See Robert Heilbroner, *An Inquiry into the Human Prospect* (New York: W. W. Norton & Company, 1974). See also by the same writer "Second Thoughts on the Human Prospect," *Challenge*, May/June 1975, pp. 21–28.

notes to chapter 2

1. See Herbert Gans, *More Equality* (New York: Pantheon Books, 1974).

2. Paul A. Samuelson, *Economics*, 9th ed. (New York: McGraw-Hill Book Company, 1974), p. 828.

3. Gerald R. Ford, *The Economic Report of the President*, February 1975, pp. 276, 300.

4. Thomas Kuhn, *The Structure of Scientific Revolutions* (Chicago: University of Chicago Press, 1970).

5. Ibid., p. 11.

6. George Cooper et al., *Law and Poverty*, 2nd ed. (St. Paul: West Publishing Company, 1973), p. 887.

7. See for the figures cited in this paragraph Winifred Bell, Robert Lekachman, and Alvin L. Schorr, *Public Policy and Income Distribution* (New York: Center for Studies in Income Maintenance Policy, New York University, 1974), pp. 5–6.

8. *Toward a Social Report* by the U.S. Department of Health, Education and Welfare with an Introductory Commentary by Wilbur J.

Cohen (Michigan: Ann Arbor Paperback, The University of Michigan Press, 1970), p. 44.

9. Milton Friedman, *Capitalism and Freedom* (Chicago: University of Chicago Press, 1962), p. 192.

10. Richard M. Nixon, *Setting the Course—The First Year* (New York: Funk & Wagnalls Publishing Company, 1970), pp. 52–53.

11. See *The Public Interest*, no. 4 (Summer 1966), pp. 38 ff.

12. See Stephen K. Bailey, *Congress Makes a Law* (New York: Vintage Books, 1964). The quotation is from p. 57.

13. Ibid., p. 74.

14. Ibid., pp. 137–38.

15. Ibid., p. 228.

16. *Washington Post*, May 30, 1975, p. A 25.

17. *American Economic Review* 65, no. 2 (May 1975): 5–6.

18. John Maynard Keynes, *The General Theory of Employment, Interest and Money* (New York: Harcourt, Brace & Company, 1936), p. 374.

notes to chapter 3

1. Thomas Robert Malthus, *An Essay on Population*, Everyman's Library (1914), pp. 69–70.
2. John Stuart Mill, Autobiography (London: Oxford World Classics, 1924), pp. 88–89.
3. John Stuart Mill, *Principles of Political Economy* (New York: Longmans, Green, 1909), p. 242.
4. Ibid., p. 177.
5. Ibid., p. 191.
6. David Ricardo, *The Works and Correspondence*, 10 vols. ed. Piero Sraffa (New York: Cambridge University Press, 1951–55), 1: 290.
7. Mill, *Principles*, p. 110.
8. Ibid., p. 751.
9. Ibid., p. 748.
10. Ibid., p. 808.
11. Ibid., p. 764.
12. Ibid., p. 950.
13. Ibid., p. 233.

14. Quoted by J. M. Keynes in vol. 10 of *The Collected Writings of John Maynard Keynes* (London: Macmillan & Company, 1972), p. 171.

15. Milton Friedman, *Essays in Positive Economics* (Chicago: University of Chicago Press, 1953), p. 4.

16. Adam Smith, *The Wealth of Nations* (New York: Random House, Modern Library, 1937), p. 56.

17. George J. Stigler, *Essays in the History of Economics* (Chicago: University of Chicago Press, 1965), pp. 59–60.

18. *Public Papers of the Presidents, Richard Nixon 1972* (U.S. G.P.O., 1974), p. 111.

19. Campbell R. McConnell, *Economics* (New York: McGraw-Hill Book Company, 1975), p. 166.

20. Quoted by the *New Statesman* (London, England), January 10, 1975, p. 48.

21. Edwin Mansfield, *National Output, Income, and Employment* (New York: W. W. Norton & Company, 1974), pp. 142–43.

22. See *The Public Interest*, Summer 1967, pp. 15 ff.

23. Ibid., p. 33.

24. Ibid., pp. 6–7.

25. Ibid., p. 7.

26. *The New Yorker*, June 16, 1975, p. 78.

27. *International Encyclopedia of the Social Sciences*, 12: 590.

28. See *Yale Law Journal* 73 (1964): 733 and 74 (1965): 1245.

29. George Cooper et al., *Law and Poverty*, 2nd ed. (St. Paul: West Publishing Company, 1973), p. 323.

30. Ibid., p. 330.

31. Philip Areeda, *Antitrust Analysis* (Boston: Little, Brown & Company, 1967), pp. 785–86.

32. Ibid., p. 805.

33. Edwin Mansfield, *Economics* (New York: W. W. Norton & Company, 1974), p. 523.

34. Thurman Arnold, *The Folklore of Capitalism* (New Haven: Yale University Press, 1937), p. 212.

35. See Richard Titmuss, *The Gift Relationship* (New York: Pantheon Books, 1971).

36. Smith, *Wealth of Nations*, p. 737.

notes to chapter 4

1. Richard J. Barnet and Ronald E. Müller, *Global Reach* (New York: Simon and Schuster, 1974), p. 16.

2. *Fortune*, May 1975, pp. 208 ff.

3. Anthony Sampson, *The Sovereign State of ITT* (New York: Stein & Day Publishers, 1973), p. 85.

4. *New York Times*, June 19, 1975, p. 35.

5. *Wall Street Journal*, June 20, 1975, p. 1.

6. I follow Anthony Sampson's lucid chronology in *The Sovereign State of ITT*, see n. 3 above.

7. Edwin Mansfield, *Economics* (New York: W. W. Norton & Company, 1974), p. 505.

8. John von Neumann and Oskar Morgentern, *Theory of Games and Economic Behavior* (Princeton, N.J.: Princeton University Press, 1944).

9. Jerry Cohen and Morton Mintz, *America, Inc.* (New York: Dial Press, 1971).

10. Peter Drucker, *The Concept of the Corporation* (Boston: Beacon Press, 1960).

11. See also the work of Robin Marris.

12. John Kenneth Galbraith, *The New Industrial State* (Boston: Houghton Mifflin Company, 1967).

13. *New York Times*, June 29, 1975, Section 2, p. 1.

14. *American Economic Review*, vol. LXIII, no. 1 (March 1973): 6.

notes to chapter 5

1. Paul A. Samuelson, *Economics*, 8th ed. (New York: McGraw-Hill Book Company, 1970), p. 567.

2. Ibid., p. 568.

3. Milton Friedman, *Capitalism and Freedom* (Chicago: University of Chicago Press, 1962), p. 124.

4. Adam Smith, *The Wealth of Nations* (New York: Random House, Modern Library, 1937), pp. 66–67.

5. Ibid., p. 98.

6. *Wall Street Journal*, September 28, 1971, p. 3.

7. *New York Times*, September 1, 1971, p. 1.

8. *Washington Post*, September 21, 1971, p. A 16.

9. Sar Levitan, *Blue-Collar Workers* (Baltimore: Johns Hopkins University Press, 1969).

10. Andrew Levison, *The Working Class Majority* (New York: Coward, McCann & Geoghegan, 1974).

notes to chapter 6

1. Joseph A. Schumpeter, *History of Economic Analysis* (New York: Oxford University Press, 1954), p. 42.

2. Adam Smith, *The Wealth of Nations* (New York: Random House, Modern Library, 1937), p. 128.

3. Ibid., p. 428.

4. Ibid., p. 625.

5. Ibid., p. 421.

6. Ibid., p. 326.

7. Ibid., p. 13.

8. Ibid., p. 15.

9. Ibid., p. 409.

10. Ibid., p. 404.

11. Ibid., p. 429.

12. Karl Marx, *The Economic and Philosophic Manuscripts of 1844* (New York: International Publishers Company, 1964), pp. 110–11.

13. Ibid., p. 111.

14. Friedrich Engels and Karl Marx, *The Communist Manifesto*, 100th ed. (New York: International Publishers Company, 1962), p. 9.

15. Karl Marx, *Capital* (New York: Random House, Modern Library, a reprint of the 1906 edition issued by Charles H. Kerr & Company), p. 787.

16. Ibid., pp. 836–37.

17. *Selected Correspondence of Karl Marx and Friedrich Engels* (New York: International Publishers Company, 1942), p. 518.

18. Friedrich Engels, *Herr Eugen Dühring's Revolution in Science* (New York: International Publishers Company, 1939), p. 309.

19. Karl Marx, *Critique of the Gotha Program* (New York: International Publishers Company, 1932), pp. 29–31.

20. Ibid., p. 31.

21. Marx, *Capital*, p. 42.

22. Joan Robinson, *An Essay on Marxian Economics* (London: Macmillan & Company, 1947), p. 221.

23. Marx, *Capital*, p. 495.

24. Ibid., pp. 953–54.

25. Thorstein Veblen, *Theory of Business Enterprise* (New York: Charles Scribner's Sons, 1906), p. 6.

26. Ibid., p. 237.

27. Ibid., p. 394.

28. Thorstein Veblen, *Theory of the Leisure Class* (New York: Random House, Modern Library, 1931), p. 190.

29. Veblen, *Business Enterprise*, p. 316.

30. Ibid., p. 397.

31. John Kenneth Galbraith, *The Affluent Society* (New York: Houghton Mifflin Company, 1958), p. 253.

32. John Maynard Keynes, *The Collected Writings of John Maynard Keynes*, 16 vols., *Essays in Persuasion* (London: Macmillan & Company, 1931), 10: xvii.

33. Keynes, *Collected Writings*, *The Economic Consequences of the Peace*, 2: 11–12.

34. Ibid., p. 13.

35. John Maynard Keynes, *The General Theory of Employment, Interest and Money* (New York: Harcourt, Brace & Company, 1936), pp. 383–84.

notes to chapter 7

1. Alexis de Tocqueville, *Democracy in America*, 2 vols. (New York: Alfred A. Knopf, 1945), 1: 3.

2. George Cooper et al., *Law and Poverty*, 2nd ed. (St. Paul: West Publishing Company, 1973), p. 880 ff.

3. I have followed the account of the Berkeley affair in *The New York Times*, March 5, 1975, p. 36.

4. A. C. Pigou, *The Economics of Welfare* (London: Macmillan & Company, 1920), p. 89.

5. See John Rawls, *A Theory of Justice* (Cambridge, Mass.: Harvard University Press, 1971).

6. Ibid., p. 75.

7. The author of the estimate is Joseph Pechman, a liberal tax specialist at Washington's Brookings Institution. See *The Washington Post*, July 18, 1975, p. A 2.

8. Ibid.

9. *Newsweek*, July 14, 1975, p. 71.

10. *New York Times*, June 24, 1975, pp. 41, 43.

index

305

about the author

Robert Lekachman is the author of *The Age of Keynes, History of Economic Ideas, Varieties of Economics: Documents, Examples and Manifestoes,* and *Inflation: The Permanent Problem of Boom and Bust.* He is currently Distinguished Professor of Economics at Herbert H. Lehman College, City University of New York.